ROUTLEDGE LIBRARY EDITIONS:
ECONOMICS AND SOCIETY

Volume 5

BRITAIN 1906–1951

BRITAIN 1906–1951

A Welfare State

PETER TEED

Routledge
Taylor & Francis Group
LONDON AND NEW YORK

First published in 1963 by Hutchinson Educational Ltd.

This edition first published in 2026
by Routledge
4 Park Square, Milton Park, Abingdon, Oxon OX14 4RN

and by Routledge
605 Third Avenue, New York, NY 10158

Routledge is an imprint of the Taylor & Francis Group, an informa business

British Library Cataloguing in Publication Data
A catalogue record for this book is available from the British Library

ISBN: 978-1-032-97576-4 (Set)
ISBN: 978-1-041-13476-3 (Volume 5) (hbk)
ISBN: 978-1-041-13479-4 (Volume 5) (pbk)
ISBN: 978-1-003-67000-1 (Volume 5) (ebk)

DOI: 10.4324/9781003670001

Publisher's Note
The publisher has gone to great lengths to ensure the quality of this reprint but points out that some imperfections in the original copies may be apparent.

Disclaimer
The publisher has made every effort to trace copyright holders and would welcome correspondence from those they have been unable to trace.

PETER TEED

Britain 1906–1951

A WELFARE STATE

HUTCHINSON EDUCATIONAL

HUTCHINSON EDUCATIONAL LTD
178–202 Great Portland Street, London, W.1

London Melbourne Sydney
Auckland Bombay Toronto
Johannesburg New York

★

First published 1963

Reprinted 1964

Reprinted 1965

This book has been set in Times New Roman, printed in Great Britain on Donart paper by The Anchor Press, Ltd., and bound by Wm. Brendon & Son Ltd., both of Tiptree, Essex.

Acknowledgements

For permission to reproduce illustrations the author is indebted to the following: Air Ministry, Architectural Press, Associated Press, Beaverbrook Newspapers, British Museum, Crawley New Town Commission, *Daily Herald*, Hulton Picture Library, Imperial War Museum, London County Council, London Transport, *Mirroscope*, Mr Roland Penrose, Power Collection of the London Museum, Surrey County Council, Tate Gallery, *The Times* and Messrs Tooth.

Preface

This book seeks to fill a gap, by providing some account of recent British history. It tries to provide some of the very special kind of information dear to the hearts of G.C.E. O level examiners, while at the same time keeping Britain in a world perspective and showing something of the forces of social change. Any book will reflect the prejudices as well as the ignorance of the author and this is true *a fortiori* for a period as recent as this. But I hope that some at least of these have been mitigated by the unsparing help and advice of Mr J. P. T. Bury of Corpus Christi College, Cambridge, Professor C. L. Mowat of the University of Wales, and Mr C. P. Hill of the University of Exeter, to all of whom I owe most grateful thanks. I would also like to thank my colleagues Mr R. W. Cady, for his work on the maps, and Mr F. H. Mitchell for reading the proofs. Above all my debt is to my pupils and to my family who have had to put up with me.

Wallington PETER TEED

Contents

PART ONE

1906–1914

1 Introduction 15
2 The Liberal achievement 1906–1911 36
3 The Liberal triumph and the approach of war 52

PART TWO

The First World War 1914–1918

4 The First World War: its causes 69
5 The First World War: its course 84

PART THREE

Between the wars 1918–1939

6 The war ends 109
7 Coalition, Labour, Conservative 124
8 The General Strike, Labour and the Depression 137
9 The twenties: a survey 151
10 The National government and recovery 164
11 The National government 1935–1939 and rearmament 178
12 Foreign affairs 1930–1939 190
13 The thirties: a survey 208

Contents

PART FOUR

The Second World War 1939–1945

14 The Origins and early stages of war 225
15 Enlargement into world struggle 238
16 The war at home 251

PART FIVE

Britain and the post-war world

17 Home affairs 1945–1951 271
18 Empire into Commonwealth 289
19 Foreign affairs 1945–1951 308
20 Britain 1906–1951: prospect and retrospect 321

TEN POCKET BIOGRAPHIES

Henry Herbert Asquith 335
David Lloyd George 338
Ramsay MacDonald 340
Stanley Baldwin 342
A. Neville Chamberlain 344
Ernest Bevin 347
Aneurin Bevan 349
Clement Attlee 351
R. Anthony Eden 353
Sir Winston Churchill 355

Appendix I: President Wilson's Fourteen Points (a brief summary) 363
Appendix II: The Atlantic Charter (a brief summary) 364

Index 365

Illustrations

1906 election hand-bills	18
A Salvation Army meeting, London, 1906	20
Providence Place, Middlesex Street, 1908	23
Old Regent Street	32
Maurice Farman Longhorn	35
Mass drill in Gopsall Street School, 1906	39
Recruiting for Haldane's army, 1914	46
Great London Railway Strike, 1911	55
A suffragette arrested, 1914	61
A protest poster, 1913 (The Cat and Mouse Act)	62
The Bunny Hug, 1913	62
Derby Day, 1912	66
Belligerents and Neutrals in Europe 1914–1918	77
The Declaration of War, London, 1914	82
The Western Front	85
Turkey and the Middle East	88
Troops landing at Anzac Cove, Gallipoli	89
The mud in Flanders	92
An air-raid in London, 1917	95
The Italian Front	104
War in Ireland following the settlement of December 1921	115
Aldgate, 1920	121
Coal Strike at Wigan, April 1921	125
A London department store in 1922	131

Illustrations

The Royal Empire Exhibition, Wembley, 1924 134
General Strike, 4 May 1926 138
General Strike, 10 May 1926 143
The Last Supper by Stanley Spencer 161
'The Flapper Vote' by Strube 163
Unplanned housing development in Surrey between the wars 170
Jarrow marchers nearing Bedford, October 1936 173
'You know you can trust me' by David Low 185
Gas-masks being fitted and issued 189
Rhineland reoccupied 195
Franco's troops in northern Spain 198
'What, no chair for me?' by David Low 204
Derby Day, 1936 212
Elephant and the Celebes by Max Ernst 216
Fascist demonstration, October 1928 220
Hungarian Jews by Vicky 226
Crowds waiting for news, London, September 1939 231
An air-raid in London, 1941 233
The situation in November 1941 236
The Far East 239
The Mediterranean 242
Normandy Landings, June 1944 244
War in the West 1944–1945 245
L.D.V. troops inspected, July 1940 256
Evacuees awaiting transport from London, September 1939 262
Tube Shelter Perspective by Henry Moore 265
Danebury School 272
Crawley New Town 281
New flats in Stepney 283
Mahatma Gandhi's funeral pyre 296
Jewish terrorists blow up the offices of the *Palestine Post*, February 1948 303

Illustrations

U.S. troops on North Korean front 315
H.M.S. *Mauritius* anchored off oil refineries, Abadan 319
The jitter-bug 322
The Festival site on the South Bank in London, 1951 326
'Must I teach you another lesson?' by Vicky 332
'On the way to Nowhere' by Will Dyson 337
'All behind you, Winston' by David Low 346
'The Bevin Boys' by Vicky 349
'The Hot Seat' by David Low 361

PART ONE

1906–1914

1

Introduction

Death of Queen Victoria

Queen Victoria died on 22 January 1901, having reigned since 1837; most men then living had never known another sovereign. Her son Edward VII, who had been rigidly excluded from state affairs when a young man and whose social connections had been frowned on by court circles, succeeded. He was now an elderly gentleman of sixty, inclined to be irascible and with a very large appetite. His reign was not to see any obvious and immediate changes in the patterns of social behaviour, even though under the apparent calm new forces were at work. The upper-middle class still lived remarkably opulent and comfortable lives. Huge houses in Knightsbridge and Kensington flourished, with their armies of servants: cooks, butlers, coachmen, gardeners, maids and odd-job men. The country-house habit was possibly at its peak, especially as the motor-car began to speed up travel. Power—political, social, economic—resided with that large wealthy class whose ladies visited each other in the afternoon according to an elaborate code, and whose gentlemen, changing each night into evening dress, would solemnly pass the port round their dining-room tables and puff their cigars, before deciding that they should 'join the ladies'.

Something like universal male suffrage for Parliamentary elections had been won in 1884. Although this in itself could not immediately break down the class patterns of Victorian England, yet slowly they were to change, and the turning point was possibly the collapse of the Conservative government in December 1905.

Party political background to 1905

The middle years of Victoria's reign had seen the emergence of the modern two-party system. With the election of 1868, two highly organized, heavily financed and brilliantly led parties faced each other: Gladstone's Liberals and Disraeli's Conservatives. In the previous year all town householders had won the vote and in 1884 rural householders were to do so as well. With their two opposed leaders and wide public interest in Parliamentary debates, these were the classical years for the House of Commons. In 1880 Disraeli was defeated in a general election and he died the next year, Lord Salisbury becoming the leader of the Conservative Party. In 1886 the Liberal Party was split over the issue of Home Rule for Ireland. A rebel group, who wished to stand by the Act of Union, formed a splinter-party, the Liberal-Unionists, under the great radical Joseph Chamberlain. By 1895 this group had become affiliated to the Conservative Party and as Colonial Secretary, whose responsibility included South Africa, their leader was one of the most powerful members of the Conservative/Unionist cabinet formed in that year. Thus the Conservatives had absorbed a group which stood for improved social conditions at home and forceful imperialism abroad. For two decades they were uncompromisingly wedded to a policy of maintaining Catholic Ireland within the United Kingdom, whatever the cost.

This Conservative government 1895–1902 fought and won the Second Boer War in the years 1899–1902 and, soon after the Peace of Vereeniging, Lord Salisbury resigned as Prime Minister. He handed over to his nephew A. J. Balfour, whose government fell in December 1905.

Other parties, apart from the giants, existed at this time. There were two small groups representing Labour and there were eighty-two Irish Nationalists who were dedicated to Home Rule for Ireland. Both these will be discussed at greater length later.

Reasons for Liberal victory

The results of the election in 1906 were as follows: 377 Liberal; 157 Conservative/Unionist; 83 Irish Nationalist; 29 Labour Representation Committee, which became the Labour Party; and 24 'Lib-Labs', miners and other independents who supported the Liberals. How can we explain the swing of the electorate, which, after ten years of Conservative rule under Salisbury and A. J. Balfour, had swung back so strongly to Liberalism?

The most important and immediate cause was undoubtedly a difference of opinion within the Conservative ranks between the followers of Free Trade (an accepted doctrine of both parties since the 1860's), and a revived protectionist group, led by Joseph Chamberlain.

Protection v. Free Trade

In 1903 Chamberlain had resigned from the government of Mr Balfour and formed a Tariff Reform League. He did this in the first instance because of his concern over imperial trade. He had been convinced by the Fourth Colonial Conference in 1902 that Free Trade would no longer work in an Empire whose members sought protection for their own young industries in Canada, Australia, South Africa and New Zealand. To help her colonies Britain should therefore introduce some system of imperial preference. At the same time such a system would protect those British industries which were suffering from the competition of America and Germany. The great industries of iron and steel, coal and cotton, were not yet involved, but much secondary industry was, and Chamberlain's scheme won the support of many British manufacturers who claimed their industries were dying. By it primary products from the Empire would be free of tariff, but a large tariff wall would be erected for other goods and the income obtained would be made available to finance social reforms and naval expansion. In this way direct taxation could be kept down while two causes (the Empire and social welfare) dear to Chamberlain's heart would be financed. Many Conservatives and more Liberals

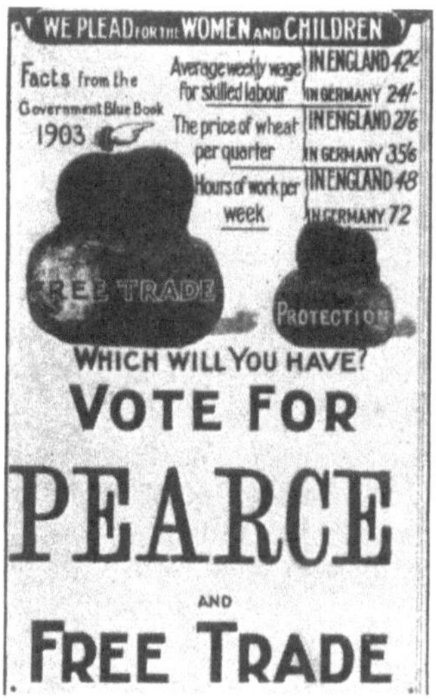

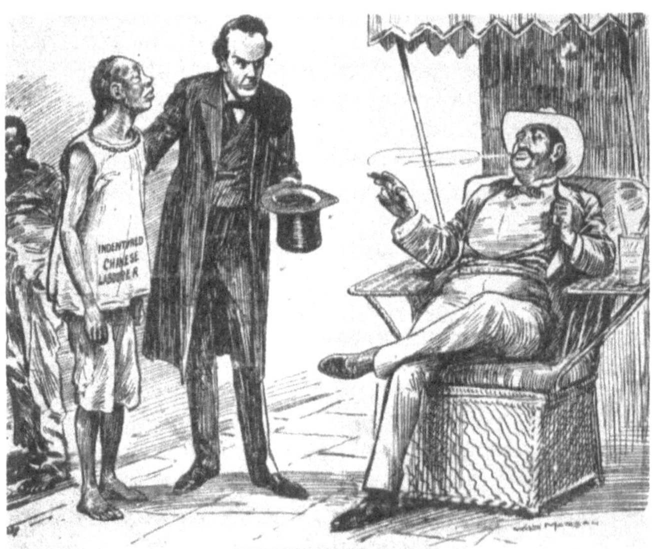

THE RANDLORD'S AGENT.

1906 election hand-bills

argued, however, that the scheme was no more than big business trying to increase, or at least preserve, its profits, at the price of a rise in the cost of living for the working man. Winston Churchill was among those who at this time changed his party, Conservative to Liberal, for this reason. Chamberlain's scheme was put forward in private opposition to the government, and when Balfour resigned in December 1905 the Liberals might possibly have won the election on this issue of Free Trade alone. Other reasons, however, helped to make the victory a landslide.

Imperialism

Britain had recently acquired huge tracts of Africa. Yet an increasing number of voters were swinging away from the crudely aggressive imperialism of the last years of the nineteenth century and in 1905 there was very strong feeling in Labour circles over a government scheme to ship Chinese labour to work in the South African mines. Some 67,000 of these unfortunates were placed at the disposal of mine-owners in 1904–1905 for work exclusively underground in terrible conditions. British organized Labour was shocked at what it called 'Chinese slavery' and the issue certainly seems to have contributed to Balfour's failure to win the election.

House of Lords and democracy

Another issue being debated was how complete should democracy itself be? Should the elected representatives of the people in the House of Commons have supreme power, or should they be checked, if not by the crown, by an hereditary aristocracy of 'elder statesmen'? The Liberals believed in making the doorway to power open to all and opposed the Conservative policy of resisting complete democracy.

Social reform

The social conscience of the country had recently been stirred by revelations of the conditions which still existed among perhaps a third of the population, especially in the slums of the great cities. Victorian humanitarianism had done a very great deal: in the mines, in the factories and in the slums. But an enormous amount remained to be done. Between 1892 and 1903 Charles Booth had published his seventeen-volume book *Life and Labour of the People of London* and its effect had been profound. In the same years General William Booth's Salvation Army was making inroads into the underworld, which had now been revealed,

A Salvation Army meeting, London, 1906

and in 1905 G. B. Shaw published his Salvation Army play *Major Barbara*. He was one of the greatest members of the Fabian Society, which for twenty years had been seeking reform by stirring up public opinion and thus exerting pressure on government. The rich were apparently getting richer in these halcyon days of Edwardian prosperity, but were the poor not getting poorer? asked the Fabians, as prices rose faster than wages. If so who was responsible? The poor themselves or society? These questions Shaw discusses in *Major Barbara*.

The state and the individual

Another question which the Fabians asked themselves was how far ought the power and influence of the state to be extended over the life of the individual? Ever since Mr Gladstone's ministry of 1868–1874 it had been extending its powers in various fields 'for the greatest good of the greatest number'. Even before this, government had begun to interfere between factory-owners and their employees, between mining companies and miners, for the welfare of those employed, factory inspectors having been first appointed in 1833. But now the question was, should there be a limit to this sort of activity? Or is the state morally bound to maintain to the maximum possible extent the welfare of its inhabitants, both when at work and also when they are incapacitated, through infancy, sickness, unemployment or old age? If the answer to these latter questions is yes, then how should this be financed? What methods of taxation, by which the state takes back for its use the earnings of an individual, are justifiable?

Socialism

These last questions tend today to be connected particularly with socialism. We have already mentioned the influence of the Fabians, a society founded by a group of young and brilliant intellectuals in 1884 for 'the advancement of socialism by democratic means'. Among the early members were G. B. Shaw, Sidney Webb, Graham Wallas and H. G. Wells. At the same time, in the 1880's, working-class socialism had begun, with such groups as the Social Democratic Federation to which belonged the old Etonian H. M. Hyndman. Nevertheless the word socialism remained a rude one for all Conservative and many Liberal Englishmen, conjuring up visions of cloak-and-dagger anarchists and revolutionaries, for whom in 1848 Karl Marx had written his famous *Communist Manifesto*. In actual fact the majority of the self-educated and earnest members of the British Labour groups at this time could have hardly been further from revolution, with their solid nonconformist backgrounds and their sincere patriotism, even though some of their leaders may have sought revolution through violence. Only after the mass sacrifices of the First World War was English middle-class opinion gradually to realize this.

The Labour Party

The great dock strike of 1889 had been something more than just an industrial dispute. It had shown what might be politically possible, given the continued co-operation between the brains of a handful of devoted intellectuals and the votes of the workers. In 1893 Keir Hardie founded the Independent Labour Party and during seven years it campaigned solidly among the unions, which were rapidly developing. Yet its success was limited and in 1900 the Labour Representation Committee was founded. It was less rigid and doctrinaire than the I.L.P., its aim being limited 'to establishing a Labour Group in Parliament'. Its finances were to come from the Trade Unions: 10*s* per 1000 members. Its membership was deliberately drawn from both intellectuals and working-men, Fabians and Trade Unionists. Its first secretary was J. Ramsay MacDonald, later Prime Minister in 1924 and 1929–1935. In 1906, when it won twenty-nine seats, it changed its name to the Labour Party.

The foundations of the Welfare State 1868–1880

The first great Liberal ministry of Mr Gladstone had come to office in 1868 and had laid many important foundations. Primary education became universal; the ancient and cumbersome legal system was reformed and its many courts amalgamated and rehoused; important army reforms took place and the modern civil service was created. The Conservatives under Disraeli (1874–1880) had an equally impressive record, particularly in extending the power of the state in various social matters: giving further protection to trade unions; giving municipal authorities powers over housing; protecting the consumer against chemicals in food and drink; making some effort to conserve the remaining common lands; interfering to protect the merchant seamen against exploitation; further extending the body of law concerning public health and further regulating factory conditions.

Decline of the family

Before the nineteenth century the family (grandparents, parents, children, numerous cousins and 'connections') was the essential social unit. The state was personified in the

Providence Place, Middlesex Street, London, 1908

monarch, but he had very considerable restrictions on his activities. It was the family which educated its children, looked after the sick and gave a home to the aged. Heads of families in the seventeenth century and earlier would have regarded it as an intolerable interference in their liberties if government had claimed rights here. But this was in an essentially rural England. With the growth of the factory and the extension of commerce (and we must remember that in the early days factory and office hours were often over twelve hours a day for a six-day week); with the appearance of the town tenements in sprawling, insanitary and overcrowded conditions; or, higher up the social scale, with the appearance of the semi-detached villa dedicated to respectability, but unable to house a large family; with these social changes crisis was imminent. A patriarchal rural society having given way to a modern industrial and urban one, a new social system had to be created. It is this which was realized with increasing clarity by these early architects of the Welfare State in the last years of the nineteenth century.

Education

One of the ideas behind the new concept of the state as it was emerging is that the education of the next generation is basically a responsibility not of the parent, who may be both unable to afford to buy it and unable to give it to his children himself, but of the state. Of course, there were opponents of this idea. They feared indoctrination and they disagreed violently over the question of religion. Before 1870 most education, which was not self-education or which was not bought at one of the exclusive preparatory and public schools, had been provided by the churches. But with the pressure of population the latter were increasingly inadequate, and by 1868 the idea of some system of state education was broadly accepted by both parties. The basis of our present system of state education was then laid by a series of important acts. In 1870 the Liberal W. E. Forster introduced a Bill providing for public elementary schools run by elected School Boards in places where voluntary (church-provided) schools did not exist already. Attendance at elementary school was made compulsory up to thirteen by two Acts passed in 1876 and 1880; parents would be free to contract out of religious instruction for their children and parents unable to afford fees would receive assistance. In 1891 fees were abolished by Salisbury's Conservative government.

In 1902 came a second great Act, the Balfour Act, passed again by a Conservative government. Both board schools and voluntary schools were placed under Local Education Authorities, responsible to the newly created County Councils, with financial support for both. By preserving this 'dual system' the Act was unpopular, since many people did not see why church-provided schools should be supported by public funds, and this unpopularity contributed to the Conservative defeat in 1906. Secondly this Act gave the power and indeed the duty to County Councils and County Boroughs to draw up schemes for secondary schools and found new ones where necessary, where existing grammar schools were inadequate. Many of the latter were to receive financial aid in return for providing a percentage of their places to scholars from the elementary schools. But for most children a grammar school still cost money and it was not until 1944 that free secondary education was to be offered by the state to all children.

Sickness

So much for the children, what of the sick? There had long existed various forms of Friendly Society and private insurance schemes, whereby a man could receive financial aid to defray medical expenses. In 1897 there had been passed the Workman's Compensation Act, by which an employee could obtain compensation for injury at work without having to prove negligence by his employer. But insurance against illness was the exception rather than the rule. Fear of illness, its costs and the possible dismissal from work which might result remained to haunt British working families until Lloyd George and later legislation.

Old age

As with sickness, so with old age; the state as yet took no responsibility. If a man had failed to provide for his old age, and his family either refused help or could not give it, he might find private charity coming to his aid. There were many ancient foundations of alms-houses and some modern ones, many of which still in our own time provide homes for old people. In 1892 Charles Booth had suggested one possible state old-age pension scheme, on the lines of that introduced by Bismarck in Germany. In 1895 Joseph Chamberlain had promoted a Royal Commission to investigate the problem and in 1900 a select committee of the House of Commons had recommended adopting a scheme similar to one introduced by New Zealand in 1898. The Liberals promised in 1906 to adopt the recommendations of this committee, if elected.

Poor Law and unemployment

For the unemployed there were the workhouses. In 1834 the Elizabethan system of outdoor poor relief provided by parishes had been replaced by a system of workhouses based on groups of parishes, whereby the inmates should receive a bare minimum of relief for a maximum of work. Life in such institutions was to be deliberately so unpleasant that the inmate would do his best to get out and into a job. This Poor Law system represents one of the more inhumane sides of life in Victorian times and had been under steady attack by the Fabian Society and others for a quarter of a century. It was not going to be altered much by the Liberals but would be partly superseded by the old-age pension and national insurance schemes. The underlying assumption that somehow it was immoral to be poor and unemployed was, however, gradually to disappear.

Measures for education, sickness, old age and unemployment represent one side of the Welfare State. Another is the state's action as arbitrator in certain human relationships, where the scales seem unduly weighted in one direction.

Slum clearance

It was the Conservative government of Disraeli which in 1875 had first recognized that government on occasions may have to interfere in the relations between landlord and tenant, on behalf of the latter. Many of the tenement houses which had been provided by private speculators for the new industrial towns and suburbs earlier in the century were in an appalling condition. Many had not received a coat of paint since they were built and few had more than one running-water tap per street. Yet before 1875 even a go-ahead city or town corporation was powerless to enforce improvements on landlords. Some of the necessary powers were first given by two Acts: the Artisans Dwellings Act of 1875 and the Public Health Act of 1876. This completed what the Public Health Act of 1848 had begun and laid the foundations of public health work which we have inherited. By 1900 many cities, led by Birmingham, had made enormous advances. Some of the worst slums were cleared, and public baths, public libraries and public parks were provided. The process was assisted by great reforms in local government, the Act of 1888 having created the system of County Council government, including the London County Council, and County Boroughs. Once such new units for local administration existed, far greater control by government of the living conditions of the people became possible.

Trade unions

Another relationship which was also causing strong feeling in the early years of the twentieth century was that of employer and employee. Since 1824 trade unions had been legal bodies, but their powers had at first been very limited. In 1871 the Liberal government had passed the Trade Union Act, which had placed beyond doubt, it was thought, their legal status as corporations, with powers to hold corporate property and to sue and be sued in the courts. But in the same year the Criminal Law Amendment Act made peaceful picketing during a strike illegal, thus greatly reducing the effectiveness of strikes, particularly in unions of unskilled or semi-skilled labour, which is easily replaceable. This was reversed in 1875 by Richard Cross's Conspiracy and Protection of Property Act, and a great development of unskilled and semi-skilled unions now took place. As a result, there were many strikes, the most successful being that of the London dockers in 1889. In 1901 occurred a famous legal case, the Taff Vale Case. This was a judgment in the House of Lords for the Taff Vale Railway Company against a trade union, the Amalgamated Society of Railway Servants. The union was judged liable for damages to the value of £23,000 for strikes held in 1898. The unions would once more be at the mercy of the employers unless granted government protection. This was promised by the Liberals in 1905 and was to be granted in 1906 by the Trade Disputes Act.

Drunkenness

Yet another relationship, that of manufacturer or retailer with the consumer, was also in the last quarter of the nineteenth century to come under review: and in some ways this was to be the most controversial. Most were agreed that the state should intervene to prevent retailers from, for example, putting salt in the beer to make people drink more, or manufacturers from putting injurious colouring matter into processed foods. But where passions were aroused was over the question of drunkenness. Has the state the right to tell a man when he has had enough to drink? Or is this intolerable interference? Mr Gladstone himself, appalled at the incidence of drunkenness in London, initiated by the Licensing Act of 1872 a new system of licences for the sale of liquor and limited very slightly the hours of opening of public houses, but there was considerable opposition. A bishop called for 'England free rather than England sober' and there was some change of allegiance among brewers and distillers from the Liberal to the Conservative party. In 1904 a Licensing Act further reduced the number of licensed public houses, compensating persons whose licences were not renewed out of a fund levied on the entire trade, and transferred the issue of licences from special sessions to quarter sessions of J.P.s. This Act was an electoral liability, since the Liberals objected to the compensation provided.

Defence

In Europe, since the successful unification of Italy in 1860 and of Germany ten years later, there had been some important shifts of power. France in 1870–1871 had been brought crashing to the ground from her traditional place as the first land power, established by Louis XIV in the seventeenth century; the humiliation had been bitter. The two great powers of the Habsburg and Ottoman Empires were both beset with rising tides of nationalism. By 1900 the Turkish Empire had lost as independent or semi-independent states most of what had been European Turkey. At the same time a less easily definable factor continued to influence Central and Eastern Europe—the vaguer, semi-mystical force of pan-Slavism drawing the slavonic peoples towards their great neighbour, Mother Russia.

Britain in the 1880's and 1890's had tried to maintain a position of isolation. But far from being 'splendid', this could easily become dangerous. The Boer War had provoked strong feelings in Europe and had revealed Britain's weaknesses. The Conservative government of Lord Salisbury, therefore, at the turn of the century had embarked on a new policy of seeking friendships and at the same time a policy of naval expansion was begun. For a few years the Liberals were to reduce this latter as too expensive, while carrying out drastic and brilliant improvements to the army. Yet basically, on the question of foreign affairs and defence, there was no great difference between the two main parties. This was less true over imperialism, where the two topical questions were Ireland and South Africa.

Ireland

For centuries there had been an Irish problem, whose basic cause was the determination of Anglo-Saxon England to maintain some sort of control over her neighbouring Celtic island. By the eighteenth century a situation had arisen whereby Catholic Ireland was in the hands of a mostly Protestant land-owning class, who had a monopoly of political power, and whose Protestant Church was a privileged institution in a country of Roman Catholic peasants. The first half of the nineteenth century had seen the unpopular Act of Union in 1801 and the more popular Catholic

Emancipation Act of 1829, but strong currents of unrest had continued. In 1868 Mr Gladstone had proclaimed his mission to pacify Ireland. He duly disestablished the Irish Church and sought to curb the powers of the landlords. But by now even the moderates were demanding something more: the end of the Act of Union. In 1879 Charles Stewart Parnell had become leader of the Irish Nationalist Party, dedicated to this end, and by 1886 Mr Gladstone had come to accept its repeal as necessary; but his first Home Rule Bill had been defeated in the Commons in 1886 and his second in the House of Lords in 1893. Parnell, a moderate nationalist, was discredited over a divorce case in 1890 and was dead within a year. The long Conservative rule of 1895–1905 had reverted to the policy of a fair but firm paternalism. The Unionists believed in resolute government and under the Crimes Act of 1887 offences against law and order could be tried without a jury. At the same time they had made genuine attempts to ease the problem of land tenure by helping tenants to buy their farms. Two Acts had been passed in 1890 and 1891, and in 1903 George Wyndham's Land Purchase Act offered to lend £5,000,000 annually to a total of £180,000,000, to enable tenants to buy their farms from compensated and therefore willing landlords at an annual redemption of only 3¼%. Five years earlier, by an Act of 1898, Ireland had been given a system of local government based on County Councils similar to that introduced for England, Wales and Scotland in 1888. Thus the policy of resolute government had gradually been eased to one of 'kill home rule by kindness'. The French Liberal historian Halévy relates how when travelling up and down Ireland in 1903 he discovered a remarkable contentment prevailing everywhere, and he noted the warm welcome given to Edward VII when he visited the country in August of that year. It is not altogether surprising, therefore, that even among Liberals in 1906 by no means a majority was in favour of Home Rule, let alone independence. As we shall see, at first the Liberal government did little to alter the Irish situation, possibly because it knew that without reducing the power of the House of Lords nothing could be done. Only after this had been done, and when the government depended for survival on the votes of the Irish Nationalists, was a Third Home Rule Bill to be introduced.

South Africa

The Boer War, which began as a minor episode and went on to cost £250,000,000 and the lives of 22,000 British troops, had been opposed by a section of the Liberal Party in Parliament and by liberal opinion in the country. At the peace of Vereeniging promises of self-government had been made to the Boers. By 1906 £3,000,000 to restock Boer farms had been paid out, but little had been done to implement these political promises, possibly because of the imperial government's distrust of the Boer or Afrikaaner attitude towards native rights. But the Liberal Party was determined to end this situation and implement the peace of 1902. It is a tragedy of today that they were to do so at the cost of the rights of the black African, whom British missionaries had for three-quarters of a century been doing their best to protect. On other imperial questions the Liberals were content to inherit the greatest empire since that of Rome, and only a minority even of radical opinion questioned the fundamental ideas behind it. For a good Liberal, believing as he did in the superiority of his own civilization to that of 'native' and 'barbarian' races, it went without saying that for the backward and coloured peoples of the world nothing but good could come from their membership of the British Empire.

Suffragettes

The last question which was catching the attention of the press and of the man-in-the-street in the years preceding the election of 1906 was that of the franchise. The year 1884 had seen the electorate extended to include about four-fifths of the male citizens of the country, but no females. In the later years of the nineteenth century an increasing number of girls' schools were founded and the universities were opened to girls. The demand for a vote inevitably followed. In 1903 Mrs Emmeline Pankhurst and her daughter Christabel founded the Women's Social and Political Union, which was pledged to win the suffrage for women. They began by heckling and interrupting at political meetings, and in 1906 they were about to extend these activities to more violent methods. The question cut across party lines, only a handful of Liberals supporting their demands. The majority in all parties thought the whole question monstrous and absurd. It would take the war of 1914–1918 to swing male opinion over to accept the political equality of women.

Social patterns

In 1906 the whole of the front pages of such newspapers as *The Times* and the *Daily Mail* were devoted to advertising, as well as much space inside: processed foods such as cocoa, soups, teas, jams and tinned fruits; patent medicines such as Beecham's Pills ('Health restored without medicine or expense' or 'Don't grow old . . . etc.'); tobaccos and cigarettes (the habit of cigarette-smoking by men was ex-

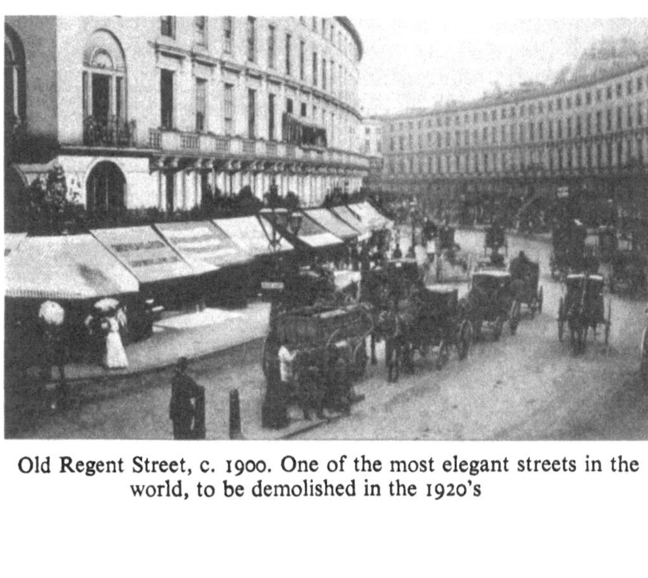

Old Regent Street, c. 1900. One of the most elegant streets in the world, to be demolished in the 1920's panding rapidly); and, above all, the new London department stores such as Selfridges, Swan and Edgar, Derry and Toms, and the Hackney Furnishing Company, which actually offered free luncheons to patrons as well as transport to and from the railway station. There is no doubt that the processes of mass-production and packaging behind these stores were of the greatest importance in determining the pattern of living which was to develop during the twentieth century. The historian Sir Robert Ensor described the Edwardian era as a 'seething and teeming' period of 'immense ferment' and 'restless fertility'. It was a time of remarkably rapid technical change which was being translated into daily economic and social life at a quicker rate than ever before. For the fox-hunting upper classes it seemed an age of calm prosperity, but for the urban middle classes it was an age of great social changes, while for the submerged millions it was an age of hope, made possible by the advances in technology.

In 1901 Seebohm Rowntree estimated that no less than 27·84% of the total population was living below a subsistence level which would satisfy bare physical needs, and this may have actually increased before 1914, owing to prices rising faster than wages. It was the advances in technology which were to enable this figure eventually to shrink. One factor was to be cheaper and more effective transport: the spread of trams, motor-buses and underground trains meant that cities could extend their suburbs and thus ease the appalling overcrowding in their central slums. This would help a nation, which had had 34·5% of its applicants for army service rejected on medical grounds in the decade 1893–1902, to begin to raise its standards of health.

Technological changes

(i) *The motor-car.* The first internal-combustion engines had been developed in Germany by Drs Otto and Rudolf Diesel. They used unrefined oil and were very heavy, but in 1884 Gottfried Daimler patented his lighter engine, which was then developed by German and French firms. In 1895 the first motor exhibition was held in London, and Britain became interested in the new means of transport. In 1896 fifty-four mechanically propelled vehicles took part in the first London to Brighton race. By 1910 the first standardized petrol-driven omnibus had appeared in the streets of London. The roads of England which had declined since the great days of the stage-coach were greatly improved, especially after the passing of the 1909 budget which provided for them. Bitumen rapidly replaced the dustier road surfaces of the nineteenth century and the roads of Britain became the best surfaced of any in the world. A revolution in transport had begun which after the war was to challenge the position of the railways. But up to 1914, to own a car was the exception; it was very expensive and was regarded by many as a symbol of the 'selfishness of arrogant wealth'.

(ii) *Electricity in transport.* At the same time electricity was being used to develop transport. Leeds was the first big city to electrify her tramways in 1891; the horse-trams gave way to electricity, just as the horse-buses were to give way to motors. Bristol, Plymouth, Glasgow and London quickly followed. In 1901 the Metropolitan District Electric Traction Company was registered, to electrify the already existing Metropolitan District Underground railway. This was rapidly to develop and expand during the years 1902–1914, becoming the Underground Electric Railway Company of London and absorbing all rivals. The turbine for generating electricity for driving a ship had been invented by Sir Charles Parsons in 1884, at first powered by coal and later by oil.

(iii) *Aircraft.* In 1905 an internal combustion engine was successfully applied to a flying machine. In America the Wright brothers flew twenty-four and a half miles in half an hour. In France and Germany the military potential of this new development was quickly grasped. The Channel was first flown by Blériot on 25 July 1909; by 1914 both countries had aircraft available for artillery spotting purposes, Germany having developed them as part of naval

Maurice Farman Longhorn, used by RFC on its formation in 1912

gunnery. In Britain a party of young officers at the War Office was strongly urging the development of this machine and the Royal Flying Corps had been founded in 1912. The commercial potential of the aeroplane was largely ignored until after the war.

(iv) *Communications.* The electric telegraph had been developed in the days of the Crimean War, the first practical version having been produced in 1837 by Cooke and Wheatstone. In 1876 Graham Bell in America sent his first telephone message. But far more important for the future was the development of radio. Marconi in 1901 transmitted the letter 'S' in Morse across the Atlantic from Cornwall to Newfoundland. Wireless telegraphy began to replace cable, all British ships being quickly equipped, so that means of keeping in touch while at sea were revolutionized. But commercial exploitation of this fantastic discovery as a means of mass communication and entertainment was not to come until the 1920's.

2

The Liberal achievement 1906–1911

Newcastle programme 1891

The year before the general election of 1892 the Liberal Party (now shorn of Joseph Chamberlain) had adopted an election programme at a party conference in Newcastle. Naturally Home Rule for Ireland had dominated this programme, but other items had included the disestablishment of the Church in Wales, further control over the sale of intoxicating liquor, one man one vote, triennial parliaments, further local government reform, an employer's liability Act and vague promises to limit working hours and to pay M.P.s a salary. Some of these items were in fact effected by the Liberal government 1892–1895, for example the Parish Councils Act 1894, though many had been vetoed by the House of Lords, for example an Employers' Liability Bill. A Conservative alternative to this latter had been passed in 1897, but in 1906 most of the other aims of the Newcastle programme remained unrealized.

There were two immediate and pressing questions: first the failure of the Conservatives to introduce an Old Age Pensions Scheme and secondly the Taff Vale decision of the House of Lords which had paralysed the trade unions. The Liberal Party had promised in the election to redress both these grievances at the first opportunity.

The cabinet

The new Prime Minister, Sir Henry Campbell-Bannerman, had available for his cabinet some very able men, nearly all of whom were men of wealth. Many were men of high ideals, such as R. B. Haldane, the Secretary for War. Two ministers only came from a background other than upper middle class. They were John Burns, President of the Local Government Board, and Lloyd George, President of the Board of Trade. Burns was a self-educated trade unionist from Glasgow, who had been prominent as an organizer of the great London dock strike in 1889 and as an early member of the Social Democratic Federation. He was to resign at the outbreak of war in 1914. Lloyd George, a much more formidable figure, had been educated in a Welsh elementary school and articled to a solicitor at sixteen. He had first entered Parliament in 1890, aged twenty-seven, and was probably the most powerful personality of this cabinet.

Early achievements

First in importance came the Trade Disputes Act of 1906. A Royal Commission in 1903 had recommended legislation and the government lawyers in 1906 drew up one Bill and the Labour M.P.s drew up another. The former was in places unintelligible to all but trained lawyers, and the government accepted the Labour Bill, which duly became law. Trade unions would no longer be financially responsible to employers for losses incurred during a strike. In the same year Lloyd George introduced a Merchant Shipping Bill, which laid down minimum conditions of food and accommodation for all ships flying the Red Ensign and also certain regulations for any ship using British harbour facilities. Next he was responsible for preparing, although not for actually steering through Parliament, an important Act for the setting up of the Port of London Authority. Also in 1906 the Workmen's Compensation Act of 1897 was extended to cover a much wider field of industry and trade including industrial diseases.

House of Lords and its veto

These early Acts were largely uncontroversial and had not been challenged by the House of Lords. But when attempts were made to realize other aspects of the Liberal platform trouble threatened. In 1906 an Education Bill which tried to remove some of the grievances of the nonconformists against the Education Act of 1902 was defeated in the Lords after a clear Commons majority; so was a Plural Voting Bill (one man one vote). In 1907 no less than four land-reform Bills, i.e. a smallholdings Bill, an evicted tenants Bill for Ireland and two Bills for Scotland, were all vetoed by the Lords.

Asquith as Prime Minister

Early in 1908 Campbell-Bannerman retired through ill-health and within a month he died. Edward VII at the time was in Biarritz and, without reference to the Liberal Party, he summoned H. H. Asquith to kiss hands as Prime Minister. Asquith was a shrewd Yorkshire lawyer who had risen to the top of his party partly through a brilliant marriage and partly through great skill in debate. Sir Robert Ensor said of him: 'From the first to the last year of his premiership he was a giant of the Commons' debates.' But behind the doors of Downing Street he was something more: a master of tact and ability in the handling of a cabinet of brilliant egotists. Lloyd George moved to be Chancellor of the Exchequer; R. B. Haldane continued his work at the War Office; Walter Runciman became President of the Board of Education and Winston Churchill President of the Board of Trade. Sir Edward Grey continued as Foreign Secretary.

Renewed veto from the Lords

The first year of Asquith's government saw a renewed clash with the House of Lords and growing government unpopularity in the country owing to a trade depression.In the budget for 1908, which Asquith had prepared and himself introduced, old-age pensions were at last provided for. To single persons over seventy earning less than 10*s* p er week, a pension of 5*s* was to be paid. To a married couple it would be 7*s* 6*d*. The House of Lords challenged the proposal, but withdrew on an assertion of privilege from the Commons. The pensions were to begin on 1 January 1909. The main domestic measure apart from this was a licensing Bill. We mentioned in the last chapter Mr Gladstone's attempt in 1872 to grapple with the problem of drunkenness in British cities, but it remained a terrible evil, which it is almost impossible now to envisage. This Bill set out to reduce further the hours of business and numbers of licensed premises. It passed the Commons, but was defeated by the Lords. There was less popular approval of their action than their Lordships expected.

Other early legislation

In 1906 the Labour Members of Parliament introduced a Bill to enable local education authorities to provide meals

Mass drill in Gopsall Street School, 1906

for poor school-children, and this became law. In 1907 the President of the Board of Education obtained an Education Act which made it the duty of education authorities to have their children medically inspected. These two Acts resulted in a vast improvement in the medical health of school-children in Great Britain, partly as a result of the brilliant work of Dr (later Sir George) Newman at the Board of Education, who encouraged school Care Committees to develop medical treatment services following medical inspection. Another important piece of social legislation was the bringing into being of a scheme, recommended by a Liberal committee in 1894, for some segregation of young criminals, to prevent them from 'recruiting the criminal class'. A Prevention of Crimes Act was passed under which a Borstal system for both boys and girls was to come into effect from August 1909. At the same time Probation Courts were set up.

The naval scare

In 1906 H.M.S. *Dreadnought* had been launched according to a programme of naval development laid down by the First Lord of the Admiralty of the Conservative government, Lord Cawdor. Battleships of this calibre would put all others into the second class, owing to their increased speed and armament. But their cost was formidable and during their first two years the Liberals had abandoned much of the expansion programme of Lord Cawdor and Sir John Fisher, the First Sea Lord. Economy was not the only motive. The Liberals hoped to persuade other powers, for example Germany and the U.S.A., to participate in active disarmament at a conference held at The Hague in 1907. But in 1908 there began a crisis in the Balkans and the eastern Mediterranean which was to prove more or less continuous until 1914. In 1905 Admiral Tirpitz in Germany had laid down four dreadnought-class ships to Britain's two, and in 1909 he proposed another four. This caused something of a panic. Reginald McKenna, First Lord of the Admiralty, replied by asking Parliament for six dreadnoughts in his 1909 estimates. Public opinion was dissatisfied. A music-hall song demanded: 'We want eight and we won't wait', and eight dreadnoughts were in fact proposed. These would cost something over £15,000,000. Thus the return of the Liberals to the Fisher-Cawdor programme could mean a financial crisis, but over an issue which was intensely popular, since public opinion was acutely sensitive to Britain's navy having pride of place.

The People's Budget and the Parliament Bill

This was the background for the most famous of all budgets: that introduced by Lloyd George for 1909. To pay for two highly popular measures, old-age pensions and naval expansion, the Chancellor introduced a number of tax innovations which between them produced a deep political crisis.

The first innovation was a motor-car licence. English roads were good, but intolerably dusty and in need of quick repair and maintenance to stand up to the growing motor traffic. There was little to fight over here. Another proposal was the allocation of £100,000 from the budget towards the setting up of a national system of Labour Exchanges. £200,000 a year was to be spent on the preservation of nature reserves and natural resources. Children's allowances were to be introduced into income-tax assessment. These proposals were not violently controversial.

The main sources of new revenue were to come from increases in current taxation and some new taxes. Increases included raising income tax from 1*s* to 1*s* 2*d*; higher death duties on estates between £5000 and £1,000,000; higher taxes on tobacco and spirits; increased costs for liquor licences. Two controversial innovations were proposed. The first was the introduction of supertax on incomes over £3000, a modest tax aimed to produce some £500,000. The second was a land-value duty to be paid by all land-owners. It was these which caused such violent feeling. The Conservative Party strongly opposed the proposals. Tariff-reform advocates realized that if they were successful, one of their main arguments (tariffs as an additional source of income) would be lost.

The unwritten convention of the British Constitution was that money Bills were not touched by the House of Lords. Up to now what this government had lacked was a popular cause and now they had one. Lloyd George had successfully manœuvred the Lords into the position where they appeared as a party of angry rich men trying to dodge their share of the nation's expenses, particularly at a time of popular naval rearmament.

The Conservative Party formed a Budget Protest League and the ladies of the party rallied to the cause. Lloyd George replied by a series of brilliant speeches all over the country, the most famous being perhaps that at Limehouse, which passed into legend and in which he ridiculed the Lords and their out-of-date claims for privilege.

Trade Boards Bill

Meanwhile during the year, while the temper of the nation grew warmer over the issue of the budget, his successor at the Board of Trade, Winston Churchill, successfully introduced his Trade Boards Bill against sweated industries. This Act marked the culmination of over ten years' agitation, led by Sir Charles Dilke and others, against appalling conditions of work among urban non-factory workers. The original Act applied to only four industries: tailoring, paper-box making, lace- and net-making and chain-making. But it was to be widely extended and was to do much towards ending the term 'sweated' in industry, as these Boards enforced minimum standards and wages.

The Budget resumed

By November 1909 the budget had reached the Lords. King Edward advised that they accept it, however bitter the pill. But it was rejected on 30 November by 350 votes to 75. Stalemate had been reached and a January election was necessary. The issue was not so much the budget itself as the question of the Lords' position in the Constitution. For almost twenty years they had been delaying or vetoing legislation which had a majority of votes in the Commons. For how long should an hereditary house retain this power? For the first time peers themselves were allowed actively to take part in campaigns for the election.

The result was a Liberal victory but no triumph. The figures were Liberal 275; Labour 40; Irish Nationalist 82 and Conservative/Unionist 273. Thus in this Parliament, unlike the last, the Liberals would depend on Irish and Labour votes.

If the Lords continued to veto the budget what then? King Edward had told Asquith that he would not follow the 1832 precedent (when William IV had agreed to create the necessary Whig peers) without a second general election on this specific issue. But this was not publicly known. Three resolutions were now presented to the House of Commons: the first concerned money Bills, the second other Bills and the third proposed that Parliament's life be reduced from seven years to five. All successfully passed the Commons by 14 April 1910 and were incorporated into a general Parliament Bill which now received a first reading. On 27 April the budget passed the new House of Commons and the next day it quietly passed through the Lords. But they were not to be spared, for the Parliament Bill was coming up to them. It would bring their status as an equal partner in the Constitution to an end.

Suddenly on 6 May King Edward died. Sir Robert Ensor said of his reign:

'Personal memories of Edward VII have transferred to it [his reign] something of the king's own character and atmosphere. Men think of the decade as one of calm and contentment, of pomp and luxury, of assured wealth and unchallenged order. Court splendours apart, it was none of these things. It was an era of growth and strain, of idealism and reaction, of swelling changes and seething unrest. At home politics had never been so bitter; abroad the clouds were massing for Armageddon.'

He was succeeded by his son, George V, whose reign was

to see both the greatest war the world had yet imagined and also the development of those new forces of radicalism and idealism which had already broken the surface calm of Edwardian England.

The Parliament Bill, which the Commons had already read once, proposed first that the House of Lords should lose all power of amending or rejecting money Bills; secondly, that any other Bill which passed the Commons in three successive sessions should become law irrespective of the Lords; thirdly that Parliamentary elections should occur at least once in five years, instead of seven.

King George's first action was to call a round-table conference: four members from each main party to meet at Downing Street. This conference held twenty-one sittings from June to November 1910. What in fact apparently baulked it finally was not so much the Parliament Bill itself as the Unionist determination to block Irish Home Rule which was now once more an issue. The conference having failed, Asquith dissolved Parliament and called for another election. The Conservatives fought it almost entirely on Home Rule. They called Redmond, Parnell's somewhat milder successor, 'the dollar dictator' because of his support from Irish Americans. The election was very close, the figures being Liberals 272, Labour 42, Irish 84, Conservative/Unionist 272.

The King opened Parliament in February 1911. Already the Liberals had their list of proposed new peers and he had agreed to the principle that it might be necessary to create them. The Parliament Bill came into the Lords in May and they returned it to the Commons in July heavily amended. Lloyd George, on behalf of the Government, now privately told Balfour and Lord Lansdowne of the King's agreement to create if necessary up to 400 new peers. The die-hard Unionists in the Commons staged violent scenes against the Prime Minister, but they knew that the game was up. The Commons rejected the Lords' amendments and in August the upper House reluctantly accepted the inevitable, many Lords abstaining. The final figures were only 131 to 114.

Britain had taken a decisive step towards becoming a fully representative democracy. The Liberal House of Commons had triumphed but the high tide of Liberalism itself had passed. Never again was the Liberal Party to win a general election. A new party pattern was about to develop: Tory democracy against some form of socialism. The Lords had fought unsuccessfully against what Oliver Cromwell had called an 'omnipotent House of Commons, the horridest arbitrariness that ever existed in the world', and their political significance was steadily to decline after their great defeat. Whatever one feels about the merit of a 'second House' in a Constitution, one might agree with Lloyd George that through its selfish attitude to his budget the British House of Lords forfeited its place in the Constitution and thus virtually committed political suicide.

Haldane's army reforms

The British tradition was a naval tradition. Only very reluctantly has a large professional army been tolerated. Before Wellington and the Peninsular War such armies were usually very temporary creations of mercenaries raised for a particular emergency. After 1815 a permanent army remained, but it was financed on a shoe-string and always more inclined to refight the last war than prepare for the next. Thus in 1854 the Crimean War revealed an army hopelessly ill-equipped and ill-trained; its effect was to produce certain considerable reforms, but by no means enough. In 1870 the new German army showed the world the kind of military machine that could now be created and the British reaction was to allow Edward Cardwell to bring about further very necessary reforms in an army which, among other duties, had an increasing responsibility for law and order in an expanding colonial empire. But Cardwell's army had taken three years to win the Boer War. A committee on the conduct of the war reported in 1904 'gross inefficiency and corruption'. It recommended among other things ending the office of Commander-in-Chief and substituting instead an Army Council.

In 1906 R. B. Haldane became Secretary for War. He had been educated at Göttingen University and was a philosopher and scholar of some standing, having translated the German philosophers Hegel and Schopenhauer. He had a considerable liking for the German people and admiration for their tremendous achievements in the second half of the nineteenth century. In 1906 he was a guest of Kaiser Wilhelm II at German army manœuvres.

As War Secretary, Haldane had two aims: to create a more efficient army and to reduce its cost, his method being to adapt much that he had observed in the German army. Conscription, however, was not possible in England. It would cost too much and the English tradition was too firmly anti-military. The alternative was a Territorial Army built around the nucleus of the Regular Army. This must be as efficient and as highly trained as possible. Behind it there should be reserves, which would be supplied both by the Territorial Army and the Officers' Training Corps. Haldane introduced his Territorial and Reserve Forces Bill

Recruiting for Haldane's army on the outbreak of war in 1914

in 1907, by which the old yeomanry and volunteer units were to be transformed into the Territorial Force of fourteen infantry divisions and fourteen mounted brigades, with their own transport and medical services, all available as a reserve. They would train one night a week and at an annual camp. The regular forces would remain on a basis of linked battalions: at home and overseas. But the home force would be organized into a potential expeditionary force of six infantry divisions, four cavalry brigades, full artillery, transport and medical units, which would make the force a self-contained spearhead in the event of an outbreak of hostilities. The old volunteer corps at the public and secondary schools was to be converted into a much more highly organized Officers' Training Corps. In Whitehall there was created an Army Council and General Staff along the lines of the German High Command. Haldane was able to make his reforms and still reduce the army estimates in the best tradition of Gladstonian Liberalism, and from 1905 to 1912 he watched over his creation. When mobilization came he was to urge the cabinet in vain to send all six regular divisions to France at once, as he had intended. Instead two were held in reserve. Because of his German connections he was to be excluded from office in May 1915, but lived to be the first Labour Lord Chancellor in 1924.

Naval expansion

In 1897 Admiral Tirpitz had become German Minister of Marine. Two years earlier, in 1895, the Kiel Canal had been opened, thus freeing the German navy from dependence on the Danish Sound. In 1898 a naval law had been passed providing for considerable naval expansion, i.e. 12 battleships, 10 large cruisers and 23 small cruisers in six years. A second law in 1900 doubled the rate of expansion. The British reaction to these laws, following the ending of the Boer War, was a vast scheme of expansion, put forward by Sir John Fisher, who became First Sea Lord in 1904, and who had earlier been responsible for advances in naval gunnery at Portsmouth.

Reference has already been made to this Fisher-Cawdor scheme. There was to be a new building programme dominated by two new classes: the Dreadnought battleship class and the Invincible battle-cruiser. H.M.S. *Dreadnought* of 17,000 tons was the heaviest steel battleship yet floated. She was the first battleship to be powered by steam turbines; her armament was of twelve-inch guns on revolving gun-turrets, which could fire from well out of range of anything submarine torpedoes could then approach. She was launched in 1906 and completed in 1907. There were to be four ships of her class laid down each year according to the programme. In addition, the fleets were to be reorganized and regrouped, concentrating in home waters. The home fleet was to consist of 6 battleships, 6 cruisers and 48 destroyers, with H.M.S. *Dreadnought* as flagship.

Germany's reaction to this scheme was a new naval law of 1906, which authorized a similar dreadnought class and the widening of the Kiel Canal to carry them, although the details of the British ships were still kept as close secrets. There followed the Liberal attempt in 1906–1908 to reduce the rate of expansion, which lost Britain two years and her clear lead in this struggle for naval supremacy. The reversal of policy in 1909 produced a neck-and-neck fight. The building programmes were stepped up on both sides, England gaining a rough lead of two to one in 1911 with no less than eighteen dreadnoughts laid down (to be ready by 1914) as against nine in Germany. In that year Winston Churchill became First Lord of the Admiralty. He was a great admirer of what Fisher, who had retired in 1910, had achieved. In 1913 H.M.S. *Queen Elizabeth* was laid down. She was to cost £3,000,000, with a displacement of 27,500 tons and a speed of twenty-five knots against the twenty-one knots of the first dreadnought. There were eight fifteen-inch guns which could fire seven-ton shells over a distance of eleven miles. Her turbines were oil-fired. Nevertheless the German development of the submarine was in fact to make such monsters almost useless when war did come.

In 1912 an agreement was made with France that her

fleets should concentrate on Mediterranean defence, while the British guarded the Channel, the North Sea and the Atlantic. By 1914 Britain had successfully maintained her numerical advantage, although in many ways the Germans were technically superior. We have just mentioned submarine development. Germany built up large supplies of mines while Britain had none. German gunnery and range-finding were more accurate and their shells more powerful. The German navy had developed aircraft for spotting purposes which the British had largely ignored. Lastly there was the question of power. Oil is 40% more efficient than coal; it enables a ship to refuel at sea; and it requires fewer men to operate it. Both navies now began to move over to it and there began the battle for the oil-fields of the world. Britain needed oil supplies both east and west of Suez. She looked to Mexico and the Caribbean for the latter and to Persia for the former. In 1914 Winston Churchill managed to obtain a Parliamentary Act to provide money to finance the Anglo-Persian Oil Company's acquisition of part of the oil-fields of Persia. Germany began seeking oil supplies in the Balkans and in the Turkish Empire. There could well develop a clash of interests between the two powers for control of Middle East oil supplies for their two expanding navies.

South Africa

This chapter will end with a brief look at the Liberal attempt to settle the South African problem. During the Boer War the British had invented the concentration camp. Thousands of Boer civilians had been shepherded into camps in order to break their resistance towards the British authorities, who, after their military victories in 1900, were trying to bring the country under control.

Terrible conditions had followed; not so much as a result of deliberate cruelty and atrocities as through sheer incompetence. Within fourteen months 20,177 inmates had died, including thousands of children. It was an Englishwoman, Miss Emily Hobhouse, backed by a relief committee, who had exposed the conditions to the world. In public the Conservative government had denied all knowledge, but in fact her work had led to great improvements being ordered by the Colonial Secretary, Joseph Chamberlain. The Liberal leader, Campbell-Bannerman, had forcefully attacked the government. Public opinion at home had at first aggressively supported Chamberlain, but the Liberal leader had won the respect of the Boers. It was said that his assertion that these were 'methods of barbarism' later made possible the Liberal attempt to implement the peace of Vereeniging. His first action in 1906 was to send a small commission to the Transvaal to investigate the possibility of self-government. Letters-patent were issued in December; an election was held and the Boer leaders Botha and Smuts came to power in the Transvaal. At the time Dr Jameson was Prime Minister of Cape Colony. He now put forward a memorandum proposing complete union of the four colonies. In 1907 the Orange River Colony once again acquired self-government. In October 1908 a convention comprising delegates from each of the four Parliaments, Transvaal, Orange Free State, Natal and Cape Colony, met at Durban to devise a Constitution for South Africa.

The British government sought to gain the maximum protection for the coloured peoples of the colonies, the vast majority, while the Boers sought to give them the least. In Cape Colony, where coloured voters already existed, they were to gain a federal vote and would be able to be deprived of this only by a two-thirds majority. Elsewhere the electorate to the House of Assembly was to be confined to Europeans. There would be a senate of sixteen, half to be nominated by the Governor-General in Council and the other half to be elected by both Houses. Certain nominated senators were to speak for the African natives, as possessing very 'special knowledge of the needs and wishes of these people'. The Convention's recommendations were accepted. An Act was passed in August 1909, the House of Commons showing little interest. General Botha's first cabinet consisted mostly of his old war comrades. It was by no means popular among the workers of the gold-mines and a South African Labour Party accused Botha and Smuts of betraying their race and selling themselves to British capitalism. The fundamental weakness of this party was its utter intolerance of by far the largest section of the South African workers, the coloured peoples. It was to be from a curious mixture of racialist and socialist propaganda that the Nationalist Boer Party of today was to emerge. What little African opinion was at that time articulate expressed itself bitterly against the Liberal Party's policy.

3

The Liberal triumph and the approach of war

Industrial unrest and syndicalism 1910–1912

The crisis over the Parliament Bill had caused bitterness, but at no time had feelings in the country been either strong enough or united enough to provoke civil war. Lloyd George had won his victory over 'the Dukes' in spite of a strong body of opinion through all classes in favour of 'elder statesmen' and suspicious of the new Liberalism. The way was cleared for a new list of Liberal reforms. But while this political tension of Commons v. Lords had developed, the turn of the first decade also saw considerable social tension and industrial unrest.

In February 1910 Winston Churchill became Home Secretary, an office he held for eighteen months, before transferring to the Admiralty, where he remained until the outbreak of war. As President of the Board of Trade he had been a highly popular figure. He had personally opened the first Labour Exchanges; he had piloted the Bill against sweated industries; he had set up arbitration machinery to try to deal with threatened strikes. But now it fell to him to deal with the worst labour troubles ever seen in this country.

The trade unions in these years strongly distrusted both Parliament and the law-courts, regarding them as little better than instruments of the class war. M.P.s were not yet paid; the legal decision in 1909 in the Osborne case, making the political levy for the Labour Party illegal, had caused deep bitterness and had seriously affected the unions' opportunities for direct political action. At the same time they enjoyed great popularity with their members, who, temporarily losing faith in constitutional action through Parliament, gave their support for direct strike action for political ends.

After the great Dock Strike of 1889 two of its leaders, Tom Mann and Ben Tillett, had gone to Australia to help the trade-union movement there. They were socialists and interested in the Syndicalist Movement on the continent. Syndicalist ideas, springing from the writings of Georges Sorel, advocated ruthless and if necessary violent strike action by the trade unions as the surest way to achieve the socialist utopia. The strike was not to be regarded as simply a means of exerting pressure on an employer to achieve better social conditions within a limited area, but as a means of exerting political pressure on government, local and national. Thus the miners called first for the amalgamation of the smaller unions, and then for all unionists to be prepared to engage 'in political action both local and national on the basis of complete independence of and hostility to all capitalist parties'. The movement was already gaining ground in 1910, when Mann and Tillett returned to England and started the newspaper the *Industrial Syndicalist*. Organized middle-class opinion as reflected by *The Times* newspaper feared 'an orgy of naked anarchy'.

Even before Mann and Tillett returned a series of non-violent labour strikes had broken out up and down the country, making 1910 the worst year for strikes yet recorded. In July there was a railway strike in Newcastle and in September a cotton strike in Lancashire, followed by a lock-out of boiler-makers, which cost the men some £800,000 in lost wages before they admitted defeat. Gradually the temper of the strikers worsened and violence began to be adopted by the syndicalist agitators, who used such arguments as 'if the peers may sabotage the Constitution for their own purposes, why may not we?' Even so, it should be emphasized that the *cause* of these strikes was not primarily syndicalist, in spite of the agitation: it was wages, hours and resentment against trade unionists being excluded from the House of Commons. As conditions improved, the rank and file showed themselves increasingly out of sympathy with Marxist and Syndicalist extremism.

Still, in November 1910 violent strikes developed in South Wales; the village of Tonypandy was looted and troops were sent by the government from Salisbury Plain. Churchill stopped the troops at Swindon while he tried to mediate with the strikers, but he failed and they were sent on to maintain order. Two months later Churchill was again involved in maintaining law and order. Two Russian anarchists, suspected of murder, barricaded themselves in a house in Sidney Street, Stepney. Two thousand troops with cannon and rifles were needed before they died in the burning house. Tom Mann wrote: 'If two men can keep 2000 men employed and hold them at bay in one street, how many men would be required to defeat two or three million men spread over the area of Great Britain?' This was a plea for the unions to unite and fight. There should be an end of the small craft unions because, wrote James Connolly, the Irish leader, 'it is an axiom . . . that they who rule industrially will rule politically' and trade unions would rule industrially once they were willing to drown petty differences and unite. Thus there should not be separate unions of engine-drivers, plate-layers, railway-clerks and porters, all of whom could be played off against each other by the employers, but one united Union of Railwaymen.

Such amalgamations of unions had in fact been steadily proceeding, and they continued, along with this series of strikes. In 1908 had come the Miners' Federation; in November 1910 Mann and Tillett formed the National Transport Workers' Federation out of thirty-six unions; in 1913 the N.U.R. was to be created, uniting three out of the four manual railway-workers' unions. These three—railwaymen, miners and transport workers—were next to form the Triple Alliance. To such a powerful pressure group governments were in fact to listen far more attentively than they ever had to individual unions. The formation in 1912 of a Labour Party newspaper, the *Daily Herald*, edited by George Lansbury, greatly helped the whole trade-union movement.

Meanwhile 1911 saw a continuation of strikes. The 14th of June was supposed to mark the beginning of an international seamen's strike. Its effect was slight on the continent, but in Britain a seamen's and firemen's strike began, which was marked once more by considerable violence. There were arson, rioting and looting in many port towns and many police were wounded. Middle-class opinion was frightened. The employers stood out as much as they could but were obliged to concede wage increases. This set a new

Great London Railway Strike, 1911

wave of strikes going: 'If the seamen can win why not we?' The Dockers obtained 7*d* and then 8*d* an hour. The London Carmen's Trade Union struck and 20,000 troops were alerted before the strike was settled. Finally in August the railwaymen came out throughout most of England—only the London and South-Western line not being involved. Rioting was not extensive except in Llanelly, but troops were widely used to overawe the strikers, who finally agreed to resume work and seek conciliation after Asquith had handed the settlement over to Lloyd George, the hero of the People's Budget. The summer of 1911 was the hottest since 1868. More strikes followed: From October 1911 to January

1912 the Miners' Federation was on strike and again in March when they achieved a Bill setting up a minimum wage machinery. In 1912 also the dockers again struck, but this time met with defeat.

Syndicalism was obviously strengthening the hand of the workers and it had shown how much could be achieved by direct action. But violence is not in the British working-class tradition, which had been so deeply influenced by non-conformism. Improved economic conditions in the two years preceding the outbreak of war, together with greater opportunities for political action through Parliament, helped to bring to an end the wave of strikes and violence. But the methods used were to be adopted by other groups: for example those for and against Home Rule in Ireland, and those pledged to Women's Suffrage.

Later Liberal legislation

It was against a background of considerable social tension, therefore, that the Liberals set about introducing their programme of further reforms. 1911 saw a number of Acts apart from the Parliament Act itself: there was a Shops Act introducing the now characteristic institution of the half-day; a Coal-mines Act; a Smallholders' Act (Scotland), much like the defeated measure of 1907; an Official Secrets Act against espionage; an Aerial Navigation Act; an Act to enable women to be elected and sit as members of County and Borough Councils; and a financial resolution that members of the House of Commons should receive £400 a year as salary.

Overshadowing all these, however, was the great National Insurance Act of Lloyd George. This was modelled on Bismarck's scheme for Germany of 1889 and sought to insure the wage-earners of the country both against sickness and unemployment. Unable to destroy the Bill constitutionally, the Conservatives resorted to methods of demagogy and threat. Meetings were held in the Albert Hall where society ladies exhorted the public not to lick the insurance stamps. Domestic servants were organized by their mistresses; doctors were threatened with social ostracism if they joined the scheme; the newspapers of Lord Northcliffe exerted their powerful influence against it. Possibly as a result of all this, but more likely through conservatism and dislike of 'bureaucracy', neither the medical profession, who would have to work the scheme, nor the workers, who would have to contribute compulsorily to it, were enthusiastic. Trade unions at this time were no more in favour of such compulsory insurance than they were of nationalization of industry. But the opposition was defeated and the Bill became law. Employers and employees alike were condemned to lick stamps.

The Bill as it finally appeared consisted of 115 clauses. All employees between sixteen and seventy would contribute to the scheme for medical benefits whether manual or non-manual, if they earned less than £160 a year. (Incidentally, this was considered a very fair wage in 1911. Many men earned no more than £1 a week on which to keep a wife and family.) This minimum was raised in 1920 to £250 p.a. The employee would contribute 4*d* a week, his employer 3*d* and the state 2*d* ('9*d* for 4*d*' was Lloyd George's phrase). In return he would obtain free medical benefits for himself and his family; additional sickness, disablement, hospital and maternity benefits might also be obtained through a Friendly Society. In the second part of the National Insurance Bill, sponsored by Winston Churchill, for seven named industries regarded as precarious (for example building, engineering and ship-building), employing some 2,500,000 men, unemployment benefits of 7*s*. a week would be paid from the second week of unemployment for a maximum of six weeks in one year, in return for additional payments of 2½*d* a week contributed. This benefit was termed a covenanted benefit. Anything the state might pay in addition to this would be at the discretion of the government. This Act marked the beginning of a replacement of the old Poor Law system of 1834; but it was only a timid and half-hearted beginning. Slowly, by a series of further Acts, it was to be developed: in 1920 the Coalition government was to extend unemployment benefits and payments to all wage-earning workers; in 1929 the Conservative government was to abolish the old 1834 Poor Law Unions, and Acts in 1948 were finally to abolish the 1834 system. The years 1912–1914 were boom years in which there was no great unemployment and also increasingly less strike agitation. This factor perhaps helped the Bill to pass and the new system of workers' insurance to be generally accepted. By 15 October 1912 there were 15,250,000 contributors to the scheme.

One effect of the Bill was the Unionist decision that 'Balfour Must Go'. They felt his opposition to the Bill had been inept. He resigned the leadership of the party in November 1911 and his place was taken by a Glasgow business man, Andrew Bonar Law. Lord Lansdowne continued to lead the party in the House of Lords.

Other legislation 1912

The year 1912 saw the Minimum Wages for Miners' Act, already mentioned, which was a result of the successful strike actions of that year incited by Tom Mann, in spite of his imprisonment in this year for a 'Don't Shoot' manifesto to soldiers. It also saw an abortive Bill for further franchise reform. The Act of 1884 had enfranchised the adult male who lived under his own roof either as a tenant or as a freeholder. Yet in 1912 over 2,000,000 male adults did not fall into this category. They might be adult sons living at home, footmen in a great house, vagrants, paupers, or members of the armed forces of no fixed address. On the other hand there were over half a million with more than one vote, through owning several properties, or through qualifying for a university vote. But the Bill was dropped because of indifference. *The Times* reporter remarked that 'quotations from Bright and Disraeli served to remind us that there had been a time when great men were interested in a Bill for Parliamentary reform'. Finally the year saw the introduction of two Bills which the government realized the House of Lords would resist for their full three years: a Bill for the disestablishment of the Welsh Church (a cause close to Lloyd George's heart) and a third Home Rule Bill for Ireland.

Wales and disestablishment

The Liberal vote drew heavily on Wales, which is strongly nonconformist in religion. There had already been a Bill in 1909 to disestablish the Anglican Church in Wales and now a second one was introduced, as a reward for the Welsh radicals who had for so long followed their devoted leader Lloyd George. The Bill provided that the four Welsh dioceses should no longer form part of the province of Canterbury; the Welsh bishops should no longer sit in the House of Lords; the Welsh Anglican Church should henceforth be governed by a representative body within the four dioceses. Most important of all, the Church would be disendowed. Certain buildings and gifts would remain in the Church's hands, but the remaining endowment would go one-quarter to the University of Wales and three-quarters to the Welsh County Councils. In spite of Unionist opposition, the country as a whole showed no strong feeling on the Bill and it was obvious that it would become law in 1914, which it did, although not coming into force until 1920.

The problem of Ireland was quite another matter, which will be discussed later in this chapter. Needless to say, the Home Rule Bill of 1912, which proposed setting up an Irish Parliament for home affairs while Westminster retained powers over imperial matters, was rejected by the Lords.

Trade Union Act

The year 1913 saw some minor amendments to the National Insurance Act and an important Trade Union Act which reversed the Osborne judgment. In 1908 the Walthamstow branch of the Amalgamated Society of Railway Servants had resented the levying of compulsory union contributions for political purposes, i.e. financial support of the Labour Party. Through their secretary, W. V. Osborne, they had sued their union. Mr. Justice Farnell had held it was illegal for a trade union to levy funds to provide Parliamentary representation and the Appeal Court and the House of Lords had upheld the judgment. The union had closed the branch and expelled Osborne, but that did not help the finances of the Labour Party and some sixteen Labour M.P.s had suffered, attempts to raise voluntary funds having failed. The Trade Union Act of 1913 gave back the right to trade unions to spend their funds for political objects, but individual members were to be free to contract out of payment if they wished. In addition M.P.s also now had a salary, introduced in 1911.

Slowly the spate of Liberal social legislation came to an end, but two major problems remained: the Suffragette Movement and the Irish question.

Suffragettes

Feminists during the last half-century had won many victories: secondary and university education; reform of matrimonial laws; greater protection of the innocent in cases of assault; and most recently, in 1911, the opportunity to take part in local government. But still the national franchise eluded them.

The Women's Social and Political Union, founded in 1903, first achieved notoriety in 1905 when Sir Edward Grey was interrupted by two girls, Christabel Pankhurst and Annie Kenney. Both were sent to prison. Christabel's mother and Mrs Emmeline Pethick-Lawrence were now brought together by the veteran radical politician Keir Hardie and from the spring of 1906 to the autumn of 1912 the two Emmelines directed the movement in harmony. Militant tactics were adopted, but at this stage no great damage was done. Political speeches were interrupted in Parliament; women chained themselves to railings and threw bricks at the Prime Minister's windows, but no more. They wanted the vote, since it symbolized equality between the sexes.

From June 1909 a greater militancy appeared. Hunger strikes were staged among imprisoned suffragettes, the authorities countering with forced-feeding through tubes. Window-breaking was increased ('The argument of the broken pane is the most valuable argument in modern politics', said Mrs Pankhurst, a view with which the

A suffragette arrested, May 1914

syndicalists agreed). Assaults on property and increasingly hysterical behaviour developed in 1910, but the Women's Social and Political Union and other smaller suffragist groups agreed to a truce during the crisis of the Parliament Bill.

1912 saw a split in the W.S.P.U. Christabel Pankhurst persuaded her mother to break with the Pethick-Lawrences and join her in organizing far more violent outrages of arson, bombing and picture-slashing. Public opinion was reacting strongly against the forcible feeding of those imprisoned. The Home Secretary, McKenna, therefore introduced the 'Cat and Mouse Act' in 1913. This enabled a prison governor to release a starving prisoner but to re-arrest her as soon as she had put on a little weight. The stigma of her death on the hands of the government would thus be avoided, but it was a very distasteful piece of legislation.

A protest poster, 1913

The Bunny Hug, 1912

In 1913 a suffragette threw herself under the King's horse in the Derby and was killed. The extremists carried on their remarkably highly organized struggle, but they began to lose support, which in the year before the war was swinging back again in favour of constitutional methods for winning the vote. It is difficult to know how the movement would have ended without war. But these upper- and middle-class ladies had certainly shown that they could play their part in the new age of violence, through direct action. In 1918 they were to achieve most of what they had fought for, and hardly anybody was to notice it.

Ireland

Feeling in Ireland had undergone a number of changes since the days of Parnell. When Gladstone introduced his first Home Rule Bill in 1886 the country was still only emerging from the terrible years of the mid-century. Gladstone's Land Acts of 1870 and 1881, followed by those of Balfour and, above all, George Wyndham's Land Purchase Act of 1903, however, had transformed the Irish peasantry. From being no more than 'half-serf, half-outlaw' rebels, they were becoming prosperous, self-respecting farmers, more interested in their new 'vested interest' of cowsheds and pigsties than in their political rights and wrongs. Similarly the leaders of the Home Rule group matured and settled into comfortable ways, reluctant to accept new ideas from young hot-heads. What had been good enough for Parnell in 1890 was good enough for his successor John Redmond in 1910. Unfortunately, just at the moment when a Liberal House of Commons and a moderate Irish leader seemed at last on the point of being able to settle the problem, extremists appeared on both sides, determined to oppose all moderate and compromise solutions. They were centred on the two great rival cities, Catholic Dublin and Protestant Belfast: Sinn Fein or Irish Republican on the one hand against the Ulstermen on the other. These were to be responsible for the horrors of civil war and the absurdity of partition, the end of which is not yet visible.

The Home Rule Bill as introduced in 1912 was envisaged by the government as the first of a series of Bills for Ireland, Scotland and Wales, by which Britain would become a federation over which the Imperial Parliament would retain supreme control and powers of decision in matters of defence. It was the Ulstermen who largely wrecked the bill.

Ulster had been settled in 1611 by Scottish and English Protestant landlords. During the fight for the first Home Rule Bill, Belfast had re-emerged as the centre of the Protestant tradition in Ireland. The ancient quarrel of the seventeenth century came to life again. Belfast, with its great industries, was determined never to submit to Catholic Dublin. The Orangemen (in memory of William of Orange, who in 1692 had granted them many privileges) would fight to the last ditch in defence of their liberties, religious and political.

In 1910 they offered the leadership of their group in the House of Commons to a Dublin Protestant lawyer, Sir Edward Carson. He at once began to lead his adopted cause with all the fanaticism of the convert. Ulster would defy Dublin's Home Rule; she would set up an alternative system of government. In 1912 the Ulstermen began to train and to drill a volunteer force. On the eve of the Bill being introduced into Parliament a review was held. Eighty thousand Ulster Volunteers marched past Sir Edward Carson, Lord Londonderry, Bonar Law and Walter Long.

Asquith made no attempt to ban what was in fact a private army. Nor did he provide in his Bill for the exclusion of Ulster. He knew that he could not coerce Ulster, but he seemed determined to ignore the whole problem and just hope that 'something would turn up', an attitude which in retrospect seems extraordinarily weak. Meanwhile Redmond was unable to make any concession to Ulster, since southern Irish opinion would not tolerate it. It is possible that if Asquith had acted more firmly, either by obliging Redmond to accept the exclusion of Ulster or by forcing Carson to disband his army, the situation would have eased. As it was, he did neither, in spite of advice from Lloyd George and Winston Churchill.

We have noted already that the leader of the Conservative Unionist Party, who was also leader of the Opposition, took the salute at the march past in 1912. He and his party continued to give unequivocal support to the Ulstermen. Speaking at a public rally in 1912, Bonar Law said: 'I can imagine no length of resistance to which Ulster will go, which I shall not be ready to support, and in which they will not be supported by the overwhelming majority of the British people.' He had pledged his party to an instrument of terror and violence.

The Bill passed the Commons in two successive sessions in 1912 and 1913. It was twice defeated by the Lords, but in

1914 it would become law. The King, George V, now tried to break the deadlock, summoning Bonar Law and Churchill to Balmoral for discussions: a series of secret negotiations followed in private, but they were unsuccessful. Meanwhile in public Carson and Bonar Law grew bolder in their determination to resist the Bill. Senior officers in the army now joined in by unofficially becoming 'advisers' to the volunteer army and by suggesting that in an emergency regular army officers should refuse 'to coerce Ulster'.

Meanwhile on the other side the situation passed more and more into the hands of the extremists. To counteract force, the Irish Volunteers were founded in Dublin in 1913 in opposition to Carson's volunteers. Redmond deprecated them but could not prevent them. An ineffective embargo on arms importation was at once imposed by Asquith's government, although the Ulster Volunteers had been arming for over a year.

Asquith now tried to compromise. He proposed that the electors of any Irish county might contract out of Home Rule for six years at a time. But this proposal was ignored and the Ulster leaders threatened in the House of Lords to refuse the annual Army Act. In the autumn of 1914 the Home Rule Bill would become law, and, to prevent violence, troops and ships were ordered to move, including troops from the Curragh, an army camp in Kildare. Officers there were advised by the Commander-in-Chief, Major-General Sir Arthur Paget, either to 'disappear' or to resign if they objected to acting against Ulster. This was the army in revolt against the government. Lord Roberts, late C.-in-C., was advising the Ulster Volunteers and Sir Henry Wilson at the War Office undoubtedly connived; both were Irishmen. Brigadier Gough from the Curragh was summoned to London, where he extracted from the War Office a promise that officers would not be called upon 'to enforce the present Home Rule Bill on Ulster'. The Prime Minister did nothing, apart from obtaining resignations from his War Minister, Seely, and two generals. He did not touch the real culprits at the War Office, nor did he dissolve Parliament, since the international situation by July 1914 was too serious. There was little, in fact, he could do. The officer class was solidly against him and both volunteer forces were now openly importing arms in spite of bans. In May 1914 there were 100,000 National Volunteers led by Redmond himself. On 18 July King George again intervened, summoning a conference of party leaders: Asquith and Lloyd George for the Liberals; Bonar Law and Lord Lansdowne for the Conservatives; Redmond and Dillon for the Nationalists and Carson and Craig for the Ulster Unionists. The conference sat for three days and broke up on 24 July, having reached no decision. The cabinet, meeting to discuss its failure, learnt of the Austrian ultimatum to Serbia. Two days later on 26 July, the first shooting broke out in Belfast, and off and on it was to continue for over eight years. The outbreak of European war a week later was to delay the implementation of Home Rule but it was not to prevent war in Ireland.

Derby Day 1912. This captures something of the carefree confidence of the pre-war era

PART TWO

The First World War

1914–1918

4

The First World War: its causes

European Civil War

In July 1914 a war broke out in the Balkans between Serbia and Austria. There had been Balkan wars in both 1912 and 1913, but this war quickly developed into a vast struggle in which all the leading European powers were involved. It never, however, became a world war in quite the sense that the struggle of 1939–1945 did, when there was hardly a nation or a people not actively involved. Admittedly, France and England used African and Indian troops; the Middle East was an important war area; and Germany lost her colonies in Africa and the Pacific. But still the vast majority who died were Europeans or of European stock from the British Empire or the U.S.A. It was currently described in India as the European Civil War, which is essentially what it was: a vast struggle within Europe for power within Europe. It ended by the total power of the European nations being so drastically reduced as to mark the beginning of the end of European world hegemony.

Anti-German feeling

The purpose of this chapter is to try to see why this Balkan war developed and why Britain entered the struggle. After it was all over the victorious Allies decreed that it had all been the fault of Germany and of the German Kaiser. Germany must therefore be 'squeezed until the pips squeaked' and the Kaiser must be hanged as a punishment. Such an analysis was prejudiced and over-simplified. What it shows is the extent to which nationalist hatred had developed during the war. It had become unpatriotic in Britain to keep a dachschund, listen to the music of Beethoven or to drink German wine. To have visited Germany or to have married a German meant that one was almost certainly a German spy. In Western Europe such virulent feeling was more a result than a cause of war. In Central and Eastern Europe, on the other hand, it was another matter; there aggressive nationalism was undoubtedly a prime cause of fighting.

Why did Britain enter?

In Britain during August and September 1914 the newspapers were filled with cartoons: poor little Belgium, a maiden in distress, being bullied by the German Kaiser; gallant Albert I of the Belgians fighting single-handed the savage Huns from the east. Clearly at this level Britain had entered the war as an act of chivalry to rescue a gallant country from the hands of bullies. If we were to say that she had also entered to maintain the balance of power in Western Europe, by preventing the small state of Belgium from falling into the hands of the new European giant, we might get nearer the reasoning of the cabinet. Britain depended for her livelihood on her maritime trade. Any threat to the English Channel was a vital matter. In the seventeenth, eighteenth and nineteenth centuries Britain had fought many wars to prevent France from gaining this part of Western Europe. She was now equally determined to keep out Germany. The latter argued in August 1914 that she was not in fact interested in Belgium or the Channel ports but simply in attacking her old enemy France before the latter had time to attack her through the coveted Alsace-Lorraine district in the east. French forces were known to be concentrated there and so the Schlieffen Plan was to attack from the west, passing through Belgium and defeating the French army from the rear.

After the war Sir Edward Grey remarked: 'I used to think that I was meant to keep the country out of war. But perhaps my real business was to bring her into it unitedly.' He did this by the skill with which the Belgian question was presented. Were there, in fact, any other reasons why Britain entered the struggle? Indeed can the real cause of the cataclysm itself yet be detected? After 1918 a movement known as 'revisionist history' swept Europe and America, at least exonerating Germany from sole responsibility. This was in reaction to the Versailles Treaty, which had 'punished' Germany for her war-guilt by various impositions and confiscations.

In 1914 Lloyd George had remarked that Europe 'stumbled and staggered into war' and the more historians examine the causes, the more do they seem to agree with this simple analysis. Yet we cannot altogether dismiss social, economic or imperialist factors, if only because the revisionists between the wars spent so much time considering their importance.

Economic rivalry

In the years before the war the German economy was expanding at a formidable rate. British expansion, though steadier, was also taking place. The slump of 1910–1912 was overcome and the British economic position in 1914 seemed healthy, admittedly partly due to rearmament. In at least one area, the Middle East, economic rivalry between the two powers might well develop owing to the increasing need for oil. Yet in 1914 itself an agreement over Middle East oil was made between Britain and Germany. Since the mid-1880's Britain had steadily been withdrawing her traditional support from Turkey and from the 1890's German banking interests increasingly sought to develop Turkey as a field for profitable investment. But as yet there was little overt rivalry. Britain in 1914 still had the largest share of Turkish trade, while the railway development (the Berlin to Baghdad railway) was not planned as an anti-British move. By 1914 this had not been completed, while numerous invitations had been made to British capital to help finance it; moves which the British government had supported, but which the financiers had opposed since 'they disliked putting up money for a railway when they did not provide the steel' (A. J. P. Taylor). In July 1914 Britain and France reached agreements with Germany over the use of this railway and other Middle East matters. When war came, British interests in Persia and German interests in Mesopotamia may have faced each other, but they were not its cause. In other areas, too, economic rivalry between the powers was relaxed in the years just before the war: in Egypt between Britain and France; in Persia between Britain and Russia; in Morocco between France and Germany. In Africa, Britain and Germany came to an agreement over the division of Portuguese Africa, which was thought to be about to collapse.

International socialism

Just before the war business men and politicians in Britain and all the West European countries were increasingly frightened and preoccupied by socialism, and the syndicalist movements in Britain and France in the years preceding war had increased this fear. There have been historians who have argued that some politicians indeed feared socialism more than war, which they positively welcomed in 1914, since they calculated that national sentiments would overwhelm those of International Marxist Socialism. But the British Foreign Secretary was certainly not among these. He feared socialism, but his greater fear was of universal war 'with all its horrible and revolting consequences'. These included socialism, for war would mark the 'greatest step towards socialism that could possibly have been made'. Its result would be 'Labour governments in every country after this'. Most business men agreed that war would be bad for trade and 'would inevitably encourage socialism'. Thus, although we cannot deny that the business boom of the pre-war years was partly the result of the armaments race, it is not possible to regard the war as directly the result of capitalism. Rather did the capitalists seek to avoid it.

Imperial rivalry

Colonies in 1914 were still thought of by many as existing primarily to provide essential raw materials and opportunities for investment for the mother country, as well as a ready market for consumer goods; for example, Lancashire cotton. It was thought essential that they be tied politically to the mother country in order to exclude rival European nations. Further, colonies dotted over the world gave useful naval stations and also great prestige. Britain and France were the two greatest colonial powers. Germany was one of the smaller ones, although one of the more efficient. She had received her part at the share-out of Africa at the Conference in Berlin in 1884, although less than either Britain, France or Belgium, which in 1908 formally annexed one of the richest and largest areas of tropical Africa, the Congo, without German opposition. Kaiser Wilhelm II was not interested in the 'crazy vision of an African colonial empire'. He was obsessed by the 'yellow peril' of the Far Eastern peoples and looked to Britain to co-operate in dealing with the 'sick man of the Far East', China, whose government collapsed in 1911. Austria-Hungary was never a colonial power outside Europe. Thus no specific or deliberate imperialist cause can be detected for the war, although undoubtedly German naval expansion had been regarded by the British as a possible threat to their empire.

Alliances

To say that the great powers entered the war because of their alliances would be too naive. No power in modern times has not been capable of dishonouring an alliance, or of reading into an agreement only that which satisfies its self-interest. Nevertheless the broad pattern of alliances and ententes was reflected in the final line-up of the powers in 1914, and some survey of their development is therefore necessary. In 1879 Bismarck had made an alliance with Austria-Hungary. This ran counter to his earlier non-committal policy, but he hoped that it would keep the Habsburg Empire friendly. In fact it was to draw Germany more and more into the Balkan maelstrom. In 1882 this Dual Alliance was converted into the Triple Alliance by the addition of Italy, resentful against France over the latter's acquisition of Tunis. In 1883 Roumania also acceded to the alliance. By his policy of limited liability and his skilful diplomacy Bismarck kept Europe relatively stable. But in 1890 he was dismissed by the young Kaiser Wilhelm II.

In 1885 Britain's Prime Minister, Lord Salisbury, had declared that in supporting Turkey all these years Britain had in fact been 'backing the wrong horse'. Turkey began to move into the orbit of Austria-Hungary and Germany, while on the other hand Imperial Russia, a traditional rival of France in the Middle East earlier in the century, in 1891 began to seek the friendship of Republican France. An alliance resulted, which became public in 1893. Britain's policy of isolation continued, although at least up to 1895 she leaned more to the Triple Alliance than to Russia or France, fearing the former in the Far East and France in Egypt. (War with France was very narrowly averted in 1898 over the Fashoda incident, when the two countries quarrelled over the control of the head waters of the Nile.) In 1896 Kaiser Wilhelm telegraphed President Kruger of the Transvaal, congratulating him on successfully defeating an attempted invasion, 'the Jameson Raid'. This telegram and the naval policy of Admiral Tirpitz after 1898 led to a drift away from traditional British sympathy for Germany. But it was very gradual. Even in 1901 Joseph Chamberlain was feeling for a *rapprochement* with Germany, who invited Britain to join the Triple Alliance. Lord Salisbury felt that this would involve too great a liability and there followed instead the Anglo-Japanese Treaty of 1902, marking the end of British isolation, and negotiations with France which ended with the Entente Agreement in 1904. This latter tidied up a number of imperial problems, but it only committed the two nations to mutual friendship. It was not a military alliance.

Moroccan crises

In 1905 there occurred the first Moroccan crisis. France was seeking to complete her control over Morocco, which separated her territories in West Africa and Algeria. Morocco had an Atlantic coastline and Britain was interested in any power asserting itself here, for naval reasons. Included in the Entente was an agreement that Britain should have a free hand in Egypt, and France one in Morocco. Of this latter Germany pretended to disapprove. Kaiser Wilhelm II visited Tangier in March 1905 and recognized the Sultan of Morocco as independent. He demanded an international conference to discuss France's behaviour in Morocco. Delcassé, France's Foreign Minister, favoured standing firm against German intimidation, but his cabinet colleagues accepted a conference and Delcassé resigned. When the conference met at Algeciras, France triumphed. Admittedly she had to agree to certain compromises: Morocco would remain nominally independent, with France and Spain responsible for 'policing the Sultan's territory'. But her position in Morocco was vindicated. Italy supported this, although she was a member of the Triple Alliance, and Russia too was obliged by French pressure to withdraw her support for Germany, who had thus suffered a considerable diplomatic defeat.

Britain now began to conduct secret military discussions with the French General Staff and felt her way towards friendship also with Russia. The defeat of the latter by Japan in 1905 had shown her weakness and she was just emerging from her revolution of that year. Sir Edward Grey at the Foreign Office therefore felt that the traditional fear of Russia in the East was out of date. Thus in 1907 Britain and Russia made an agreement: they recognized the independence of Persia in which there should be limited 'spheres of influence' for the two powers; Russia agreed that Afghanistan was of special interest to Britain; Tibet was to be a buffer state between India and Russia under Chinese suzerainty. Germany felt that this Anglo-Russian convention threatened her. In fact it was entirely negative in character. It swung Russia a little nearer the Entente, but it did not necessarily prevent her from maintaining good relations with Germany if she chose to.

In 1909 Germany agreed to recognize French political power in Morocco and in return France agreed to protect German economic interests there. But two years later, in 1911, French troops were openly moved into Fez, the capital, allegedly to protect Europeans there but contrary to the Agreement of Algeciras. Germany decided to demand some compensation for allowing France a free hand in Morocco. She asked for a large slice of the French Congo and sent the gunboat *Panther* to Agadir, a naval base and Atlantic port in Morocco. France sought Britain's support and Lloyd George made a powerful speech at a Mansion House lunch: Britain was unwilling to see interference with her 'vital interests'; blackmail would not be tolerated. In fact it was. The *Panther* was withdrawn, Germany received a strip of the Congo, although not as much as she had demanded, and in return recognized France's position in Morocco. During the fracas Italy took the opportunity to occupy Tripoli, a Turkish province which the Turkish government was too weak to defend. Italy thus moved a stage further from the Triple Alliance, which she was going to desert in the coming war. As for the Moroccan crises, they can scarcely be regarded as direct causes of that war, even though they left a legacy of suspicion and strengthened Britain's relationship with both France and Russia.

East Europe

It has been said that to call Turkey the sick man of Europe at the end of the nineteenth century was to ignore the Habsburg Empire (ruled by the Emperor Francis Joseph from 1848 to 1916). Early in 1914 the German Secretary of State, Jagon, compared the prospects of the two empires, Ottoman and Habsburg, as a race 'between two empires which goes to pieces first'. Throughout Austria-Hungary nationalist agitation was strong: in Bohemia, in Hungary and in the Polish, South Tyrolese and South Slavonic provinces. Everywhere there were agitators, the only answer to whom was a ruthless, corrupt and inefficient police. Something of the atmosphere of 1914 can be felt in the classic novel *The Good Soldier Schweik* by Haroslav Hasek. At the same time, if the Habsburg Empire was unstable that of the Romanov's in Russia was little better. Under her ineffective Czar Nicholas II (1894–1917) Russia had been defeated by the Japanese in 1905 and had then suffered a

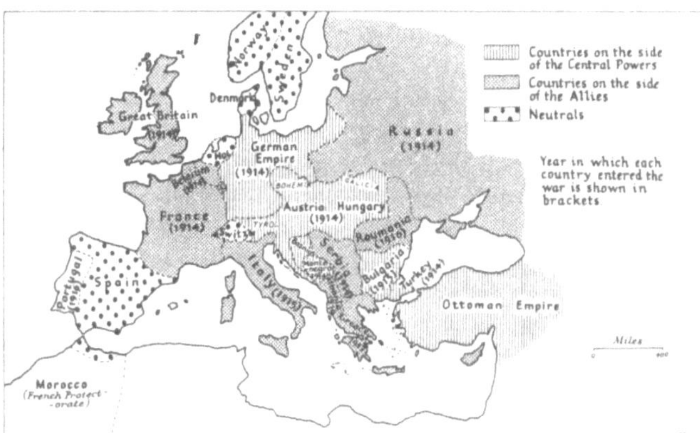

Belligerents and Neutrals in Europe 1914–1918

revolution. This had been overcome by a mixture of compromise and ruthless suppression, financed by enormous overseas loans, largely from Paris. These, incidentally, had given France considerable powers to influence Nicholas, for example in 1905–1906, when he was obliged to abandon his treaty of friendship with Kaiser Wilhelm II, drawn up at Bjorko. But Russian internal instability only seems to have aggravated the traditional Russian interest in expansion, particularly towards the Balkans and Constantinople.

The Ottoman Empire

In 1908 had occurred the revolt of the Young Turks: a prototype revolution, which has been followed many times since by aspiring young nationalists all over Asia and Africa. A group of ardent young Turkish nationalists, many educated in the West, were seeking to Westernize and liberalize the government of Turkey. Sultan Abdul Hamid at first capitulated and proclaimed himself a constitutional monarch. But within a year he tried to reverse this. He was deposed and replaced by his brother, Mohammed V. Turkey was plunged into an internal struggle between liberals and reactionaries. The latter gradually gained the upper hand until after the war, when the movement was finally to triumph under Mustafa Kemal Ataturk.

Meanwhile Austria-Hungary and Russia decided to get what pickings there were to be had from Turkey, while Balkan nationalism also advanced its claims. Austria-Hungary annexed the two provinces of Bosnia and Herzegovina, which she had in fact controlled since 1878. Bulgaria proclaimed herself completely independent, with her own Czar, Ferdinand. Austrian negotiations to build a railway to Mitrovitza in Turkey alienated Serbia and ended the period of Austro-Russian co-operation in the Balkans, begun in 1897.

Balkan Wars 1912–1913

In 1912 a League of four Balkan states was formed: Greece, Serbia, Montenegro and Bulgaria. It received the blessing of Russia. This League at once decided to dismember as much of Turkey in Europe as possible. War was declared, although without Russian approval, in 1912. Bulgaria and Serbia had divided the spoils that they expected to get, while Greece and Montenegro had agreed to extend their frontiers. Turkey would be expelled from Europe. During the summer (1912) Turkey suffered some severe defeats and an armistice conference met in London in December. The great powers decided to recognize the independence of a new Balkan state, Albania. Thus Serbia would be excluded from the Adriatic in spite of her victories. This was a triumph for Austro-Hungarian diplomacy and was violently resented by Serbia. A few weeks later a crisis developed over the frontier of Albania and the London conference was recalled in May 1913, when peace was agreed upon. Serbia and Bulgaria were delegated by the conference to work out the partition of Macedonia, but they now quarrelled. Bulgaria attacked Serbia, which was joined by Greece, Turkey and Roumania. A short war returned Adrianople to Turkey and brought southern Dobrudja to Roumania. Austria had encouraged Bulgaria against Serbia, but Germany had worked in this crisis alongside Russia and had disapproved of her ally, Austria-Hungary. One of the few consistent factors to emerge from these wars of 1912–1913 is the growing hatred between Serbia and Austria-Hungary. The chancellors of both Germany (Bethmann-Hollweg) and of Russia (Sazonov) had contributed to keeping tension from reaching danger point. Many Serbs lived in annexed Bosnia and Herzegovina and it was the declared policy of nationalist Serbian propaganda to seek to gain control over these two states. Serbia was allied to Russia and Russia was allied to France.

In the autumn of 1913 the Serbs were slow in withdrawing troops from northern Albania according to the London agreement. On 18 October Vienna issued an ultimatum. Germany supported her and Serbia backed down. Also at the end of 1913 a new and large German military mission was sent to Turkey to rehabilitate her army. The news that a German general was to command the Constantinople army corps was a shock to the Russians, even though a British admiral held a similar post in the Turkish navy. The German appointment thus worsened German-Russian relations, but the military mission to Turkey did not appreciably alter German policy: the Kaiser still talked in terms of the two powers Germany and England 'standing shoulder to shoulder' in world affairs. At the same time it seemed generally agreed early in 1914 that the most crucial factors on the European diplomatic chessboard were the ripeness of the Habsburg Empire for dissolution; the expanding force of Yugo (South)-slavism; and the preponderance of the German military machine, which in terms of fire-potential was superior to all. Lastly it should be noted that ever since the congress system had broken down after the Napoleonic Wars there had been no recognized system of dealing with a crisis between powers, except for an *ad hoc* conference convened by the powers interested. This absence of established international machinery may well in the end be accepted as the actual reason why the Serbian crisis of July 1914 led to war.

Events leading to war

On 28 June the Archduke Francis Ferdinand, heir to the throne of Austria-Hungary, was assassinated in Sarajevo, the capital of Bosnia, by Gavrilo Princip, a member of a Serbian secret society, Crna Ruka (the Black Hand). In the crises of 1912 and 1913 Austria had been deterred from intervention by the risk of Russian action and the uncertainty of Germany. This time her government seems to have decided from the start to use the murder as a *casus belli.* The German Kaiser was about to go off on a three-week cruise. Before he did so he gave vague assurances of readiness 'to stand loyally on the side of Austria-Hungary'. He obviously expected the little power of Serbia to back down to the great power of Austria-Hungary, as she had done over the frontier crisis the previous autumn.

Three weeks went by. The Serbian government failed to take proper action against the Black Hand, probably for fear of too many disclosures, and Austria-Hungary slowly prepared an ultimatum. Neither France, Britain nor Russia during these three weeks seems to have regarded the Serbian crisis as particularly dangerous. Grey believed that 'probably Berlin was trying to moderate Vienna'.

On 23 July Austria presented her ultimatum to Serbia: a formidable list of demands. Russia warned: 'If Austria swallows Serbia we will make war on her.' But at the same time she advised Serbia to accept the Austrian terms. Serbia mobilized and then sent her reply, which was highly conciliatory, although not unconditional acceptance. Austria partially mobilized against Serbia. Yet the general reaction was one of relief. In the Kaiser's words, 'all grounds for war disappear'.

Grey now suggested a conference in order to gain time for a compromise to be worked out. Germany accepted the idea of four-power mediation but felt that Grey's specific proposals would submit Austria to a 'court of arbitration'. The Russian chancellor, Sazonov, sought direct talks with the Austrian Berchtold. He was rebuffed. Instead, Austria declared war on Serbia on 28 July.

On 25 July both Germany and Russia had begun pre-mobilization. Now on 29 July Sazonov became convinced of the need for full mobilization. Orders were given and then cancelled, being replaced by others for partial Russian mobilization, following direct contact between the Czar and the German Kaiser. Since returning from his cruise, Wilhelm had been far less bellicose now that war really threatened. But his influence, with that of the politicians, was giving way to that of the generals. In Berlin, Vienna and St Petersburg the generals were all exerting pressure. On 30 July Russia, convinced of the imminence of German mobilization, decided to reverse again the orders of the previous day. On the same day Austria extended her mobilization to all fronts. From this moment, all historians agree, there was no going back. On 31 July Germany declared a state of war emergency, began mobilization and demanded that Russian war preparations cease. War was declared against Russia on 1 August and France was asked for a promise of neutrality. Belgium and France began to mobilize and on 2 August Britain conceded a guarantee to France of her northern coastline. On 3 August Germany put into operation the Schlieffen Plan, whose purpose was to knock out France before Russia completed her mobilization. It meant the invasion of Belgium, which was at once begun.

All the great continental powers operated a system of universal military training. The General Staffs of the huge armies thus held in reserve were all equally convinced that they had perfected the 'art of war'. In spite of the German army's known superiority in fire-power, they were all equally confident of victory, provided only that they had the initiative. Hence the mad scramble to get their armies mobilized. Hence also the feeling of the American Colonel House that the temper of Europe was 'militarism run mad'.

Crowds cheering the Declaration of War, London, 1914

Britain's position during the Serbian crisis has been attacked as not being clearly enough defined. Yet Britain was allied to none of the European powers and the cabinet would not have tolerated Grey using threats as long as the quarrel seemed localized in Eastern Europe. It was the German declaration of war on France and her ultimatum to Belgium on 3 August, demanding free passage, which precipitated action. Belgian neutrality was violated and Britain entered the war: to honour the treaty of 1839; to support the Triple Entente; to forestall the growing naval challenge; to maintain her control of the Channel; to prevent her imperial and Eastern interests being threatened.

At the same time the *moral* issue of the Belgian invasion helped greatly to win the support of pacifist and isolationist groups in the country.

In fact none of the belligerents had clear-cut war aims, except perhaps France. Neither Britain nor Germany had definite imperialist ambitions; Austria was not all that interested in partitioning Serbia; she needed a foreign victory to bolster up her internal regime. Russia had expansionist aims but they were as distasteful to her allies as to her enemies. Only France, who took the least part in the diplomatic charade preceding war, had a definite aim—to win back Alsace-Lorraine. The best the other powers could do was to hasten to publish evidence that the war was both preventive and defensive. But before we condemn Britain for entering it is worth noting that had she not done so Germany would almost certainly have won and probably in less time than four years. It is hard to assess what might have been the consequences of such a victory.

5

The First World War: its course

The protagonists

The War of 1914–1918 was a relatively enclosed affair. It was primarily a war between the Central European powers of Germany, Austria-Hungary, Turkey and Bulgaria against powers on the periphery: Russia, Serbia, France, Britain, Italy and in due course the U.S.A. (European in race if not geographically). It was fought primarily on two fronts, those of France and Russia, with three secondary fronts in Italy, Turkey and the Balkans. In Turkey an extremely fluid situation developed as Allied encouragement of Arab nationalism caused increasing disintegration of the Middle East.

Britain's Achilles heel was her merchant shipping. Her economy had for a century or more been entirely dependent on her overseas trade and assets. In 1914 she grew about one-third of the food needed to maintain her population of about 45,000,000. If this supply link could be cut Britain could be made to starve and her industry crippled. This was to be very nearly achieved by German submarine warfare. On the other side, the internal lines of communication of the Central powers would be a considerable asset for the quick movement of troops; communication with outlying colonies would be difficult, but economically this was not a vital factor. The resources of Central Europe were vast: moreover, nobody envisaged a long war. Germany was at the peak of her military preparedness, even though her naval expansion was still below the rate of Britain. She was able to mobilize 2,000,000 men. Austria-Hungary raised about the same number, but they were less well trained and armed. Russia could raise about 1,500,000 at the outset, though obviously in man-power potential this represented only a fraction. France, recently torn by strikes, could still raise about 1,000,000 men. Britain, who had never had conscription, was able to muster 250,000 under Haldane's Territorial Army scheme.

The Western Front

The twenty divisions of the British Expeditionary Force were mobilized on 3 August: six regular and fourteen terri-

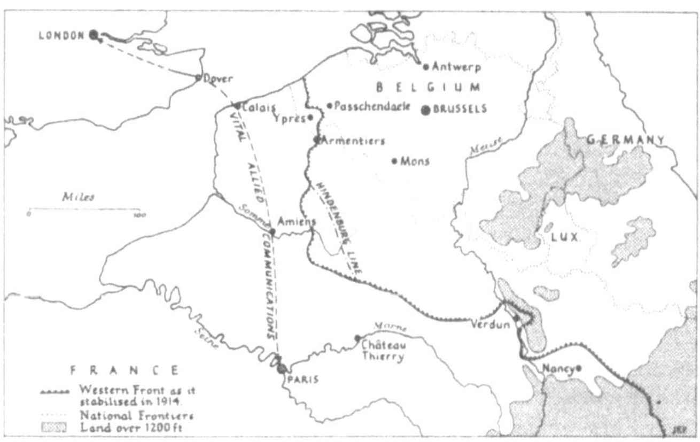

The Western Front

torial. Within a few days they were crossing to France. Within a few weeks they had suffered very heavy casualties, but the reserve force was mobilized equally smoothly. It was a triumph for Haldane and the Committee of Imperial Defence which had been set up in 1903. But it seemed at first sight utterly inadequate against the mighty army operating the plan of Count Schlieffen, Chief of the German Staff, 1891–1905.

The original plan had been in fact somewhat modified a few weeks before war by the new chief of the German Staff, General von Moltke, who never quite believed enough in the superiority of his own machine-gun emplacements against the expected French bayonet attacks. In fact this modification may well have cost him victory. The French poured their best troops into Lorraine and they were duly mown down. But the massive blow which was to have struck at the rear of the French Eastern army was weakened by Moltke. The German army advanced into Belgium and captured Brussels and Namur. Belgian troops fell back on Antwerp, whither a British force was sent to help delay the German advance. Again, instead of ignoring this, Moltke kept back two corps to deal with this flank, while sending two more corps at this late hour to the Russian Front. The spearhead pressed on. The British retreated from Mons and the Allies fell back towards the River Marne. At this point the German commanders in the field ignored their own plan and the First and Second Armies joined forces to attack Paris. They reached within twenty miles of the capital and the French government fled to Bordeaux. But this concentration by the Germans released fresh French troops and the Allies counter-attacked. German troops, who had already crossed the Marne on the way to Paris, pulled back to assist against the French attack. The French and British now had the initiative, as the German offensive had lost its momentum. Paris was saved and the Germans pulled back and straightened their line. This was the first Battle of the Marne, regarded by many historians as decisive. Moltke was replaced on the Western Front by Falkenhayn.

Antwerp now fell, but the western end of the line held on the pivot point of Ypres, where the British fought successfully during October to preserve the Channel ports and the vital rail links between them and Paris. At the cost of 50,000 men these remained open. The Dover Patrol was to ensure that during four years of war not one man nor one letter was lost as a result of German naval action in the Channel.

Russian Front

During the winter of 1914–1915 a trench-line developed on the Western Front; it was to remain static, to within twenty-odd miles, for the next four years. The Schlieffen Plan had failed and Germany had now to face war on two fronts. On the Eastern one they were more successful. After initial success the Russian army was heavily defeated at the battles of Tannenberg and the Masurian Lakes in East Prussia. Russian equipment lost at these battles was vast. Her men could be easily replaced, but arms and equipment had either to be manufactured at home in a country industrially decreasingly efficient or imported from the Allies. But here the problem of communications was vital. The northern sea route was, and is, ice-bound for most of the year. The southern route lay through the Dardanelles, which Britain had so long kept shut against Russian aggression. Now when she wanted it open to supply her ally she was to be thwarted.

Turkey and Gallipoli

In November 1914 Turkey had entered the war on the side of the Central powers. There followed a scheme which remains highly controversial. The British cabinet was split by the proposal of Winston Churchill and his ally Lloyd George to force a passage through the Straits. What might have resulted if this had succeeded has often been conjectured. If Russia and Serbia could have been kept in the war and Germany forced to continue her fight on two fronts, if the Russian army had been well supplied with equipment and ammunition, the war might have ended far sooner and there might never have been a Russian collapse nor a revolution in 1917. To speculate on the possible results of success at this point is thus a fascinating pastime. In fact the plan failed, largely because it never received the full support of either the British or the French government. Powerful groups felt very strongly that to pull troops out of France for a combined naval/military operation could be fatal, and they therefore opposed the idea.

Turkey and the Middle East

Immediately the war broke out Asquith, who had gone to the War Office himself at the time of the Curragh scandal, had invited the hero Kitchener to take over. Kitchener had won glory in the recapture of the Sudan and in South Africa in the years 1900–1902. He was a highly popular figure and his recruiting campaign was to bring some 2,750,000 men to the forces in the first eighteen months of war. It was his declared opinion that no men were available for a second front in 1915. Thus Churchill had to be content with a purely naval expedition.

In February 1915 a campaign was begun, although the Allied Commands had only allowed obsolescent ships to be used. Even then the attack might have succeeded if Admiral Carden had not been replaced through illness by Admiral de Robeck, who was convinced that without a military landing the Straits could not be forced. The fifteen-inch guns of the Allied ships were challenging the fourteen-inch Krupp guns installed in the fortresses. By 18 March the Allied fleet

Troops landing at Anzac Cove, Gallipoli

had lost three ships out of a total of nineteen, with two more, *Inflexible* and *Gambois*, badly damaged. Two thousand men had been lost and Admiral de Robeck steamed away. Kitchener now changed his mind and decided to make available some troops, both from the Western Front and from Australia and New Zealand. An expeditionary force was prepared in Alexandria, but preparations were public knowledge for weeks beforehand. The Turks massed guns and men under expert advice from their allies. On 25 April landings were made on the southern tip of the Gallipoli Peninsula under the command of General Sir Ian Hamilton. They held their bridgehead against heavy odds through the summer months, until reinforcements eventually arrived in August, when new landings were made at Suvla Bay. There were endless delays and frustrations despite much personal gallantry. Eventually the Allies, after losing three more British battleships, decided to withdraw, against the advice of Hamilton who was superseded in October. General Charles Monro was appointed to superintend the withdrawal and between 18 December 1915 and 8 January 1916 the troops were embarked and withdrawn. These same troops were later in the year to be landed at Salonika, which was to be the base for Allied fighting against Bulgaria until 1918. There had been some 120,000 Allied casualties.

Given more men, better ships and abler commanders, all of whom were available but 'could not be spared', then the Straits might have been opened. As it was, Bulgaria joined the Central powers and Serbia collapsed. Russia began her decline into the abyss of 1917. Churchill himself left the Admiralty in May 1915, disagreeing with the First Sea Lord, Fisher (who had returned at the outbreak of war), over the conduct of the campaign. In November 1915 he resigned from Asquith's government (having earlier and in secret developed the tank with Admiralty funds). The only consolation was the entry of Italy on the Allied side, out for a few more pickings from her old enemy Turkey, and possibly the Trentino district from Austria.

Disenchantment and Allied plans

1916, which opened with failure at Gallipoli, was to be a year of appalling waste on the Western Front. It was the year in which the whole tempo and attitude to war was to change in Britain. Since Napoleon, Britain had fought only local, mostly colonial, wars all of which she had won (except the First Boer War) and, apart from the Crimean War, relatively quickly and easily. In 1914 the mood was one of absurd optimism and enthusiasm. The politicians spoke, the young men came forward, the bands played and the crowds cheered as troops marched away to die. Now after two years what had been achieved? For hundreds of thousands of young Englishmen this war had meant no more than mud, lice, filth and death. At home income tax had risen to 5*s* in the £. The aims for which the Allies were fighting were increasingly obscure, and the gains no more than a few colonies in Africa and the Pacific. The new weapon of gas, first introduced by the Germans in April 1915, meant that if one survived death one might well return from the front with a constitution ruined for life. Thus the mood changed and a disenchantment developed. The flow of volunteers who had responded to Lord Kitchener's early appeal dried up and in March 1916 conscription was introduced for the first time in British history. Henceforth war lost its glamour and for most Englishmen it was to remain thus. The mood in 1939 was to be quite unlike that of 1914.

The Allied plan for 1916 was for offensives on three fronts, France, Italy and Belgium. But the Germans largely forestalled this by their decision to mount an all-out offensive of their own early in the year on the centre of the Allied Western Front at Verdun. The struggle on this section was to last from February to December; during it France lost the pick of her army. The Verdun attack began in February 1916 with the biggest artillery barrage yet fired. By March the first impetus had been held by General Pétain's arrival with reinforcements. From April to June the German offensive was at its most fierce and they captured Douaumont and Fort Vaux. French counter-attacks resulted in

Stuck in the mud in Flanders—note the blasted landscape

appalling losses. German casualties were some 300,000 men and the French as great or greater. In June a new Russian offensive was launched between the Pripet and Pruth into the Balkans against Austria. Four German divisions under Ludendorff were sent in four days from France. The Austrians retreated to the Carpathians, a quarter of a million prisoners and much equipment being captured by the victorious Russians. The pressure had been taken off the French, and Russia regained some of her lost prestige. But later in the year, with the collapse of Roumania, Falkenhayn was to reverse this Russian advance and win a series of crushing victories. Meanwhile, on 1 July, the British and French launched their attack on the Somme and the German pressure on Verdun at last relaxed: they had gained twelve square miles and two shattered fortresses.

General Sir John French had commanded the British troops in France since 7 August 1914 when they first landed. It was widely felt in 1915 that he had failed to show enough initiative, and he had been replaced by one of his corps commanders, Douglas Haig, in December 1915. Haig's theory was that given enough preparation, enough men and enough guns a break-through was inevitable. For two years he was to be allowed to keep on trying. Sir Winston Churchill (at this time in command of a regiment in France) has described how a great battle developed. It was impossible to maintain secret the site chosen; railways were at once built by both sides and mountains of shells brought up for months ahead. In this case the bombardment began on 24 June, the greatest Allied bombardment yet. On 1 July the troops went over the top, their objective the German trenches. 52,000 tons of shells had been fired at the Germans, but still 60,000 Allied troops were killed, wounded or captured on that first day. Only on the French end, where an attack had been least expected, was any progress made at all. But that did not deter the generals. More men and more ammunition were expended and the battle raged through the summer until the winter rains set in. In Churchill's words, 'a vast sea of ensanguined mud . . . replaced the blasted dust' until finally the weather brought an end. The British casualties for this Battle of the Somme amounted to some 500,000 men. In the late autumn of 1916 the French resumed the attack on the Verdun sector and drove the Germans back a mile or so. For such losses and gains were the lives of so many men lost. It seems incredible now that the generals of both sides could have been so barbarous and so lacking in the ability to find means whereby the deadlock of trench warfare might be broken. Even when offered the tank the Allied High Command could not see its potential and squandered its surprise value by using it too soon to no purpose.

Government changes and D.O.R.A.

Kitchener had died in June 1916 when, on his way to Archangel to confer with the Russians, his ship H.M.S. *Hampshire* was mined. He had been replaced at the War Office by Lloyd George, until he resigned on 5 December. By now public opinion had been brought to such a point of irritation with the continuing failure of the war that the Prime Minister, Asquith, felt that he too must resign. This was a personal triumph for Lloyd George, who was now invited to form a government (see the short biography of Asquith below). Only Asquith himself emerges honourably from the intrigues which had been afoot to force this resignation. Undoubtedly the press lords, William Aitken (created Lord Beaverbrook by a grateful Prime Minister in 1917) and Alfred Harmsworth, Viscount Northcliffe, made their contribution. Possibly they wielded more power in British politics at this time than they or their successors have ever done since. The Coalition cabinet formed in May 1915 had consisted of 12 Liberals, 8 Conservatives and 1 Labour member, with Lloyd George as Minister of Munitions. Now the latter formed his own Coalition, with its high-powered War Cabinet of six members; himself, Bonar Law, Lords Curzon and Milner (all three Conservatives), Henderson for Labour and later General Smuts from South Africa.

The new government was ruthless; Lloyd George brought into politics business men such as Sir Eric Geddes, who were determined to bring to the winning of the war the same kind of skills they had used for gaining their industrial wealth. Into the government in July 1917 was to come Winston Churchill, Lloyd George's old colleague, as Minister of Munitions. He was to be an outstanding success. At the same time new ministries such as those for Food and Shipping, Labour, National Service and Reconstruction were set up. The War Cabinet and its committees, with a vast secretariat, had a firmer control over the country's economy than any government had ever done before. This was now total war. The powers for such mobilization of the country's resources had been granted earlier in the war by the Defence of the Realm Act (D.O.R.A.); only now was this fully drawn upon.

This Act, passed in November 1914, gave the government powers of internment and trial without jury in matters of security and also the right to take over any factories or workshops thought necessary for war production. In May

1915 it had been extended to give greatly increased control over the sale of intoxicating liquor, something the Conservatives had for long resisted in peace-time.

War in the air

Before the war Germany already had a commercial airship service developed by Count Zeppelin, while British airship experiments had not been successful and were only to succeed after 1916 with the capture of a complete Zeppelin. Zeppelin air-raids reached their peak in that year, mostly over London and the Eastern counties but some reaching Cheshire and Scotland. Losses were increasingly high as searchlights, barrage-balloons and guns were developed: in October 1917 only four out of eleven airships returned from a raid. There were approximately fifty airship raids from which a total of 1913 casualties were either killed or

An air-raid in London, 1917. Note the comparative weakness of the bomb-blast—a small crater, no structural damage to buildings

wounded. Their effect was more one on morale than of material damage. There were also scattered aeroplane raids on Kent, Essex and London throughout the war, the worst being two raids on 13 June and 7 July 1917 when 844 casualties were either killed or wounded. There was a heavy raid on London on 28 January 1918 when Odhams Printing Works, which was being used as an air-raid shelter, was hit and twenty-eight people killed and ninety-seven injured. London eastern residential areas suffered most, damage to railways or industry not being very great, although the Central Telegraph Office, Charing Cross Hospital, St Pancras Station and Somerset House were among the public buildings hit. An air-raid on 19 May 1918 met with such resistance from anti-aircraft guns, machine guns and fighters that eleven machines were lost for about twenty-nine bombs dropped, and this was the last effective raid. By the end of the war the R.A.F. was carrying out bombing raids in reprisal as far as Frankfurt and Stuttgart and planning a major raid on Berlin when the armistice was signed.

War at sea and American entry

During the winter of 1916–1917 Britain faced her greatest challenge. Russia was exhausted and her army had begun to disintegrate. In the Middle East the British failure in April 1916, when 9000 men had surrendered at Kut, had not been reversed. At sea the Battle of Jutland in May had been inconclusive. The vast battle-fleet under Admiral Sir David Beatty from December 1916 continued to glare across the North Sea at its rival the German High Seas Fleet. Meanwhile the submarine war continued. During the first months of the war German submarines had fired indiscriminately. Then on 7 May 1915 had come the sinking of the *Lusitania*, when some 1198 passengers and crew were drowned, including 124 Americans, and public opinion in America had veered strongly towards the Allies. As a result, U-boat warfare had been eased in May 1915, but on 31 January 1917 the Germans took a gamble. They decided to resume unrestricted U-boat warfare, even though this meant that America might enter the war. Britain was prepared. All ships were armed and travelled in convoy; hydrophones were used for detection and depth-charges for destruction of U-boats; Q-ships (armed naval ships disguised as innocent merchant ships) were used to act as decoys. Nevertheless, of ships leaving British ports in April 1917, one in four was sunk, a total of 800,000 tons of Allied shipping being lost in that month. But, following renewed American losses from submarines, President Wilson now succeeded in persuading the U.S.A. to enter the war, which she did on 6 April with the slogan 'that the world must be made safe for democracy'. On 16 March the Russian revolution had begun and the Czarist regime ended, being replaced at first by a Parliamentary democracy.

For almost a century America had been isolated from European wars, since the treaty of Ghent in 1814, which had ended a war against Britain, caused among other things by British blockade methods. During the century America had been the 'melting-pot of Europe', receiving many millions of migrants from Ireland, Germany, Poland, Italy, Russia and Scandinavia. Naturally these or their descendants would not all feel equally sympathetic to the British cause. Indeed in the early days of the war there was considerable anti-British feeling, due once again to her blockade methods. But slowly American opinion came to favour the Allies. Partly this was a victory for British propaganda methods; partly a result of German errors, as in their intrigues in Mexico and their resumption of submarine warfare; partly it was the personal achievement of their President, Wilson (President 1912–1920), who really did see this war as a great struggle for the submerged peoples of Europe (especially Central and Eastern Europe) to throw off their 'imperial masters' and emerge as sovereign, independent nations. The withdrawal of Czarist Russia helped him in putting his case for democracy, but Wilson had war aims quite different from the original Allied ones of balance-of-power politics: aims which were consolidated into the Fourteen Points published in January 1918 (see appendix). In

Britain, too, war aims were increasingly necessary to keep up the spirit and level of sacrifice; the war was proclaimed a 'war to end wars' and Britain was going to be 'a land fit for heroes to live in'.

Labour and war

In spite of much international co-operation among labour movements before 1914 it was obvious in August 1914 that the bulk of organized Labour would support the war, the Labour Party pledging support, although not the much smaller Independent Labour Party. The T.U.C. was officially pro-war and Lloyd George as Minister of Munitions tried to enforce a policy of no strikes. Most of the trade unions co-operated although the miners never fully accepted this. From June 1915 the Labour Party was part of the Coalition Government and it remained so until November 1918. Up to 1916 Labour rank and file followed their leaders without question, but with conscription for military service, followed in December 1916 by an abortive German peace offer and in 1917 by the Russian revolution, which strongly appealed to working-class imagination, the enthusiasm declined. There grew up a new note of 'militant revolutionism' on the Left and in 1917 and 1918 there were some unpleasant strikes. The official leaders of trade unionism were tied down, but shop stewards became key figures in these strikes of the later war years.

State control over labour and industry was very extensive by the end of the war: the railwayman, the miner, the munition worker and the merchant seaman were all virtually state employees. The government was the largest single consumer, controlling purchases and production in spheres of the economy not directed to war effort. Price control and licences were extensive, for example most foodstuffs, and such essential items as paper, glass, picric acid, iron and steel, as well as fuel, were all subject to restriction. As the end of the war approached, Unions pressed for some kind of guarantee against post-war dilution of labour, which had increasingly occurred since conscription, and for the retention of a great number of controls. On the whole they were to be unsuccessful, although promises were conceded.

The employers had formed the powerful Federation of British Industries and they wanted the maximum of freedom as soon as possible. This they were to get, in spite of the advice of such bodies as the Whitley Committee which reported to the Ministry of Reconstruction recommending the claim of the workers for a 'share in the control of industry'. It is true that in 1918 a Trade Boards Act greatly extended the work of the Act of 1909, bringing several million more workers under the protection of the minimum legal wage. But long before the slump of 1921–1922, when the employers were able to use the plea of redundancy to weed out obnoxious elements, the relations in industry were to be restored to those of straight bargaining between trade unions and employers. Many members of the Shop Stewards' Movement, disillusioned with the Labour Party, joined the British Communist Party founded in 1920. The question of the dilution by women operatives was to be left to sort itself out. The greatest employer of such labour, the munitions industry, was to contract almost to nothing within months of the armistice in 1918.

Agriculture

Another section of the population from which much was asked in the war years was the farmers. After the great crash in agriculture in the 1870's, there had been a considerable recovery since about 1895. Corn production had given way to grass; livestock, fruit, vegetables and dairy farming had replaced wheat. Although the total acreage devoted to agriculture had declined only from 47,300,000 acres to 46,800,000 acres, the labour force had declined by some 600,000 men. These changes and decline were accepted as inevitable, given free competition with the vast prairie production of the New World. Nobody had any real conception of total war and its consequences. In 1903 a Royal Commission had agreed that even during a maritime war there would be no material diminution in the volume of imported foodstuff, particularly corn. It was agreed that Britain would need to rely on importing about two-thirds of her food supplies.

When war began there was some early submarine activity, but after the *Lusitania* incident this was reduced and home harvests in 1914 and 1915 were good. In May 1915 Food Production Committees were set up for England and Wales, Scotland and Ireland, and County Agricultural Committees were formed.

1916 again brought a change in attitude. Overseas and home harvests were poor; shipping losses began to go up; the area under plough had actually decreased since 1914, owing to labour shortages; thus Lloyd George's new government had to make rapid changes. A Food Production Department was set up in January 1917 to ensure better distribution of labour, machinery, feeding-stuffs and fertilizers. Sixty-one County Agricultural Executive Committees were formed, with considerable powers to compel farmers to plough up grassland. In 1918 3,000,000 acres more were ploughed than in 1916. The increase in production in terms of calorific value rose by 24% in the year 1917. It was a remarkable achievement made possible by a mixture of compulsion, high prices and high wages: the Agricultural Wages Board guaranteed the latter.

Nevertheless the food situation in 1918 was extremely serious as stocks declined. In 1916 a Food Control Board had been set up. In 1917 standard bread was introduced and sugar rationing began (incidentally the sugar beet industry now came into its own). Food prices had risen by some 130% and many foods had completely disappeared from the shops when Lord Rhondda, the Food Controller in 1918, greatly extended rationing and price control. Sugar, butter, eggs, margarine, lard, meat, jam, cheese and tea were among those foods now rationed. This together with the successful efforts being made against the submarines enabled the country to survive. The question for the farmers in 1918 was, how would the peace affect them? Would the depressed years of 1875–1895 return? What guarantees could be extracted from the government for the sacrifices made in war-time?

Extension of the franchise and emancipation of women

Approximately one in four adult males in 1914 still had no vote. If Britain was to become a land fit for heroes, they must at least be given the vote. This is the background to the Fourth Reform Act of 1918. As early as 1916 a Bill was tabled in Parliament 'to amend the Representation of the People'. It was itself to receive a great number of amendments before becoming law in 1918. Originally designed simply to provide means of registration for voters who had changed addresses or entered the Services, it ended by granting the vote to women over thirty (some 6,000,000) and to all men over twenty-one except peers, lunatics and felons (some additional 2,000,000). Plural voting was restricted to two votes. Candidates for election would need a deposit of £150 which they would forfeit if receiving less than one-eighth of the votes. The contribution of women to the war had been considerable. From the start they had supplied the bulk of the nurses for the many thousands of casualties, being organized as Voluntary Aid Detachments. In 1916 there had been formed women's units in the services: the Women's Auxiliary Army Corps and the Women's Royal Naval Service. Women had worked in thousands in factories, in agriculture, as policewomen, as bank clerks and as railway porters. The Second World War was to see much the same pattern. But it was from 1916 onwards that the place of women in society was to begin to change profoundly, bringing about the 'emancipation of women' and their gradual acceptance into nearly all professions.

Education

The Education Act of 1918, introduced by the Oxford historian H. A. L. Fisher, then Minister of Education, has been attacked often enough since as no more than political bribery; 'keep up the morale of the parents by making, for the education of their children, promises you have no intention of keeping'. This is unfair. Fisher himself, a devoted Liberal, was completely committed to the Act and much of it was at once implemented, even though some sections were to be left for another generation to complete. It was introduced 'with a view to the establishment of a national system of public education available to all persons capable of profiting thereby', i.e. it aimed to provide schools for all from nursery to the age of fourteen and part-time education up to eighteen for those not receiving secondary education. At least it succeeded in stopping the loopholes in the system as it existed for those under fourteen. It provided for physical education in schools and the setting up of a number of technical schools. Unfortunately most of its other items were to be 'axed' in 1922 when, with the first post-war slump, a great economy drive was to be introduced. One permanent result was the setting up of the Burnham Committee for negotiating Teachers' Salaries.

The war 1917–1918

1917 was to prove a very grave year indeed for the Allies. The full war-potential of America would take many months to realize. Meanwhile British shipping losses remained alarmingly high and were only gradually brought under control. In fact the only positive Allied successes of the year were in the Middle East where T. E. Lawrence, operating with Arab nationalist forces, successfully covered the flank of General Allenby who advanced from Egypt to Jerusalem (December 1917) and from there on towards Damascus which was reached in October 1918.

Elsewhere on the two main fronts of France and Italy there were disasters. In France the new Commander-in-Chief, Nivelle, planned a vast offensive. His opponent, Ludendorff, who had replaced Falkenhayn in August 1916, decided to avoid this by a tactical withdrawal to a prepared line of greater strength. The French attacked in April and had to advance across a desert of pock-marked and useless wasteland. The result was appalling disaster and mutinies within the French army. Pétain replaced Nivelle and the British promised to relieve the pressure.

This was the origin of the prolonged British offensive which ended with the Battle of Passchendaele. It began as early as April when the Canadians successfully captured Vimy Ridge. In June they took Messines Ridge. From 31 July until November the British attacked from Ypres towards what had once been the small town of Passchendaele, which they did actually occupy for a while. General Haig believed that he had the men and the shells he needed and he poured them into the autumn rains. Some 300,000 British casualties were sustained, many men being literally drowned in the blood-soaked mud. Only one small break-through was achieved, and this by the tanks in November around Cambrai, when, for 1500 casualties, the British captured some 10,000 prisoners and 200 guns. But the essential lesson of this episode, the need for greater mobility and fluidity, was even now not fully grasped by the Allied High Command.

Caporetto

On the Italian Front the autumn of 1917 saw another Allied disaster. The mountainous nature of this area had prevented trench warfare developing in quite the way it had done in flattened Flanders. This was much more a front of pill-boxes, fortresses, mountain passes and river approaches. In October the Austrians, using a plan of Ludendorff's and reinforced by troops from the Eastern Front, punched a great hole in the line on the north-east frontier around the fortress town of Caporetto on the Isonzo River. A chaotic retreat followed (brilliantly described in E. Hemingway's novel *A Farewell to Arms*) until floods and bad weather finally brought the advance to a stop somewhere along the Piave River. Fifteen thousand guns and about 250,000 men had been lost. But during the winter the Italians recovered under their new commander, Diaz, and 1918 was not to see the expected break-through. Instead, Hindenburg in Berlin planned a final breach of the French line before American troops began to become effective.

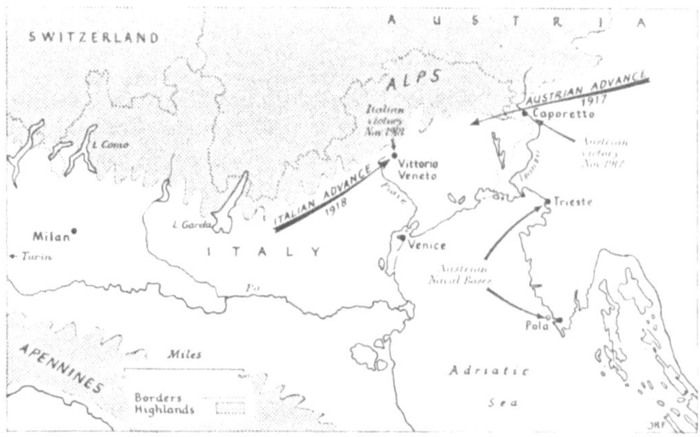

The Italian Front

He was in fact already too late. Not only were American destroyers breaking the submarine menace, but American troops were being landed in France in increasing numbers, the first having landed in June 1917. In March 1918 80,000 were landed; in April 118,000; in May 245,000. On her side Germany concluded the treaty of Brest-Litovsk with Bolshevik Russia on 3 March 1918, liberating men for the last great struggle.

The German offensive begun on 21 March was aimed at the British sector. They captured 90,000 prisoners within a week and the British 5th Army pulled back. (Haig became adamant: 'There must be no retirement,' he ordered.) A second offensive pushed the line from Ypres to Armentières. Now the Allies at last agreed in April to subordinate all their forces, French, British and American, under one supreme commander, General Foch, who had one great quality: he believed in mobility in war. His ideas were to save the day, but only because he had fresh American troops at the critical moment. This was at Château Thierry, where the American 1st and 2nd Divisions held the bulging Allied line.

In June there had been a new German attack, bringing

them once again to the Marne and nearly to Paris. On 15 July they had launched the fourth phase of their offensive, but again it was held. Three days later Foch counter-attacked, taking the Germans by surprise. Using two American divisions and one French-Moroccan one, he drove a wedge into the German line. In August the British attacked with 450 tanks near Amiens. From now on, brilliantly using air reconnaissance, the Allied armies rolled up the German front.

The Italians now attacked on the Austrian Front and avenged Caporetto at Vittorio Veneto. The troops, who had been sitting in the Allied beach-head at Salonika since 1916, advanced into Bulgaria; she sued for peace, an armistice being signed with the Serbs, Greeks, French and British on 20 September. Turkey withdrew from the war on 30 October as Allenby drove beyond Damascus. The Austro-Hungarian Empire now broke down into its component national parts, an armistice being signed on 4 November after the Italians had captured some 300,000 men and 600 guns. On 13 November Austria became a republic. Four days earlier on 9 November the German fleet had mutinied at Kiel, the revolution spreading to Berlin and to southern Germany. The Kaiser fled to Holland and an armistice was signed on 11 November. On 21 November the German High Seas Fleet sailed under British orders to Scapa Flow, where it scuttled itself the following June. Meanwhile Allied preparations were being made for the occupation of the Rhineland (on strong pressure from the French) and for putting into practice President Wilson's Fourteen Points, which had become the official war aims of the Allies. Somewhere between 10,000,000 and 25,000,000 people had lost their lives as a result of the fighting and of disease during these four years.

PART THREE

Between the Wars

1918–1939

6

The war ends

The War of Allied Intervention in Russia

In 1917, when the moderate Russian revolutionary Kerensky was trying to establish himself in power in Russia, Lloyd George sent Arthur Henderson, the Labour cabinet minister, to establish contact with him. His purpose was to keep Russia in the war. Henderson became interested in the possibility of peace with both Germany and Russia and supported a move for a Socialist Peace Congress in Stockholm. The rest of the cabinet considered that he had let them down and forced his resignation. The Labour Party continued to support the war but there was some decline in enthusiasm within the Labour Movement, and Lloyd George agreed to the idea of formulating war aims. Meanwhile in November 1917 Kerensky fled from Russia, Lenin brought about the Bolshevik revolution and Russia signed the peace of Brest-Litovsk in March 1918 with Germany.

An attempt to keep the new Bolshevik government in the war having failed, the British cabinet now made a fateful decision. It agreed to support the enemies of the new regime who were attempting to regain control. These were a very varied lot, ranging from extreme royalists to socialist revolutionaries, who had been expelled with Kerensky. Thus began the War of Allied Intervention. Its main areas were: the extreme north around Murmansk: the Ukraine, the Crimea and Transcaucasia; and thirdly the Far East from Vladivostock, which was held by socialist revolutionaries. In addition Poland, newly recreated, attacked in 1920 from the west.

In February and March 1918, even before the Brest-Litovsk negotiations were completed, a British force landed at Murmansk, being joined by French and American forces. At first the Bolsheviks accepted this, but later demanded their evacuation. The Allied aims were declared to be the prevention of the sale of large stocks of material to Germany. This force, incredibly badly handled, now made ineffective incursions southwards, in an attempt to link up with Czechoslovak troops (liberated prisoners of war) who had advanced to the Urals from Siberia.

In July a British force was sent from Persia to Transcaucasia. There, with the help of Cossacks from the Ukraine, who were determined to retain independence from the new Bolshevik regime, it inflicted a considerable defeat on the local Bolsheviks. Baku was occupied and for a while British military rule prevailed in this remote corner of Europe, regarded by the cabinet as vital because of its nearness to Afghanistan and India. However, within a month, on 17 August 1918, the British had to evacuate and retreat to Enzeli on the south of the Caspian Sea, from where eventually they were to be withdrawn into Persia.

In the Far East a British contingent reached Vladivostok on 3 August 1918 to be joined there by Japanese, French and Americans. Their aim was to contact and assist the Czechoslovak force now operating far to the west on the Volga River. Again chaos resulted, as the force was far too small to be effective.

This is no place for a detailed discussion of the events of the next two years. Gradually Britain and the Allies realized the bankruptcy of their policy. The anti-Bolshevik parties were too diverse and too corrupt ever to become an effective force for victory. But it was the Allied decision to intervene which undoubtedly prolonged the fighting and most authorities now seem to agree that it enabled the Bolshevik regime to become internally established. The counter-attacks against them simply made Lenin and Trotsky more ruthless in their policy of centralization. By playing on the dangers of the situation, with Russia besieged and ruin imminent, the regime was able to win support, in spite of the policy of terrorism now begun in a revolution which at first had been conspicuous for its moderation. The Russian peasantry, at last possessed of their land, were determined at all costs to prevent its restoration to its former owners and they gave their loyalty to the new regime. At the same time the ancient appeal to defend their mother soil from the invader brought not only peasant support. Especially after Poland entered the war, many ex-Czarists rallied 'to preserve the independence of Mother Russia', perhaps the most famous example being General Brusilov's decision to give support. He had been one of the most successful generals opposed to the Germans in 1914–1917. Now he issued a proclamation urging all Russian officers to support the Red Army.

Britain withdrew from Vladivostok in 1919 and from Archangel in February 1920. In July 1920 the Crimea, the last refuge of the Allies in the south, was lost to the Bolsheviks. Still there were powerful advocates, led by Churchill, now Secretary for War, for active intervention in Poland. The Russians invaded newly liberated Poland in July 1920 and the Poles appealed for Allied help. The French General Weygand, at that time in Warsaw, assisted the Polish army, which successfully held the Russian advance. Poland then reached a frontier agreement at the treaty of Riga and the danger of a renewal of the War of Intervention had passed.

Nobody can estimate how many millions died during these three years, from atrocities, battles, disease, cold and starvation. For two whole years Moscow and Leningrad workers never received a daily ration of more than one-eighth of a pound of black bread, and even that was half bran. They often received less. By 1921 the area under crops was 60% less, and the yield 50% less, than before the war. Output of heavy industry was only 13% that of pre-war and of light industry 44%. The physical and financial blockade imposed by the Allies until 1921 brought Russia to the edge of collapse. But by the ruthless determination of her rulers she had survived and the Allied attempt to prevent the revolution had failed. The Allies had, however, forced the Bolsheviks to compromise with their own principles and abandon the idea of spreading the revolution through Europe and to this extent they had been successful.

By the end of 1921 the war was over. The Communist government had established authority over what remained of Russia, large parts having successfully broken free, including Finland, Poland, Latvia, Lithuania and Estonia. British intervention had produced an exaggerated fear in Russia of British Imperialism and in Britain of Bolshevik Communism.

The establishment of the Irish Free State

The great struggle in the nineteenth century of Irish Nationalists drew its strength from the peasantry. But the long years of Conservative rule before 1906 had done a great deal to produce a prosperous, reasonably contented countryside of small farmers. The twentieth-century struggle was largely an urban one. Above all it was a struggle between Catholic Dublin, traditional capital but lacking any heavy industry, and violently Protestant Belfast, rapidly expanding as a great industrial centre. We have already traced one line of this struggle and noted the appearance of the Ulster and Irish Volunteers by 1914. But many of the latter belonged to a secret society called Sinn Fein (not to be muddled with the earlier Fenians).

Sinn Fein means 'We ourselves'. It was a movement of young nationalists who wanted something more than Home Rule. They wanted to re-create the legendary land of the Celts. This meant an absolute political, social and economic breakaway and also a positive cultural rebirth. The movement began in 1902, started by Arthur Griffith, an Irish journalist of those brilliant Dublin years before 1914 immortalized by James Joyce. In 1906 Griffith started a newspaper called *Sinn Fein*, which at first appealed mostly to students and intellectuals. Gradually the movement became more popular, and when the Ulster Volunteers began, Sinn Fein actively supported the creation of the Irish Volunteers to oppose them. In 1914 Asquith was saved from the dilemma of his Home Rule policy by war. John Redmond, the moderate Irish nationalist, pledged Ireland's support for the war. But already there had been isolated incidents of shooting between Irishmen and Ulstermen and in 1916 came the Sinn Fein rising in Easter week in Dublin.

The details of this incident are still disputed; for example was Sir Roger Casement travelling from Germany to Ireland (by submarine) in order to join the rebellion or to try to discourage it? In any case, during the week, extremist members of Sinn Fein tried to seize Dublin and proclaim a Republic and they were put down by the army, after bloody fighting and some 450 deaths. Several hundred arrests were made and some fourteen executions followed, including James Connolly, the self-educated Irish trade unionist, and Patrick Pearse, who was Commandant-General of the Irish Republic Army and President of a provisional Republic of Ireland. An Irish-American, Eamonn de Valera, was imprisoned, but not executed; Griffith was arrested, although not actively involved in the rising; Casement was tried and executed for high treason in England. The bloody methods of suppression helped to swing Irish opinion behind Sinn Fein.

In 1917 the British government sought to ease the tension by a general amnesty. De Valera, among others, was released and immediately elected as M.P. for East Clare and secretly as President of Sinn Fein. In May 1918 he was rearrested and imprisoned in Lincoln. Later that year attempts to enforce conscription in Ireland greatly aggravated an already tense situation.

In December 1918 came the Coupon Election. John Dillon, who had succeeded Redmond, was defeated and the old Irish Nationalist Party was nearly obliterated, winning only seven seats. The seventy-three elected Sinn Fein members who were not in prison refused to take their seats in

Westminster. Instead they set up in secret their own Dail Eireann in Dublin, with Arthur Griffith and Michael Collins as ministers. The latter, as Minister of Finance, raised money for the importation of arms for the Irish Volunteers, or Republican Army as they were now called. Collins had active supporters among the Irish police, Post Office and Customs officers. He organized a sort of 'scarlet pimpernel' service to enable prisoners to escape, his most daring success being to get De Valera out of Lincoln prison in February 1919. He was spirited to Dublin and thence to the U.S.A. in order to raise money.

All effective government now tended to break down, especially in and around Dublin and Belfast. The Coalition cabinet decided to meet force with force. The new secretary for Ireland, Sir Hamar Greenwood, revitalized the Royal Irish Constabulary by recruiting into it the toughest elements he could find. These were the Black and Tans. They were assisted by a force of unemployed officers, the Auxiliaries. Lloyd George, Winston Churchill and Lord Birkenhead, the three strongest men in the Coalition, seemed to have been persuaded by their C.I.G.S., the Ulsterman Sir Henry Wilson, that force was the only answer.

A terrible year of atrocities now followed: kidnapping, midnight raids, ambushes, torture, shootings and reprisals. These were used by both sides. Black and Tan parties would roar into a quiet village in the middle of the night; turn all the occupants out of bed and out of the village; kill all their animals and burn down their buildings on the mere suspicion of 'sympathy for the Irish boys'. In retaliation the I.R.A. would force their way into buildings and shoot their way out again. On Bloody Sunday, 21 November 1920, members of the I.R.A. forced their way into fourteen houses and hotels scattered through Dublin. They hauled from their beds and shot fourteen British officers and civilians, in some cases in the presence of their wives.

Such a war of mutual hatred could not go on for ever. Already, at its height, the Westminster Parliament passed a Bill partitioning Ireland into six northern counties and twenty-six southern, granting Home Rule to both. Thus Northern Ireland, which had so violently resisted Home Rule in the years before the war, began its Home Parliament in June 1921 with Sir James Craig as Prime Minister. In the south an armistice was arranged on 11 July, both sides being exhausted and British public opinion having turned against the bloody guerilla war. Prolonged negotiations followed, encouraged by George V, who pleaded for

War in Ireland following the settlement of December 1921

conciliation. De Valera and Lloyd George met, and then in December 1921 Griffith and Collins were sent to London. A treaty was signed on 5 December creating the Irish Free State which would have the same status within the Empire as dominions such as Canada then had. Griffith, Collins and William Cosgrave all agreed to the treaty, but De Valera opposed it and a civil war now ensued between the two Irish groups. After Griffith's death and Collins's death in an ambush in 1922, Cosgrave became head of the government.

Throughout 1922 and early 1923 the civil war continued, but gradually it subsided, until in April 1923 De Valera decided to make it a constitutional struggle rather than a military one. His group became a political party, the Fianna Fail or Republican Party. In 1932 they were to triumph at the elections and De Valera became Prime Minister. The Irish Republican Army went underground, to fight for the ending of partition and the reunion of Ireland. Gradually the Irish Free State was to move step by step to being a fully independent Republic outside the Commonwealth, which was finally proclaimed in 1949 (see Chapter 11).

Labour Party programme and Constitution 1918

In February 1918 the Labour Party had acquired its present Constitution and a new programme based on the pamphlet *Labour and the New Social Order*, by Sidney Webb. The Constitution converted the party from being no more than a loose affiliation of trade unions and various socialist societies into a centrally organized political party, with wide membership, but maintaining a close link with the T.U.C. with whom the party shared headquarters. There were to be annual Party Conferences, but the day-to-day management of policy would be by the national executive of the party. Labour M.P.s would belong to the Parliamentary Labour Party, whose representatives would sit on the National Joint Council of the whole party. The new programme can be summarized as follows:

1. Universal enforcement of a National Minimum, i.e. further social security and greater use of public works to ensure full employment.
2. Democratic Control of Industry, i.e. some degree of nationalization, particularly of coal, electricity, railways, breweries and insurance companies, and possibly even land.
3. Revolution in Finance, i.e. greater equality of sacrifice through taxation, including a capital levy.
4. Surplus Wealth to be devoted to the Common Good, which summed up all the other points.

Arthur Henderson had already left the Cabinet, and it is not surprising that, with a programme like this, the Labour Party on 14 November 1918 decided to withdraw from the Coalition and fight the coming election on its own.

Coupon Election and the Coalition

Lloyd George had announced on that day an immediate election, which was to be held on 10 December. The Liberal Party was split, there being Asquith Liberals and Lloyd George Liberals and no love lost between them. For Lloyd George, to vote for the Coalition meant to vote for a candidate who had received a letter from himself and Bonar Law giving their support. The result was a victory for the Conservatives and the Lloyd George Liberals who between them obtained 484 seats. The Asquith Liberals got 26 seats and the Labour Party 59. This split of the Liberal Party was to prove fatal.

The new cabinet contained Lloyd George himself, of whom, for all his failings, Winston Churchill has said, 'he was the greatest master of the art of getting things through that I ever knew'; Bonar Law as Lord Privy Seal; Lord Birkenhead as Lord Chancellor; Austen Chamberlain as Chancellor of the Exchequer; A. J. Balfour as Foreign Secretary; and Churchill as War Secretary. It was a powerful team, mostly of Conservatives. We have already noticed two of its main tasks: the finding of solutions to the international problem of the Bolshevik Revolution and to the Sinn Fein movement in Ireland. At home its main task was demobilization and a return to peace-time without undue social upheaval. The government exaggerated the Bolshevik danger at home and consequently was anxious to maintain the restrictions imposed by D.O.R.A. Nevertheless, in these bleak winter months, with the influenza plague claiming 150,000 victims and coal alarmingly short for power and heat, there were no grounds for complacency. Churchill faced the question of demobilization with characteristic energy. Basing his scheme on length of service and number of wounds, he demobilized at the rate of 10,000 men a day for nearly six months. Of the 4,000,000 men released, most at first obtained employment in the immediate post-war boom. Women in the services were all released, but the number of women in employment rapidly fell. In fact by 1921 the proportion of women to men in employment had actually fallen below that in 1914.

Industrial unrest

In spite of this relatively easy first transition from war to peace, there was much industrial unrest, particularly in Scotland, where on 31 January 1919 occurred the 'Battle of George Square' between troops armed with tanks and machine guns and a crowd of 30,000 strikers 'armed with no more than Red Flags and bottles of soda water'. In August 1919 there was a police strike and a railway strike in September and everywhere the government sniffed Bolshevism. This was apparently confirmed when in September 1920 Labour was remarkably united in its opposition to government plans to intervene on behalf of Poland, and when in the same year the British Communist Party was formed, from discontented elements in the trade unions and Labour Party. In fact Bolshevik activities, as far as they existed, were never more than on the fringe of Labour. During the year 1920–1921 strikes were fewer and labour as much as capital enjoyed the short post-war boom while the government had been busy appointing commissions and enquiries which it was hoped would gain the time necessary for tension to relax. The recommendations of the Whitley Committee to the Ministry of Reconstruction during the war for greater participation of workers in the government of industry, were partly adopted by the setting up of numerous Whitley Councils of employers and trade-union representatives. Unfortunately, many, though not all, of these were to die within a few years.

Immediate post-war legislation

During the year of industrial boom two important pieces of legislation were introduced of considerable social importance: the Housing and Town Planning Act of 1919 and the Unemployment Insurance Act of 1920. The Housing Act of 1919, often known as the Addison Act, after Dr Christopher Addison, its author and the first Minister of Health, gave powers and subsidies to local governments to begin to erect council houses. Under this Act, towns and villages throughout the country acquired rows of terraced and semi-detached council houses with subsidized rents. They were to provide far better living conditions for more people than any previous housing schemes had done and the Ministry of Health thus became in part a ministry of housing. Under the Act some 171,000 houses were built in the years 1919–1923.

The Unemployment Insurance Act of 1920 greatly extended the provisions of 1911. During the war munition workers had qualified for assistance and after 1918 an out-of-work donation (the dole) had been provided to ex-servicemen and munitions workers not yet employed, on a non-contributory basis. This scheme ended in November 1919 and there was considerable agitation for the scheme of 1911 to be completely recast. As a result, a government Bill was introduced in Parliament which would cover nearly all workers earning under £250 a year except domestic servants, agricultural workers and civil servants. It provided weekly benefits of 15*s* for a man and 12*s* for a woman for fifteen weeks in any year after twelve contributions, provided the Labour Exchange could not provide employment. In this way the benefits of 1911 were extended, although there was as yet no provision for family allowances or for the destitute poor on a non-contributory basis. Possibly it would not have become law if 1920 had not been a year of full employment.

The next year was to see the beginning of the post-war economic troubles which were to last off and on until the next war. First, in 1921 the government, against the advice of a commission which had recommended nationalization, handed back the coal-mines to the owners: secondly it decontrolled the railways, after grouping them into four large systems: G.W.R.; L.M.S.; S.R.; L.N.E.R.; thirdly, the drinking restrictions of D.O.R.A. having come to an end, the hours of opening of licensed premises, controlled as before the war by local magistrates, were to remain heavily restricted and they have been ever since.

Post-war agriculture

In October 1919 Lloyd George announced his agricultural policy: greater home production and some form of protection of farmers against violent price fluctuations due to foreign competition. In 1920 an Agriculture Act was passed, guaranteeing prices of wheat and oats. But unfortunately this Act could not stand the slump which at once followed; wheat prices going from 80*s* 10*d* per quarter to 42*s* 2*d* by 1923. It was repealed in 1921 and the guarantees removed, except for current crops, it being argued that the Treasury could not hope to meet bills of somewhere between £15,000,000 and £35,000,000. The Agricultural Wages Board, with its minimum wage, was abolished and wages fell from 42*s* for a 48 hr. week to 36*s* for a 50 hr. week. There were some strikes and the overall effect was for the decline of the amount of land under plough, begun long before the war, to be resumed. By 1931 it was to stand at 1,197,000 acres, the lowest figure ever recorded. Only the new industry of sugar-beet survived the cuts. This continued to obtain protection and in the Second World War Britain was to be able to depend almost entirely on home production of sugar. It is grown in wheat-producing East Anglia.

By the Smallholdings Act of 1908 and the Acquisition of Land Act 1919 County Councils were empowered to buy, in some cases by compulsion, land to be sold or let in small units as smallholdings. Some 16,000 such units were created immediately after the war; farms for chickens, fruit and vegetables. Some 24,000 ex-servicemen put all their savings and borrowed capital into their ventures, but many of these, perhaps a quarter, were unable to survive the fall in prices and the return to *laissez-faire* for agriculture. They joined the 2,000,000 unemployed who were outside the Labour

Exchanges by the spring of 1922. Later governments of the 1920's were to try to grapple with the agricultural problem and there was to be a new smallholders Act in 1926 which would try to ease their problem, but it remained a depressed industry throughout the decade.

Treaty of Versailles and the League of Nations

Meanwhile in Paris the Peace Conference had taken place, having assembled on 12 January 1919. The demands for hanging the Kaiser were receding, but there was still a strong determination that 'Germany must pay'. This was strongest in France and among the Conservative back-benchers in England. Delegations from the victorious Allies installed themselves in the hotels in Paris and the map of Europe was redrawn. In Central Europe the empires of Austria, Russia and Turkey had gone and Germany was turning herself into the Weimar Republic. The principle of

Aldgate, 1920. Post-war London had many more buses as well as trams

monarchy was at a discount; the principle of self-determination, as put out in the Fourteen Points of President Wilson, was to be the means by which the new nation-states were to come into being. In multi-racial districts the majority was going to have to decide by plebiscite.

A Council of Ten (two representatives from Britain, France, Italy, Japan and the U.S.A.) was entrusted with working out proposals. In fact the Big Three (Wilson, Lloyd George and Clemenceau) did all the work. Wilson fought for all his fourteen points, while Clemenceau was interested only in the subjection of Germany and the extraction of reparations, and was bored by Wilson's liberalism. 'Mr Wilson bores me with his fourteen points; why, God Almighty has only ten.' At the same time Clemenceau firmly believed that the future of France lay in maintaining her links with the Western powers. Wilson accepted the principle of German disarmament and an unspecified bill for reparations, in return for the setting up of a League of Nations. Germany was to be required to admit her war guilt, to be stripped of all her colonies, to return Alsace-Lorraine to France, to restore the Belgian frontier, to hand back her Polish provinces to the new Poland, to give to the Allies the coal from the Saar basin, to accept military and naval disarmament and to pay reparations: five billion dollars as an immediate indemnity and a future sum not yet decided. The Rhineland was to be occupied by the Allies for fifteen years, a clause later to be abandoned at Locarno in 1925 in favour of 'demilitarization'. German colonies were to become mandated territories, looked after by the victorious powers, Britain and the Commonwealth receiving the lion's share. East Prussia and West Prussia were to be separated by a Polish corridor leading to the German city of Danzig which was to be internationally controlled.

A Reparations Commission was to be set up to decide final figures. Lloyd George is often today attacked for following the policy of 'squeezing the German orange until the pips squeaked', but at the time much opinion in Britain regarded him as too lenient. He was attacked by Lord

Northcliffe's newspapers *The Times* and the *Daily Mail*, and 233 Conservative M.P.s tried to exert pressure on him. Nevertheless the treaty was drawn up and presented for signature to the German delegates on 7 May 1919, in the Hall of Mirrors at Versailles. The Conference continued to sit through 1919 working out subsidiary treaties, but President Wilson returned to the United States an overworked man. He fought hard for his achievement, but the Senate refused to ratify the Treaty of Versailles and the U.S.A. returned in part at least to her traditional policy of isolationism, which was to continue until 1941.

The League of Nations came into being in 1920: the Council first meeting in January and the Assembly in November. None of the three great powers, the U.S.A., Russia nor Germany, was represented. As long as Lloyd George remained in power it tended to be bypassed and replaced by a series of conferences, twenty-three of which met in the years 1920–1922 in the pleasure resorts of Europe. All were dominated by the British statesman, now the only war leader still in office. After the fall of the Coalition government in 1922 this form of diplomacy declined.

7

Coalition, Labour, Conservative

Slump and unemployment

A serious trade decline followed the immediate post-war boom. In 1921 both export and import trade was only 60% of that in 1920 and wage rates sank by nearly 100 points. Unemployment figures rose from 1,355,206 in December 1920 to 2,171,288 by March 1921, ship-building, iron and steel, and engineering being the hardest hit. Inevitably such unemployment caused demonstrations and even a threatened general strike growing out of a coal strike, to counter which the government formed a special Defence Force whose aim one of its members said was 'to get the working classes back to their kennels. Back to cheap labour. Back to discipline'. A general strike was narrowly averted, following Black Friday, 15 April. Earlier Lloyd George had offered mediation to the miners, which they rejected on the morning of the 15th. They appealed to the Triple Alliance of trade unions for support for a general strike to start at midnight. This they failed to achieve and the strike was called off. Great bitterness resulted and the Triple Alliance, formed in 1914 following the pre-war labour troubles, dissolved. Labour leaders such as J. H. Thomas and Ernest Bevin had felt that such a general strike would be pandering to the extremists in the trade-union movement while at the same time giving a government, ready for a showdown with labour, too easy a way out. Thus little occurred except an increase in membership of the Communist Party.

Coal Strike at Wigan, April 1921. An agitator holding a meeting

Government measures:

(*i*) *The Dole and Family Relief.* More constructively the Coalition government tried to wrestle with the problem in three ways. First there was introduced a series of unemployment Acts consolidated as the Unemployment Insurance Act of 1922, which not only continued payment of relief benefit to those who qualified by the earlier Act of 1920 but made its receipt general for an unlimited period for all unemployed. This was known as unconvenanted benefit; it was often resented by those who were obliged to queue each week to collect their 'dole' and by the middle classes who considered it demoralizing.

It was partly an insurance benefit and partly a contribution made by those who were fit and in employment towards helping those who were ill and out of work. A second government measure was the provision of family relief. The Unemployed Workers' Dependents Act of November 1921 gave relief for wives (5*s* per week) and children (1*s* per week). From this stemmed a whole system of allowances, but no general family allowance until 1945. Inevitably there remained cases of hardship and these continued to be dealt with by the older nineteenth-century system of Poor Law Guardians who paid out relief from local taxation. The scale of this relief varied considerably from one area to another.

(*ii*) *Geddes Axe.* Thus one answer was relief; another was economy. In August 1921 the government appointed a committee of bankers and businessmen to advise, the chairman being a powerful business man, the late Minister of Transport, Sir Eric Geddes. The result was 'The Geddes Axe'. The Committee recommended not higher state spending, as the economists of the American New Deal in 1933 were to do, but lower. They aimed to save £75,000,000, by economies in the government services. The armed services should be further reduced; the Education Act of 1918 should be largely scrapped, teachers' salaries reduced and the school starting age raised from five to six years old; war pensions should be cut by £3,300,000; the state's contribution to the National Health Insurance scheme should be reduced and maternity and child welfare services go; the civil service should be reduced and a number of ministries abolished.

Not all the recommendations were accepted. The Admiralty succeeded in halving their reductions and education suffered by £6,500,000 instead of £18,000,000, although this was still enough to make the Labour Party cry against 'making the children pay while the rich betake themselves to St Moritz'.

(*iii*) *Protection.* The third measure was protection: a triumph at last for the principles of the Tariff Reform League. The war had seen the introduction of considerable control over the economy, including in 1915 the McKenna duties to discourage the importing of luxuries when shipping was scarce, and embargoes on a number of other goods. A number of duties had been retained, although in 1919 import duties on goods from the Empire were reduced. But strong pressure came in 1921 from business interests that there must be further protection against 'dumping of foreign goods' and that 'key industries' must not be imperilled. The result was the Safeguarding of Industries Act of 1921 which imposed a duty of 33⅓% on a long list of 'key articles', a very heterogeneous collection of some 6500 items varying from motor-cars to dolls'-eyes. The Act was introduced by Stanley Baldwin, President of the Board of Trade. It did not have the support of a number of Liberals who clung desperately to Free Trade.

The total value of imports fell in 1922 from £1,085,000,000 to £1,003,000,000 and similarly exports recovered slightly from £810,000,000 to £823,000,000. Unemployment fell from 2,038,000 in December 1921 to 1,464,000 in December 1922, but the Coalition government did not survive. Yet its fall was caused less by this economic problem than by a crisis within the ranks of the Conservative Party. A group of rebel M.P.s threw out Lloyd George.

The Chanak Crisis

Throughout 1921 there was much muttering of possible change. A strong group of Conservatives and Liberals wanted a permanent fusion to take place to form a single party of the Right against the socialist parties of the Left. But the Free Trade issue, as well as conflict of personalities, prevented any such development. The occasion for the collapse of the government came with a crisis in Turkey.

The Sultan of Turkey had signed the peace treaty of Sèvres in 1920. But a young army officer, Mustafa Kemal, inspired by the pre-war Young Turk movement, had drawn up a document, the National Pact, rejecting much of the treaty. Allied troops were sent to Constantinople to dissolve the Parliament which had accepted this pact and Mustafa withdrew into the heart of Turkey to set up a rebel government in Angora (Ankara). He forced the Sultan to abdicate and proclaimed himself President. The treaty of Sèvres had granted Greece the western part of Anatolia, but Mustafa now expelled the whole Greek population, some half million, many of whom lost their lives. The Allies still controlled the Dardanelles and the Bosphorus and Turkish forces now attacked many of these Allied detachments. The British were stationed at Chanak on the east side of the Dardanelles and the Big Three of the cabinet, Lloyd George, Churchill and Birkenhead, decided to take a firm stand. Neither the Dominions, except New Zealand, nor France under Poincaré, were prepared to help. But Britain threatened that war would follow if Chanak was attacked. General Harington, whose troops faced those of Turkey across a thin barbed-wire fence, helped to save a delicate situation by deliberately not taking offence over a number of incidents. Diplomatic efforts brought an armistice on 11 October 1922, which was to lead to the new treaty of Lausanne in 1923. This was to recognize the New Turkey and give her control of the Dardanelles, the Bosphorus and Constantinople. But this kind of 'brinkmanship' was too much for the government's supporters. Lloyd George, backed by Winston Churchill, had stood up against an armed threat; the last time Britain was to do this until 1939. But it was also the last time that Lloyd George would wield power in Britain.

The revolt of the Conservative Party was one of young back-benchers and a few ministers. Its leader was Stanley Baldwin, now aged fifty-three and President of the Board of Trade, who instinctively disliked Lloyd George for his 'first-class brains', his 'levity and insincerity', his 'extravagance and recklessness'. He wished to 'clean up party politics' and particularly to end the open system of sale of honours, £15,000 for a knighthood, £25,000 for a baronetcy and £50,000 for a barony. (This money was paid into Conservative Party funds and a Liberal fund which later became the Lloyd George Trust Fund.)

Chanak gave the rebels their chance, the revolt being staged at the Carlton Club. Lord Beaverbrook, owner of the *Daily Express*, decided to support it, and eventually Bonar Law was persuaded too. On 19 October 1922, at the Carlton Club, where some 274 Conservative M.P.s were meeting, both Balfour and Austen Chamberlain gave their full support to the Coalition. But Bonar Law (who had previously left the Coalition government through ill-health) was enthusiastically cheered as he advocated the withdrawal of support for the government. When Lloyd George heard of the strength of this revolt against him he resigned and King George sent for Bonar Law. Lord Curzon, the Foreign Secretary who had grown to dislike Lloyd George and himself sought to be Prime Minister, left the sinking ship just in time. But Churchill, Birkenhead, Austen Chamberlain and A. J. Balfour all stayed out of office. In Churchill's phrase the Coalition was followed by 'a Government of the Second XI'.

Conservative governments 1922–1923

Bonar Law's first action was to hold a general election and the result was a Conservative Party victory. They won 347 seats; Lloyd George Liberals won 57 seats; Asquith Liberals 60; and Labour 142. During the winter of 1922–1923 Baldwin as Chancellor of the Exchequer sought to ease the problem of war debts to the U.S.A. The Americans offered to fund the debt at 3·42% instead of 4·5% and Baldwin was inclined to accept the offer, but Bonar Law recalled him from America for consultations. Baldwin indiscreetly 'leaked' the American proposals to the press and the Americans felt they must stand by them. The cabinet reluctantly agreed and thus Britain was committed to an annual payment of £30,000,000 p.a. for ten years and £40,000,000 until 1985. At the same time she reduced the debt owed to her by many European countries (e.g. the French debt by 62% and the Italian by 86%) and urged a general cancellation of war debts and reparations. Neither France nor the U.S.A. would agree, although the U.S.A. did now make more generous settlements with her other debtors, without offering to revise again the British agreement. These complicated matters lost the government much support, especially among the middle classes, and they help to explain the result of the next election.

In 1921 Bonar Law had almost completely resigned from

politics due to ill-health, but, as we have seen, he had recovered in 1922 and played an active part in bringing down the Coalition. The improvement had not been permanent and in the spring of 1923 he resigned and died within a few months. King George was persuaded by a number of advisers to invite Baldwin and not Lord Curzon to form a government. The latter had travelled to London prepared to accept the office, and was bitterly mortified to learn that the King was convinced that membership of the House of Commons was nowadays essential for a Prime Minister. He agreed all the same to stay on as Foreign Secretary and Baldwin's cabinet remained much as that of Bonar Law.

French occupation of the Ruhr

During 1923 relations between France and Germany badly deteriorated and a strong current of feeling grew up in Britain hostile to French militarism and sympathetic to the new German Weimar Republic. On 9 January the Reparations Commission declared Germany in default on deliveries of coal for reparations and on 11 January French and Belgian troops occupied Essen and the Ruhr Valley, the most heavily industrialized part of Germany. The troops were supposed to support the efforts of a civilian commission charged with obtaining 'production pledges' for reparations. Britain disagreed with France's policy but did not seriously attempt to prevent it, French troop-trains being allowed to cross the British-occupied section of the Rhineland on their way to the Ruhr. Labour attacked the Conservative government for not taking a firmer stand against France's refusal to accept reconciliation, but the occupation undoubtedly helped British industry, since for a year strikes and inflation raged in Germany, until France eventually accepted the bankruptcy of her policy. Incidentally it was in these conditions that the Nazi Party was first formed in Munich.

General election 1923

By the autumn of 1923 the economic situation was again worsening, with the import bill rising and also unemploy-

A London department store in 1922. Note the fashions and the interior decoration

ment. Exports were only very slowly advancing and Baldwin decided that a full programme of protection was now needed; but he felt bound by Bonar Law's pledge not to introduce further protection. He later said that, with his thoughts 'day and night for long past' on the problem of unemployment, he now decided 'that the only way of fighting this subject is by protecting the home market', but that he felt bound first to seek from the country a mandate to reverse Bonar Law's policy. This time both Austen Chamberlain and Lord Birkenhead of the Coalition fought alongside Baldwin's Conservatives. On the other side the Liberal split between Lloyd George and Asquith Liberals was healed. Churchill stood by his old chief as a Liberal but failed to be elected for Leicester. The Liberals won 158 seats, Labour 191 and the Conservatives 258.

At first Baldwin's government tried to survive in the new Parliament. But Asquith decided to work with the Labour

Party, which was strongly against protection, to bring it down. Thus came into being the first Labour government, although, dependent as it was on Liberal votes, it could not hope to implement much of the 1918 programme. Ramsay MacDonald formed a cabinet of moderates, only five of his cabinet of twenty members having been trade unionists and Lord Haldane becoming Lord Chancellor. Nevertheless the moment did mark something of a revolution. John Clynes, the Lord Privy Seal, remarked that he could not help marvelling 'at the turn of fortune's wheel', which had brought 'MacDonald the starveling clerk, Thomas the engine-driver, Henderson the foundry labourer and Clynes the mill-hand, to this pinnacle'. Fears that the new government would not even know how and when to wear formal clothes proved unfounded.

Labour's achievement

The government formed in January 1924 survived for less than a year, its achievements being few. Some adjustments were made over the payment of unemployment benefits. County Agricultural Wages Committees were set up again. Some of the worst economies of 1922 in education were removed and permission was given to progressive education authorities to advance their schemes. Some steps were taken to create public works schemes, to the sum of £28,000,000, in the hope of reducing the high unemployment figure of about 1,260,000. A Housing Act, the Wheatley Housing Act, 'the basis of a vast expansion in municipal building', was introduced, subsidizing by £9,000,000 annually for forty years houses built at controlled rents, some 521,000 houses being built under the Act before the ending of the subsidy in 1933. Philip Snowden as Chancellor of the Exchequer reduced duties on sugar, tea, cocoa and coffee and, to the delight of all Free Traders, a number of the 1921 duties which had been imposed by Baldwin.

Foreign affairs and the Dawes Plan

In foreign affairs the Labour government was more important and MacDonald won the title 'the peacemaker'.

Relations with France, which had been very strained since the war, were greatly improved. Gustav Stresemann, who now dominated German affairs as Chancellor and Foreign Minister, was anxious for Germany not only to recover economic stability but also to be once again received into the European concert of nations, and with MacDonald's help he succeeded. Stresemann broke the wave of anti-Allied strikes in the Ruhr district, and MacDonald proposed and the U.S.A. accepted a new committee on the problem of German reparations. This was under the chairmanship of the American General Dawes and made far-reaching proposals: that a permanent committee be set up which should decide each year just how much Germany could afford to pay towards reparations and that America should make substantial loans to Germany to get her economy working again. The Dawes proposals were accepted by all countries concerned and loans were floated in the U.S.A. for German aid. The European and world economies entered a new period of recovery and prosperity which was to last until 1929.

MacDonald at the League of Nations, where he personally led the British delegation, succeeded, with Henderson and Lord Parmoor, in bringing into being the Protocol for the Pacific Settlement of International Disputes. By this, such disputes would be brought before the Permanent Court of International Justice and, if that failed, sanctions would be applied automatically by the Council of the League. Unfortunately the government was to fall before Parliament could ratify this protocol and it was to be annulled by the succeeding Conservative government.

Fall of the Labour government

What brought the government to the ground was its attempt to follow up its promise to establish 'normal relations with Russia'. Two treaties were drafted in August 1924 dealing with compensation for holders of pre-revolutionary bonds and a possible loan to Russia. These treaties were attacked not only by the Conservatives but by Lloyd George and

The Royal Empire Exhibition, Wembley, 1924

many Liberals. *The Times*, reflecting middle-class opinion, criticized the proposed loan as 'Bolshevist'. In October the government fell, the actual incident which led to its fall being the withdrawal of the prosecution of the editor of the Communist newspaper *The Workers' Weekly* for an inflammatory article. The third general election in three years was held on 29 October 1924.

A. J. P. Taylor has pointed out that in 1924 a fully planned economy was not yet part of classical socialism and that very few of the Labour Party, which incidentally at this time included Sir Oswald Mosley, yet believed in a full programme of public works and of 'sheltering the poor from the storm and hang the expense'. The economic theories of John Maynard Keynes, which were to become part of Labour economic theory in the 1930's and 1940's, were still in conception. The Labour Party had had no solution to the economic problems of 1924 and it fell. It failed to be re-elected fundamentally because of this fact, but it put the blame on the famous Red Scare.

The Red Scare and the Zinoviev letter

The press, apart from the *Daily Herald*, was strongly against the Labour Party. *Punch* carried a cartoon of an obviously Russian sandwich-man carrying the placard 'Vote for MacDonald and Me'. *The Times* followed, four days before polling, with the 'Zinoviev letter'. This was a document allegedly signed and sent by Zinoviev, President of the Presidium of the Communist International in Moscow, to the British Communist Party. It was a general concoction of exhortations to the British proletariat to work for revolution, to support the projected loan to Russia and to oppose the foreign policy of MacDonald. *The Times* took it seriously, as though it were an official document, but the whole thing may well have been a piece of brilliant forgery. Whatever MacDonald tried to do, the Zinoviev letter was accepted and taken to show the dangers of the Labour government's attempts to establish relations with 'Russian Bolshevism'. At the same time it now seems clear that Baldwin's campaign calling for 'a sane, commonsense government' was already winning over the electorate before the scare and that the most the letter did therefore was to gain the Conservatives a bigger majority.

Amongst those returned to Parliament was Winston Churchill, once again a Conservative. Asquith was defeated and in 1926 was persuaded to resign the leadership of the Liberal Party. The figures were 415 Conservatives; 152 Labour; and 42 Liberal.

Return to gold

Into Baldwin's new cabinet came Churchill as Chancellor of the Exchequer; Austen Chamberlain as Foreign Secretary; Lord Birkenhead as Secretary for India; and Lord Curzon who became Lord President of the Council. Churchill's appointment was the least expected and the most controversial. It was he who introduced the return to the gold standard in his budget of 1925, ending the war-time and post-war prohibition on the export of gold. The economist J. M. Keynes opposed the proposal, which had come from the banks, on the grounds that the differences in prices between England and America would lead to further deflation and unemployment. London was aspiring to return to its position as the financial centre of the world and for a while it succeeded. The pound was again able to 'look the dollar in the face' even though, when the great 1929 American crash came, London was to follow Wall Street. Before that however there was to occur the General Strike, which was partly precipitated by the fall in prices and the threatened reductions in wages, themselves partly due to the return to gold.

Baldwin as Prime Minister

Meanwhile Stanley Baldwin was now firmly established as Prime Minister and for the next twelve years he was to be the dominant figure in politics. 'Always opposed to socialism, I yet determined to make the Conservative Party look left' was his own version of where he stood. The short life at the end of this book gives some of the details of his career. Son of a Midland iron-founding family, he was always determined to remember that the Conservative Party depended as much on working-class as middle-class votes. His policy was essentially similar to that of the moderate trade unionists: 'to lower the temperature of politics at home and abroad'. The public image of him: the plain man in politics, slow, not very clever, but sincere, was obviously an exaggeration; for he was a master politician, ruthless when necessary and shrewd. But it did reflect his antipathy to intellectuals, to those 'too clever by half', and to unconventionality in thought or behaviour. The historian Robert Blake has described Baldwin as 'very emphatically a man who belonged to the Establishment'. As such he was to be faced with two crises of a very different kind: the abdication of Edward VIII in 1936 and the General Strike in 1926. In his handling of both he showed a masterly ability to alienate as few sections of the population as was possible.

8

The General Strike, Labour and the Depression

Locarno

One of the first actions of Baldwin's cabinet, in which Austen Chamberlain was Foreign Secretary, was to end all negotiations with Russia. This was followed by a repudiation of the Geneva Protocol on which MacDonald had put such high hopes. Many observers since have considered that the decline of the League of Nations dated from this action. In its place was to be an alternative pact negotiated privately outside the sphere of the League: the Locarno Pact. On the relaxing shores of Lake Maggiore statesmen from Germany, France and Britain (Stresemann, Briand and Austen Chamberlain), as well as from Italy, Belgium, Czechoslovakia and Poland, came to a series of agreements on 16 October 1925. France on her own supported the eastern countries, Czechoslovakia and Poland, against possible German action there, at this time Britain being unwilling to enter into commitments in Central Europe. The treaties greatly reduced tension. The Rhineland was to be gradually evacuated and demilitarized and the Allies agreed to support Germany's bid to enter the League of Nations as an equal power. The signing of the treaty 'ended the First World war; its repudiation eleven years later marked the prelude to the second' (A. J. P. Taylor, *The Origins of the Second World War*). It marked the beginning of a brief period of European prosperity; loans to the sum of

£750,000,000 poured into Germany, mostly from America; reparations payments were paid to Britain and France who in their turn made annual repayments on their debts to the U.S.A. The industry of the Ruhr came to life again; but one country to suffer from the competition was Britain, whose intermittent prosperity since the war had been partly aided by the collapse of German industry.

Origins of the General Strike

The General Strike of 1926 centred around the coal industry. But its roots lie in the steady decline of a number of Britain's basic industries since even before the war. Such

General Strike—scene on the Embankment, 4 May 1926. It was 'private enterprise' in the form of the motor-car which ensured the failure of the strike

industries as iron and steel, coal, cotton and shipbuilding had been at the heart of the great industrial expansion of the nineteenth century. Now they were challenged by other nations and they were beginning to contract. Secondary industries, such as the motor-car, clothing, processed foods and other consumer goods industries, were replacing them, dependent often on newer forms of power, for example electricity, and centred in newer areas. It was in the areas of heavy industry and the textile industry, particularly in South Wales, Lancashire, the Clyde and Tyneside that the unemployment figures had been consistently high, and here they were to remain until 1940.

One remedy of the Conservatives in 1925 for this problem of contracting industry had been to restore those 'safeguarding of industry' duties which Snowden had reduced the previous year. A second remedy was convertibility: to re-establish the pound on the gold standard at the pre-war rate in relation to the dollar, thus keeping export prices high in comparison with those of other countries. The third main solution offered was to encourage the reduction of wages.

The coal industry

The coal industry in the 1920's had ceased to expand. It was only slowly adopting mechanization and many of the seams being worked were increasingly remote and thin. Underground transport was still primitive and, incidentally, was mostly to remain so until the 1940's. Whoever was fortunate to own land above a coal seam, owned the coal and received a royalty on each ton raised, it being mined by private companies. In 1919 the Coalition government had appointed the Sankey Commission to investigate the industry. Half its membership had been drawn from the labour side and its findings were that some other system of ownership must be substituted for the current system: 'either nationalization or a method of unification by national purchase and/or joint control'. The coal-owners on the Sankey Commission had dissented from this view and urged the government to restore their freedom, for the mines were still under war-time government control. Lloyd George accepted the principle of 'nationalization of royalties', but it is not clear whether he intended to do anything about it. A Coal Mines Act of 1919 and a Mining Industry Act of 1920 resulted in a seven-hour day and some improvement in safety conditions, as well as improved mines amenities, such as baths, clubs and canteens. In 1921 the owners triumphed and the mines were restored to their control. They immediately reduced wages. As we saw, the miners urged the Triple Alliance of Trade Unions to support a general strike, but on Friday 15 April this was turned down to the disgust of many in the Labour movement, by whom it is still remembered as Black Friday. The miners tried to continue to strike on their own, but by July they were obliged to accept the wage cuts, determined district by district.

During 1923 German industry was at a standstill, but from 1924 it began to recover and the British mining industry faced a new crisis. The owners demanded a new reduction of wages and a return to the eight-hour day. The T.U.C., with its membership of some 8,000,000, was determined that there should be no repetition of 1921. They pledged 'all such moral and material support' as was possible. Baldwin, faced by united union opposition, agreed (31 July 1925) to appoint a new Commission and meanwhile to subsidize the industry (in the event by some £23,000,000). He justified such 'surrender to union intimidation' as the Conservative press called it, by three arguments: hard times; the suffering a general strike would cause; the fact that public opinion was not yet ready to face the consequences fo such a strike. Like Lloyd George after the war, he was buying time.

Thus the Royal Commission, whose chairman was the Liberal, Sir Herbert Samuel, was appointed. Plans, meanwhile, were made by the government in case a general strike should after all occur. Twelve leaders of the Communist Party were arrested and sentenced under the Act of 1797 for Incitement to Mutiny.

The Commission's report appeared in March 1926. It

supported neither nationalization nor subsidization. On the long term it recommended nationalization of royalties, reorganization of the industry, greater modernization and research, and better relations between employers and miners through greater welfare. On the short term it argued that the men must be prepared to accept lower wages. Both sides rejected the proposals, the miners adopting the slogan 'not a penny off the pay, not a minute on the day'. The government persuaded owners and men to meet on 22 April, but to no effect. Neither side would move and on 1 May the miners stopped work, their agreement of 1925 having run out. On the same day the government declared a general emergency. Negotiations continued between the government and the General Council of the T.U.C. for two days and then the cabinet broke them off, apparently out of pique at the unilateral action of the printers of the *Daily Mail* who had refused to print an editorial calling the proposed strike a 'revolutionary movement'. Baldwin the peacemaker had thus been precipitated by those in the cabinet who wanted action: Churchill, Neville Chamberlain, Douglas Hogg and Leo Amery. Baldwin remarked 'everything I care for is being smashed to bits at this moment'. The process was to last nine days, and he was to emerge victorious, but at heavy cost. The coal industry was not to recover fully for a decade and class bitterness was gravely aggravated.

The General Strike

On 4 May the General Strike began. It included all transport workers (railwaymen, dockers, bus and lorry-drivers) and much of heavy industry. Journalists, sailors, firemen and electrical engineers did not support the strike, but the printers did, and newspapers practically disappeared. Into the gap came the volunteers. University undergraduates took a week off from their books to work in the docks, railway stations and on the buses. Society débutantes and the 'bright young things' of the upper middle class greatly enjoyed trying to keep the essential services going: delivering milk, driving buses and dustcarts and attempting to drive trains. It was all 'great fun and a lark'. But it was also blacklegging and provoked a certain amount of bitterness; there being a number of incidents, particularly involving buses which were overturned. Probably, though, it is true to say that in most areas good-humoured tolerance dominated. Possibly the comradeship of the war years now helped to bridge the gap between the employed wage-earners and the salaried staffs, who mostly sympathized with the employers.

The government had had six months to prepare. The navy operated many vital services and troops were moved to London and key industrial areas. There was much steel-helmeted and armoured-car display, but it was not necessary. Over 130,000 special constables were recruited and the government gave notice that any action taken 'to aid the Civil Power' would 'receive the full support of His Majesty's Government'. Luckily this too was largely unnecessary. This notice appeared in the *British Gazette*, the one newspaper to appear throughout, printed under Mr Churchill's supervision and violently unsympathetic to the 'hold-up of the nation by the T.U.C.: this Soviet'. The T.U.C. themselves tried to reply through a paper, the *British Worker*, but without much success. The B.B.C. greatly extended its influence at this time, when newspapers, especially in the provinces, almost disappeared (London began to receive a *Daily Mail* printed in Paris and flown in). The Director of the B.B.C., John Reith, resisted strong pressure from the government that it should be commandeered. He allowed both sides to broadcast, but inevitably leaned towards the government, if only to protect the Company's freedom.

Meanwhile behind the scenes negotiations went on continually. For the sober trade-union leaders it was as much fear of their revolutionary extremists as anything else which prompted them to seek a compromise. Baldwin in a skilful broadcast did much to win the moderates to his own opinion that 'he was a man of peace'. King George exerted pressure against the extremists in the cabinet not to provoke the strikers 'who until now had been remarkably quiet'. Sir Herbert Samuel meanwhile did his best to break the deadlock and by 10 May he persuaded the General Council of the T.U.C. to reopen negotiations for a mining settlement and to call off the General Strike. Against the wish of the miners, therefore, the Council on 12 May informed the Prime Minister that they wished to call it off. It was in fact near surrender, Ernest Bevin failing to persuade Baldwin to promise that there would be no victimization. The *Daily*

General Strike, 6th day, scene at Hyde Park at 6 a.m. showing armoured cars and troops ready to escort London's great food convoy

Mail exulted over the 'Surrender of the Revolutionaries' and Baldwin confirmed that no conditions had been agreed to. Victimization and reprisals began at once and great bitterness resulted: of the workers against the employers; of the strikers against the T.U.C.; and of the Labour movement against the government. On 13 May, as the strikers went back to work to be faced with threats from the employers, there followed more incidents and police savagery than throughout the previous nine days and there were several short-lived attempts by the men to resume the strike unofficially. Again the King tried to reduce tension and Baldwin now promised to try to prevent employers using 'this present occasion for trying in any way to get reductions in wages'. Slowly tension relaxed and the men went back to work. All, that is, except the miners, whose strike dragged on bitterly until the autumn.

In June Baldwin introduced through Parliament an eight-hour instead of a seven-hour day and a levy on coal royalties for miners' welfare. The Industrial Christian Fellowship tried now to intervene in the miners' strike through such men as William Temple from the Church of England and the Quaker philanthropist Seebohm Rowntree. But their offers of help were rejected. By the autumn the miners were starting to return to work and in December they capitulated to the owners' demands. They had to accept lower wages, while the government had enforced longer hours. The amount of suffering by miners' wives and children during the later months is impossible to estimate. The Samuel Commission's suggestions for improving the industry were nearly all quietly shelved. Baldwin had achieved something of a victory, but unfortunately for him he was to lose much popularity by allowing the extremists in his party to take their revenge in Parliament. On the other side the strike can be regarded as a failure for the revolutionary extremists in the Labour Party, while at the same time it strengthened the moderate working man's allegiance to that party.

Trade Disputes Act

In May 1927 the government introduced the Trade Disputes and Trade Union Act. In part it represented a deliberate attempt by the right-wing of the Conservative Party to gain revenge against the Labour Party. First it sought to make strikes aimed at 'coercing the government' and all kinds of intimidation illegal. In other words another general strike would be illegal. Secondly it forbade civil servants to form effective trade unions. Thirdly, and most controversially, it aimed to make it necessary for a trade-union member to 'contract in', by giving written notice of his desire to contribute through his union to Labour Party funds. Since 1913 such contributions had been automatic unless a man 'contracted out'. The prediction was that, human nature being what it is, the majority of moderate unionists would not bother to exert themselves and thus the Labour Party would be reduced financially to dependence on a devoted minority. To some extent this was proved wrong, although the Labour Party's income did fall. The Act was to be totally repealed in 1946 (see Chapter 17).

Break with Russia

Meanwhile the extremist Home Secretary, Sir William Joynson-Hicks, remained fearful of the 'Bolshevist Bogy'. His crude handling of relations with Russia caused great resentment in the Labour Party, which was intensely interested in and sympathetic to the Russian experiment at this time and strongly deplored the crude anti-Russian propaganda of right-wing Conservatives. In May 1927 the police raided the buildings housing a Russian Trade Delegation, allegedly looking for some documents. Nothing was found, and to cover up the blunder Baldwin decided to recall a British Trade Mission which was then in Moscow and to end diplomatic relations with the U.S.S.R., which were not restored until October 1929.

Welfare legislation

Yet not all actions of this government were unpopular. Neville Chamberlain, as Minister of Health, and Churchill, as Chancellor of the Exchequer, did something to extend the operation of the Welfare State, particularly by introducing in 1925 a widows, orphans and old-age contributory pensions scheme: 10*s* a week for insured workers from sixty-five, 10*s* a week for a widow and 7*s* 6*d* for an orphan child. The non-contributory pension at seventy which had been raised in 1919 to 10*s* would continue for those workers who had not been insured. An Unemployment Insurance Bill in 1927 tightened up and readjusted the system of paying benefits.

Reform Bill 1928

In 1928 was introduced the Representation of the People (Equal Franchise) Bill, which granted the vote to the 'flappers': that is all women over twenty-one, subject only to three months' residence. Plural voting continued. Possibly Baldwin hoped to win the 2,000,000-odd votes which were now added to the electoral rolls. If so he did not succeed at the general election next year.

Local Government Act 1929

In November 1928 Chamberlain introduced his Local Government Bill, which became law just before the election. It was a very complicated measure, containing some 115 clauses, and was partly the result of a Royal Commission set up in 1928. Its main point was to abolish the Poor Law Unions and Guardians set up in 1834 and now partly overlapping with the social services which had been developing since 1911. Powers of poor relief were transferred to the County and County Borough Councils; Urban and Rural District Councils were to be regrouped; County Councils were to receive additional powers for such things as roads, town-planning and child welfare, and also additional grants from the Treasury. There was much reassessment of rateable values. The Bill was not violently challenged by the Labour Party.

Foreign affairs

In foreign affairs since Locarno only two events need perhaps be mentioned. In 1926 the Imperial Conference made recommendations which were ultimately to lead to the Statute of Westminster and the redefining of Dominion Status (see Chapter 18). In 1928 the government subscribed in Paris to the Kellogg-Briand Pact, along with fourteen other nations, solemnly renouncing all war, except wars of self-defence. It was a pact of singularly little significance.

General election 1929

As the law stands a general election must be fought at least every five years and the parties were now preparing. Lloyd George was the leader of the Liberal Party and he made available his considerable funds (the Lloyd George Trust Fund) for propaganda purposes. A number of books and pamphlets appeared which sought to give the Liberal Party a new programme. The most important of these were *Britain's Industrial Future* and *We can conquer unemployment*, which together urged far greater government control over credit and an expansion of national development schemes such as roads, houses, garden-cities and afforestation. At the same time Free Trade remained a basis of the party's programme.

Within the Conservative ranks many of the old die-hards were now retiring, and a group of young men, such as Robert Boothby and Harold Macmillan, were urging much the same kind of extended control over the economy as was Lloyd George, and were profoundly dissatisfied with Baldwin's Micawber-like attitude to the continuation of high unemployment (some 1,330,000).

The Labour movement was split between the small left-wing Independent Labour Party (founded 1893) and the more orthodox and moderate Labour Party (founded 1900). The latter drew up a pamphlet *Labour and the Nation* in 1928 affirming that it was a socialist party and that its aim was to end the capitalist dictatorship 'in which democracy finds everywhere its most insidious and most relentless foe'.

In May 1929 the general election took place. Unemployment and world peace were the two main themes and the Conservative call was for 'Safety First'. They were defeated, gaining 261 seats against Labour's 287. The Liberals, in spite of great propaganda efforts, were the greatest losers, winning only 59 seats. Once more Ramsay MacDonald formed a Labour government which depended for survival on Liberal votes, the cabinet inevitably therefore reflecting the right rather than the left wing of his party. Lloyd George pledged Liberal votes for any moderate legislation to put into effect his own programme. In fact most of this government's time was to be spent wrestling with the greatest depression the world had yet seen.

The American crash came in October 1929. In one week securities on Wall Street fell by some $15,984,000,000. The German economy, almost entirely dependent on American loans, therefore quickly collapsed as well. The primary producing countries, particularly those of the British Empire, now faced ruin and British export trade was bound to suffer. Exports fell from £839,000,000 in 1929 to £461,000,000 in 1931. Unemployment rose from 1,164,000 in June 1929 to 2,500,000 in December 1930.

Mosley memorandum

Early in 1930 Oswald Mosley, assistant to J. H. Thomas, Minister for Unemployment, produced his own proposals, which included protection for home and empire producers and greater public control of industry and of credit and banking. His memorandum was rejected and Mosley resigned, MacDonald reshuffling his cabinet. Philip Snowden remained Chancellor of the Exchequer, believing in Free Trade but not socialism. Mosley tried unsuccessfully to steal the leadership of the Labour movement and then moved on to form The New Party, which soon became the British Fascist Party.

Before the crash came the government had tried to right what it considered to be various wrongs. The Unemployment Insurance Bill had increased slightly the benefits obtained by young persons and wives. The Coal Mines Act of December 1929 had restored the working day to seven and a half hours and had tried to reach some compromise agreement on prices and wages. Various other Bills had been introduced, such as one to raise the school-leaving age from fourteen to fifteen and one to repeal the Trade Disputes Act. They had either been killed by Liberal Amendments or by the House of Lords. Meanwhile the financial crisis worsened and unemployment continued to rise. Snowden's budget of 1930 had satisfied nobody and early in 1931 MacDonald agreed to the forming of a Committee on National Expenditure under the chairmanship of Sir George May. Unemployment was over 2,700,000.

May Report

In August the May Report appeared when the government deficit was running at some £120,000,000. To meet this, the report recommended raising taxation by £24,000,000 and introducing economies to save £96,000,000; £66,500,000 of this should come from reducing unemployment payments. The Report itself greatly worsened the situation since foreign investors now seriously lost confidence in the British economy.

Crisis worsens

Heavy foreign withdrawals of funds thus took place in London, aggravating the situation, the Bank of England beginning to lose gold at the rate of £2,500,000 a day. London bankers claimed that the trouble was the lack of confidence felt by foreign firms and banks and urged that a 'National Government' be formed to face the crisis. Therefore on 13 August MacDonald and Snowden met the other party leaders: Baldwin and Neville Chamberlain for the Conservatives and Sir Herbert Samuel and Sir Donald Maclean for the Liberals. Lloyd George was ill at the time.

By 19 August the cabinet had agreed on some £56,500,000 economies to offset the deficit. Gradually, however, it began to split, largely over unemployment payments. 'Cut the talk and get on with it,' called the *Daily Mail* on 22 August. MacDonald and Snowden realized that only reduction of benefits would satisfy the Opposition and restore confidence abroad. A small majority of the cabinet accepted the cuts, but a strong minority, as well as Bevin and Citrine of the T.U.C., were determined against them. The Opposition accepted that £12,500,000 must come off unemployment benefits. The Bank of England was seeking a loan from New York, and MacDonald feared that the only terms they would be able to get would be heavier economies yet.

The National government is formed

He proved right. On 23 August the New York bankers stated that before they would help, 'Parliament should have already enacted legislation which had the approval of the Bank of England and the City'. The Prime Minister knew that this would mean more economies and that the further £12,500,000 must be saved from unemployment benefits. This split the Cabinet and MacDonald asked for the resignations of all. The King now urged him to form a new Coalition government with the help of Baldwin and Samuel, which he did. The new cabinet consisted of MacDonald as Prime Minister and three other Labour men, including Snowden and Thomas; Baldwin as Lord President and three other Conservatives; and two Liberals. Thus the National government was formed in the middle of this acute financial crisis which had created the most powerful atmosphere of national emergency since 1914.

9

The twenties: a survey

The 1920's are popularly thought of as a 'gay decade': jazz, gin and sports cars; the movies, cloche hats and endless parties; yachts, the Riviera and the craze for air-travel. One could continue the list. But in fact few of these aspects of it ever affected the vast majority of middle- and lower-class people for whom it was simply a decade of slowly improving living standards, provided one was successful in avoiding the spreading shadow of unemployment. The acquisition of a wireless set, a family car and even possibly a new suburban villa on a hire-purchase loan, marked the limits of aspiration for the great majority, for whom often only the first was a practical possibility.

The remarkable thing really about the 1920's is the social and political conservatism of the period. In politics safe men of the right and centre held firm control even in 1924 and 1929 when the Labour Party was in office. The press may have become increasingly sensational, but its influence was solidly on the side of conservatism. In art and architecture traditionalism held its own in spite of what happened on the continent. Only perhaps in the 'smart set' of Mayfair, where the night-club habit was growing, and in a small fringe of the middle class, did the decade seem one of change and to some of decay.

For those who looked for it, truth, particularly religious truth, was even harder to find than it had been when religion was under attack in the nineteenth century. The writings of the psychologist Freud, the anthropologist Malinowski and the physicist Einstein were popularized, and they challenged many accepted ideas about character, behaviour, reasons, space and time. But such relativity, both in the social and physical sciences, hardly affected the general patterns of behaviour. Outside London, provincial codes and traditions were not easily broken down.

Distribution of income and standard of living

Socially England remained chronically class-conscious. Nevertheless the difference in material standards of living between England rich (the governing and professional classes) and England poor (the lower-middle and working classes) became less. The proportion of the national income going to super-tax payers showed a slight decline from 8% in 1911 to 5·5% in 1924, while the total number who paid the tax slowly increased during the decade. Of course, there was considerable unemployment, fluctuating between 1,000,000 and 2,500,000, but the average wage of those in employment rose and so did their standards of living. Even including unemployment figures the decade saw a rise in real earnings of 5%. A number of the great town and country houses of the aristocracy were closed, allegedly because of high taxation. Some were pulled down; some became institutions; few were yet 'given to the nation'. At the other end of the social scale, water, gas and electricity moved into many rural cottages and pylons, carrying the Electricity Grid System, started to spread over the countryside. Elaborate rehousing schemes were planned and carried out on the outskirts of many cities, new suburbs being carved out of the green fields around them. For the middle classes faster train services meant that suburban dormitories spread further away from the big cities. London and the more prosperous Midland counties gained most from the housing boom; the industrial cities of the north, where most of the unemployment was to be found, the least. Seaside resorts and the fringes of provincial towns and villages all acquired a rash of that characteristic building of the 1920's, the bungalow. Domestic servants decreased in number and were replaced by many labour-saving devices such as the vacuum-cleaner.

Methods of transport

One phenomenon of the decade was the growth of motor-transport and the relative failure of the railways to maintain their position. Before the war, as we have noted, motor omnibuses were arriving in the cities and during it motor taxi-cabs increased greatly in number. Now were developed the cheap family car for the middle-class pocket, together with road haulage and long-distance motor-buses. The number of licensed vehicles rose in the decade from 975,783 to 2,251,142 and problems of traffic control became acute, 72,000 cars passing Hyde Park corner in twenty-four hours in 1929 (in 1960 the figure was to be 95,106 from 8 a.m. to 8 p.m.) The over-all effect was for country life to be brought into much closer contact with the cities; for the week-end habit in the Home Counties to extend from the upper to the middle clasess; and for 'stock-broker Tudor' architecture to spread out into the country for the wealthier city workers. Deaths from road accidents in 1929 were 6,896; the figure in 1959 was in fact to be lower, 6,520, as a result of better traffic control.

Although considerable progress was made in repairing the ravages of war-time neglect and in developing new classes of locomotives, the railways began to lose custom to the roads. Many lines around London were electrified and they played their part in the growth of suburbs, but the main-line stations remained dirty and uncared for; more and more freight as well as passengers went by road; some remoter rail services were reduced; there was little electrification outside the London area and no development of the diesel except in Ireland.

Some went by air, since commercial aviation had quickly developed after the war. Many saw a future in the airship as well as the aeroplane, and the Admiralty Airship R34 crossed the Atlantic in 1919. Only with the disaster in France of the R101 in 1930 did airship development cease. In that year

Miss Amy Johnson won £10,000 from the *Daily Mail* for her solo flight to Australia in twenty days. Commercial air-links were established with Paris and the continent and from London to Cairo and on to Karachi. But not even in the 1930's was an Atlantic passenger service to be developed. The seaplane seemed at first to have a great future. R. J. Mitchell's Supermarines won the International Schneider trophies in 1927, 1929 and 1931 and the Supermarine S.6B created the record of 407 m.p.h. later in 1931. Only after the Second World War were seaplanes to be abandoned, with the development of fast jet airliners. But air-travel hardly affected any but the very rich and a few government and business officials in a hurry. It speeded up mail delivery with the continent, but in no revolutionary way. High operating costs meant that as yet it could not easily compete with older methods of transport.

The class structure and education

In the 1920's many were seeking to up-grade their class, but at no time did the existence of the different classes, nor the subtle taboos which went with each, suffer serious inroads. Provincial speech remained one form of class barrier, although it began to break down at the end of the decade with the spread of 'B.B.C. English'. The real barrier into the upper reaches remained education. To be accepted as a member of the upper class, as against being tolerated for one's wealth, still necessitated a public-school education and if possible an Oxford or Cambridge degree.

After the Geddes Axe, state education fell on hard times, only 0·4% of the elementary-school children ever reaching a university. State scholarships began in 1920, but only 200 were given each year. County Councils even before 1914 had begun to offer a very few scholarships to the universities, while a handful of 'guinea-pig' places were made available at public schools for scholarship boys. The later years of the decade were to see some improvement and in 1926 appeared an important book by Kenneth Lindsay, *Social Progress and Educational Waste*, and the Hadow Report, which recommended great changes in the elementary schools from which the primary and secondary schools of the 1940's were to develop. There were also several new grammar schools, the number of which rose during the decade from 1205 to 1307.

The ancient public schools, such as Eton, Winchester, Westminster and Shrewsbury, had during the nineteenth and early twentieth centuries been increased to over a hundred in number, many old-established grammar schools being up-graded into the select band by incorporating some boarders and then somehow managing to get the headmaster elected to the Headmasters' Conference. During the 1920's a number of completely new independent schools were founded, including Bryanston, which was to be a pioneer in new ideas. Teaching in the public schools remained very formal, with still a heavy emphasis on the classics and, for a technological century, surprisingly poor science teaching. Character training was regarded as their main purpose by most of these schools. But to generalize further is dangerous. Of many it has been said that 'such words as psychology and psychiatrist were ostracized' and that 'games and O.T.C. were regarded as the most serious activities in the school'. Graves and Hodges, in their book *The Long Week-End*, maintain that in the public schools the Spartan virtues of 'modesty, reticence, endurance, courage, generosity, loyalty, personal cleanliness and general decency' were rigidly enforced by Houses, but that with them went 'the Spartan prejudice against all things artistic, eccentric, abstract, poetic, studious, foreign or feminine'. This is undoubtedly unfair to many of the best schools, where one of the finest educations in the world was to be had. Any community will have misfits, eccentrics and round pegs in square holes. The best public schools of this era sought to tolerate and to help the latter, while giving each individual boy a personal attention impossible in the state grammar schools. But it is probably true to say that a great number of the less good schools were extremely narrow in their outlook.

To move on to Oxford or Cambridge from a public school was still relatively easy: it was arranged between one's housemaster and the tutor of a college. Other universities were still regarded as socially and educationally inferior. These ranged in size from Manchester with 1748 students to Reading with 558. Three new university colleges were opened during the decade at Swansea, Leicester and Hull.

The 1920's saw many new ideas on child psychology and education. Infant schools operating Froebel ideas ended some of the repression formerly used and made school something to enjoy rather than dread. There was considerable debate on how much punishment children should receive, A. S. Neill founding a school at Summerhill, specializing in 'problem children of problem parents', where no discipline was imposed at all. Private preparatory schools varied considerably from the traditional Victorian pattern to something much more free and easy, but the vast majority of children being educated in state elementary schools continued to receive a fairly traditional training in the three R's, hampered always by poor and shabby buildings and a lack of finance.

Religion

Some kind of religious instruction was given in nearly all schools, although in state schools this was not obligatory before 1944; in many public schools great efforts were made to make 'the chapel the centre of the school's life'. But it is never easy to generalize about religion, since church- or chapel-going seldom gives a clear idea about the situation. Mention has already been made of the difficulties some had in their search for religious truth. Comparative religious studies were popular and so for a time was modernist theology which took most of the supernatural out of Christianity. The decade saw the beginning of two new Church of England cathedrals and the failure in 1928 of the Church to obtain permission from Parliament for its newly proposed prayer-book. The B.B.C. became, at the end of the decade, a strong force on the side of religion, but the motor-car took many families into the country at the week-end and away from church or chapel. Two highly popular and influential men did much to bring the Church of England into closer contact with the man-in-the-street: the Rev. Dick Sheppard of St Martin's-in-the-Fields, and Canon William Temple, who was to become Archbishop of York in 1929 and Archbishop of Canterbury 1942–1944. The two Archbishops of Canterbury of the twenties, Davidson and Lang, were somewhat remote ecclesiastical statesmen. It is estimated that the Roman Catholic Church was the only community to be expanding, possibly at the rate of 11,000 converts a year. A religious movement among the upper middle class was the Oxford Group Movement, started by an American, Frank Buchman. It became very wealthy, but it is hard to say how influential. At the universities there was a noticeable drift away from religion, many believing that modern scientific ideas had made its arguments invalid. The new suburbs seldom had churches at first, but in the older suburbs chapel-going probably declined more than church-going, since the latter was still a sign of respectability.

The press

Another such sign was to take *The Times*, the *Daily Telegraph* or the *Morning Post*. More popular newspapers were the Liberal *Daily News*, the Asquithian Liberal *Daily Chronicle*, Lord Beaverbrook's *Daily Express* (whose circulation in 1919 was only 350,000), and of course the *Daily Mail*, which, since before the war, had set the pace for popular journalism. Yet much of the sensationalism of the *Mail* lay more in its prizes (for sweet peas, flights to Australia, cooking recipes and sand-castles) than in its exploitation of scandal. Before the Regulation of Reports Act of 1926 the Law Courts provided even more material for the scandal reporter of divorce cases than they have done since. But, even so, it has been argued that 'the *Daily Mail* was less sensational in 1920 than the *Daily Telegraph* became fifteen years later'. The *Daily Mirror*, a conservative paper with as yet a modest circulation, pioneered in photographic 'tabloid' presentation. The *Daily Herald* was restarted in 1919 by George Lansbury as a socialist newspaper for the working classes and it was followed by the *Daily Worker*. Neither achieved large circulations in the 1920's.

The B.B.C.

The biggest competitor of the national press was the B.B.C. Before 1920 wireless communication was confined to wireless telegraphy, but in that year the Marconi Company made experiments in broadcasting music and speech. Again the *Daily Mail* contributed, sponsoring a broadcast by the opera star Dame Nellie Melba. Parallel developments were going on in America, where very quickly a chaotic state of free-for-all broadcasting developed. It was this which led the Post Office to support the idea of a broadcasting monopoly. The British Broadcasting Company thus came into existence in 1922, with a government-granted monopoly. It was promoted by the young radio industry and had the approval of many educationalists, but was attacked by some sections of the press as likely to end their own monopoly of news. Its first General Manager was a Scotsman, John Reith, aged thirty-three. He was the son of a Presbyterian minister and himself has told how he felt that God had chosen him to do 'some great work' in the world and that to him 'had been committed this tremendously powerful force, for good or evil'. Very quickly the pattern of B.B.C. broadcasts developed, Reith being given a free hand by his board of governors: weather forecasts, news bulletins, children's hour, outside broadcasts from Covent Garden, religious programmes, 'Variety', plays, symphony concerts, light music, etc. Sunday broadcasting until the Second World War was to be quite free of jazz and variety programmes. In December 1926 the Company became a Corporation, under a Royal Charter, with considerable independence from government pressure or interference. Reith may have been autocratic and have imposed his will too hard, ending the informality of the early days, but he created a remarkable institution which was to be the envy of other countries. Headphones for 'listening-in' were replaced by loudspeakers from about 1924. Experimental television programmes were first transmitted in 1929.

Mass communication and the arts

The B.B.C. was responsible for a considerable improvement in the level of musical taste and appreciation in the country. It may not have kept right up to date with current ideas in music, but the time-lag between the composer and public, which always exists, was enormously shortened. The number and standard of symphony orchestras increased, including the B.B.C's own orchestras, which developed from 1930. 'Modern' composers such as Stravinsky, as well as contemporary English composers such as Vaughan Williams, were all patronized. On the other hand, the radio play, written expressly for the medium, never developed as much as many hoped.

Was the cinema an art form? The 1920's was the decade of the silent film. Few British films succeeded and the vast majority shown in Britain were the products of Hollywood, which had become the centre of the American film industry. Most towns now had at least one cinema and 'going to the movies' became a habit along with greyhound racing, another popular form of amusement in the 1920's. The first 'talkies' appeared in London in 1929: Al Jolson in *The Singing Fool.* Unfortunately many of the screen idols of the twenties were found to be unsuitable for talkies. They had to be abandoned and substitutes trained in elocution. Greta Garbo, the legendary Swedish actress, whose first film was made in 1922, was with some difficulty persuaded to talk.

How far did the cinema kill the live theatre? West End theatre-going was highly fashionable, but more as a social occasion than as an artistic experience. In Birmingham Sir Barry Jackson had built the famous Repertory Theatre in 1913. For twenty-one years it remained one of the most creative playhouses in the country, providing fresh and forceful productions of Shakespeare, as well as other classics, and first performances of many of Shaw's plays. In 1929 he began the Malvern Festival, which has had successors in many provincial cities since. The taste for Shakespeare was to lead to improvements in the quality of productions at Stratford-on-Avon and in 1932 to the building of the new theatre there. In London the Old Vic in Waterloo Road, under Lilian Baylis from 1914, had become a centre for opera, ballet and the classical theatre. The former two were to move to Sadlers Wells in 1931, with a ballet-mistress of genius in Ninette de Valois. The decade saw the beginning of the careers of a number of outstanding players, such as John Gielgud, Laurence Olivier and Ralph Richardson. The theatre certainly needed new writers and new audiences: it did not obtain enough of either in the 1920's.

The other arts

In architecture the 1920's saw little in England which was really exciting and new. In painting public taste began to be educated to the achievements of the French post-impressionists, although something like 'a twelve-year gap' still continued. Henry Moore and Epstein, two of the greatest sculptors of the century, regularly had their work daubed or tarred and feathered. Few British painters were doing more than trying to gain a hearing for new ideas in art and breaking down the stifling traditionalism enshrined in the Royal Academy. Possibly Ben Nicholson, Matthew Smith and Stanley Spencer are the painters of the decade whose work shows most signs of surviving. Yet if the public was slow to accept new ideas it was increasingly less philistine in its attitude to painting as a whole.

It was perhaps in literature that the decade achieved most, though few of the greatest works written in English were by Englishmen. Two certainly were masterpieces: *Ulysses* by James Joyce (an Irishman), published in Paris in 1922, and *The Waste Land* by T. S. Eliot (an expatriate American), published in 1923 and perhaps the central poetic achievement of the early twentieth century. The critic Edmund

The Last Supper by Stanley Spencer

Wilson has written that this poem 'expresses the terrible dreariness of the great modern cities . . . nameless millions performing barren office routines, wearing down their souls in interminable labours of which the products never bring them profit: people whose pleasures are so sordid and feeble that they seem almost sadder than their pains'. Other remarkable Americans writing in English during the decade were Scott Fitzgerald, Ernest Hemingway, Gertrude Stein and William Faulkner. Four very powerful English novelists were also working: Evelyn Waugh, who satirized most aspects of upper-class society; Aldous Huxley, whose novels are a curious mixture of brilliant philosophy and high fashion; D. H. Lawrence, whose greatest work, *Sons and Lovers*, had been published in 1913, but who still had many pungent if increasingly bitter things to say; and Virginia Woolf, who was perhaps of these four the most interested in the style and form of the novel.

Fashion

The increase of mass-production of cheap clothes and the use of artificial silk (rayon) meant that working men and women could now have more than two outfits: one for the office and one for Sundays. Women's skirts gradually rose from below the ankle to above the knee, and from about 1924 onwards there began for women the fashions for shorter and shorter hair (the shingle and then the Eton crop); for flat chests and straight hips; for powder and lipstick, although these remained frowned on outside London as 'fast' until the next decade. Oxford bags appeared for men in 1925, strange, rather ugly trousers for informal wear, twenty-six inches at the knee and up to thirty inches at the ankle, in bright colours, green, pink, blue and mauve. 1926–1927 probably saw the furthest point women's fashions were to go away from femininity. Perhaps it is significant that once the female sex had achieved emancipation with universal suffrage granted in 1928, there began a swing back to more conventionally female clothes. In 1927 the Women's League of Health and Beauty was formed, which put the emphasis on feminine physique.

Agriculture

In 1921 Lloyd George had been obliged to break his pledges to agriculture and to abandon wage control. This was restored by the Labour government of 1924 by the Agricultural Wages Act, when County Committees were empowered to fix wages, which became stabilized at about 30*s* a week. The acreage of land under plough fell steadily and in the years 1924–1928 Britain produced only 39·3% of her food needs. The number of oil- and petrol-driven engines in use on farms rose from 6284 in 1913 to 65,725 in 1931, while the number of horses steadily declined. There was much talk of better land utilization and of properly exploiting the 32·1% of land in Britain classified as hill lands, but in fact little was done. During the decade the population employed on land fell from 1,307,000 to 1,194,000, which is just over 1%. The next decade was to see something of a recovery,

THE MANAGERS (outside): "Why, that's the very girl I've been looking for!" *October 10th, 1927.*
Theatrical Managers are much puzzled by the present shortage of leading ladies.

The Flapper Vote

but also much more breaking down of the traditional rural habits and ways of thought, as city life spread further and further out.

The end of the decade

The twenties may be judged to have ended when the fatal Wall Street crash occurred in October 1929. It had been a decade of hope and many fears unrealized. After 1925 there had seemed to be a healthier world situation, with the recovery of Germany, but this was something of an illusion. The great crash precipitated a new cycle of world crises, and the 1930's were to see democracy on the retreat in Europe, vast social and economic problems, and everywhere an increasing fear of war.

10

The National government and recovery

Ramsay MacDonald

In forming the National government as he did, when he met King George at Buckingham Palace on 24 August 1931, Ramsay MacDonald to some extent had committed political suicide. The bulk of his own party quickly disowned his action of joining the Conservatives and Liberals, and it is not altogether clear whether he did it as a genuinely spontaneous action in response to the King's appeal in the moment of crisis, or whether it was the result of a long-laid scheme. There had been talk of such a government in the influential newspapers since the spring and in banking circles through the summer. But MacDonald did not reveal anything of his intentions even to his Chancellor of the Exchequer, Philip Snowden, one of the few who elected to stay with him, although not for reasons of personal loyalty. MacDonald was certainly a man who liked political power. He increasingly resented the interference of the trade unions and despised their lower-middle-class ways. From humble Scottish origins he had educated himself to become a man of fastidious taste, who enjoyed more and more the company of cultivated society. As is often the case with political leaders, his temperament became more and more autocratic and it is possible that he relished the prospect of becoming the leader of a government containing so many members of ancient political families. He may have been joking when he referred to 'every duchess in London wanting to kiss me', but to devoted Labour followers he seemed an increasingly remote snob.

World depression

The world catastrophe, which began in October 1929, and from which the various national economies only slowly recovered during the 1930's, is obviously extremely complicated to understand in detail. It was the worst depression to have affected world trade since modern capitalist undertakings really took root in the seventeenth century. The recovery which began in 1933 in most countries was partly no more than the 'natural swing' which is a characteristic of trade cycles. Nevertheless this particular slump had some peculiar features. The most obvious is the extent to which, through the Dawes Plan, the economy of Europe had become linked with that of the U.S.A., which during the 1920's had experienced one of the most fantastic boom periods ever seen. President Harding in 1920 had proclaimed 'back to normalcy' as his election ticket, but there had in fact taken place a highly abnormal boom and an unprecedented reaction when the crash came. By 1933 in America there were 14,000,000 unemployed and hardly a bank open.

In Germany, following the crash, came the ending of reparations payments in 1932 (this meant that the Allies in the same year had to abandon war-debt repayment), high unemployment and the rise of Nazism. Further afield the collapse of world prices for primary products hit such countries as Australia and New Zealand terrible blows. In Britain the cost of production of goods for home consumption fell, as did the cost of food. But for ship-building and a number of heavy industries the collapse of world trade meant great suffering and whole towns such as Jarrow were killed by these years. Plants became idle, firms went bankrupt and their people were forced on to the dole, the cost of which was still rising as the National government took over. How would it face its financial problems? At least the loan from America, earlier refused, was now made available, since 'dangerous socialists' had been replaced by 'sound financiers', in the eyes of the lenders.

MacDonald's cabinet

MacDonald's new cabinet was small. It omitted Lloyd George, who was ill, and Winston Churchill, who was not to hold office again until the outbreak of war. Nor was Austen Chamberlain in the cabinet, perhaps one of the ablest Conservatives. Stanley Baldwin was Lord President; Philip Snowden remained Chancellor of the Exchequer; Sir Herbert Samuel (now leader of the Liberals) was at the Home Office and Neville Chamberlain again Minister of Health.

Naval mutiny and the budget

The formation of the cabinet alone could not end the crisis, although the £80,000,000 credits from America were granted to the new government on 28 August. Two weeks later there was a minor mutiny in the navy at Invergordon, as the ratings refused to accept the proposed reductions in their pay. These had been part of the emergency budget by which numerous government employees were to lose percentages of their pay. Teachers were to lose 15%; seamen 13·6%; judges, policemen, and M.P.s 10%; and admirals only 7%. The A.B.s were objecting to what seemed class discrimination. They did so in a very well-disciplined way and the cuts were revised. But news, which the government foolishly tried to censor, of a mutiny in the British Navy caused a renewed run on the Bank of England and the £80,000,000 credit was soon almost exhausted. Britain's holdings of gold fell to £130,000,000 and it was decided 'to go off the gold standard', which happened on 21 September, the value of the pound falling from $4·86 to $3·40.

The Means Test

The budget had also introduced a 10% cut in unemployment benefits so that, for example, a married man with three children would now only receive 29*s* 3*d* a week for the first fifteen weeks as 'standard benefit'. After that, in order to obtain 'transitional benefits', which themselves varied from area to area, he would have to satisfy a 'Means Test'.

Here the total income from all members of the household, together with all savings, pensions and any income from property would be taken into account by the local Public Assistance Committee. If calculated to be sufficient for the family to live on, nobody would qualify for further benefit or 'dole'. Thus a married man might be obliged to rely on his daughter or wife and himself be 'knocked off dole', although unable to get work and existing at a bare subsistence level. The system led to much family tension, daughters resentful of having to keep their parents, neighbours blackmailing and informing on any extra income not declared. The cost of transitional payments, as a result of the Means Test, fell by £24,000,000. It ensured that the unemployed would not starve, but it degraded them, while at the same time few positive efforts were made to give them work, which today is the basic criticism against the National government.

By the emergency budget the bank rate was raised to 6% to try to reverse the flow of money which had been leaving the country, but this was only a temporary measure. The new government's aim was 'cheap money' to aid recovery and by June 1932 the bank rate was down to 2%, where it stayed until 1939. The old school economists, who had prevented the Labour government from such actions, predicted still more financial chaos. But in fact 1932 marked the beginning of recovery in Britain, even though the unemployment total increased up to 1933. The reduced dole continued to be paid; wage rates for those employed remained fairly stable; and prices continued to fall slightly. What the Conservatives in the National government wanted next was protection. The Liberal Party and most of Labour were still pledged to Free Trade.

A general election was held on 27 October 1931. The Liberals remained pledged to Free Trade, and so was Snowden, the Chancellor of the Exchequer, but Baldwin was convinced of the 'supreme value of the policy of tariffs'. It was a very muddled election, with various so-called supporters of the National government supporting various conflicting policies. Robert Boothby asserted that the country was being asked to vote for the 'Boys of the Old Brigade' of the Conservative Party. True or not, the National government won a resounding victory. 472 Conservatives were elected, together with 35 Liberals (under Sir John Simon), who supported tariffs, and 13 Labour, who would also. Pledged to oppose tariffs were 33 Liberals, led by Sir Herbert Samuel; 4 Liberal seats from Wales went to Lloyd George and his family; 46 seats went to Labour, now led by Arthur Henderson.

MacDonald's second cabinet

The most striking change in the new cabinet was the promotion of Neville Chamberlain to the key office of Chancellor of the Exchequer. Snowden became Lord Privy Seal and entered the House of Lords. He was to resign in a year, together with the Liberals Sir Herbert Samuel and Sir Archibald Sinclair, when tariff reform became a reality. Chamberlain was regarded as one of the strongest men in the cabinet and it appears that he increasingly dominated it. He had at this time clear views, great energy and determination, and a ruthless lack of any sentiment. He was regarded as a cold man and it was said of him that he 'repelled Labour men by his scorn, Conservatives by the discipline he demanded of them'.

Tariffs

The Liberals in the new government were faced almost at once with a first list of tariffs. They were persuaded that duties on such items as pottery, cutlery, cotton goods and cameras were essential to surmount the crisis and they agreed at first to remain in the government. But in February 1932 Chamberlain introduced an Import Duties Bill which would impose a general tariff of 10% on nearly all imports, except from the Empire, pending an Imperial Conference to be held at Ottawa. An Import Duties Advisory Committee, under the chairmanship of Sir George May, would be created to advise on further tariffs. The widow of Joseph

Chamberlain sat in the House while her step-son introduced this bill. Twenty-nine years earlier his father had first formed his Tariff Reform League. The Bill was vigorously opposed by Liberal and Labour but it became law. The Imperial Conference followed in July and August at Ottawa. The latter produced much ill-feeling, since the Dominions were determined to protect their own secondary industries, while demanding duty-free preference for their primary products exported to Britain. On the whole Britain agreed to their terms: British exports to the Dominions were to pay tariffs, but not such high ones as those on other foreign imports. Snowden and Samuel resigned, embittered against the Conservatives. Apart from MacDonald, who remained Prime Minister (an increasingly unwell man), there was very little that was National about the government from now on.

Recovery

It is no easier completely to explain the economic recovery, which certainly was beginning by the end of 1932, than it is to explain the depression which had developed in 1929. To pretend, however, that there was *no* recovery, and that the thirties remained a 'hungry decade', is to be the victim of political passions. Ccrtain 'depressed areas' remained appallingly impoverished and in the general movement of industry from some of its earlier nineteenth-century areas a great deal of individual suffering was caused. But production rose and unemployment fell, and so for a while did prices. Thus the standard of living in general went up. The number of insured unemployed reached a peak in 1933 at 2,950,000, but by 1938 it was down to 1,180,000. If we take the unit of production for 1929 as 100, it fell to 84 in 1931, but reached 124 by 1937, before rearmament gave it a new boost.

Difficulty comes when it has to be decided how much of this was due to government policy (tariffs, import quotas, devaluation, exchange control and a policy of cheap money for loans) and how much to such factors as the fall in prices of raw material and the expansion of numerous home industries. World trade was recovering at much the same time as the internal economy. By 1935 Britain had a favourable balance of trade, although this was the only year in the decade when this was so. The Ottawa conference led to an increase of imports from the Dominions and a decrease of food imports from such countries as Denmark and the Argentine. It led likewise to an expansion of exports to the Empire from 39% in 1929 to 45% in 1938, against a decrease of exports to other foreign countries from 55% to 50%. At the same time elaborate measures of market control and increasing subsidies were introduced to aid British agriculture.

To look in greater detail at the expansion of home industry we will consider three items: housing, consumer goods and heavy industry.

Housing

Every great English city, but especially London, is stamped with the hall-mark of the thirties: its suburbs. In 1933 it was possible to build a working man's house for £300 and a somewhat smarter middle-class villa for £700 or £800. During the years 1931–1935 county and municipal schemes

Unplanned housing development in Surrey between the wars

for council houses came almost to a standstill and the Wheatley subsidies were ended in 1933, but what replaced these were the private builders, building for individual clients financed by Building Societies. Building costs were very low, wages remained stationary, and much of the building was of poor quality, but from 1934 to 1939 over 300,000 houses were built each year. On mortgages of about twenty-five years, the buyer was able to pay as little as £2 15*s* a month towards paying for his house. These were laid out in estates in much the same way as in the 1920's, overall Town and Country planning being still almost non-existent. The effect of this building boom on the general recovery of the economy was very great. It occupied much of the building industry, while at the same time it greatly helped allied industries: timber, electrical appliances, furnishings and other consumer goods.

Tertiary employment and consumer goods

Part of the slack in the economy of the 1920's was to be taken up in the 1930's by the expansion of what the economists call tertiary production: i.e. work in the Civil Service, teaching, transport, business, distribution, commerce and 'general services'; for example, entertainment, hotels, laundry and sport. At one time historians argued that the greater such activity the greater a society's decadence. But today it is agreed that with the ever-increasing efficiency of the machine a steadily increasing percentage of the population *must* be involved in such occupations if unemployment is to be avoided. This certainly happened in Britain in the 1930's, where the increase in tertiary production averaged some 4% of the total insured population.

Another way to use up the excessive productive power of a modern industrial nation is to devote an increasing section of industry to the production of 'consumer goods'; for example, mass-produced clothes, whose life will not be long, processed and canned foods, sweets and ice-cream. Secondly, by means of high-powered salesmanship, such machines and appliances as motor-cars, vacuum-cleaners, refrigerators and wireless-sets must be made to seem indispensable to modern life and a hire-purchase scheme introduced to help their purchase. Thirdly, by 'planned obsolescence', these goods must either be made so badly as actually to need replacement within a short while of payments being completed, or the buyer must be made to feel that they are out of date and unfashionable. Thus the advertising profession was to expand during the decade, one of its main functions being to foster this sense of fashion. Middle-class Britain became gadget-conscious and home-conscious. Such exhibitions as the annual Ideal Homes Exhibition begun in the 1920's all helped to increase the demands for the products of industry. Indeed the Ideal Homes Exhibition has been described as the great 'cultural achievement' of the English middle class.

Heavy industry

It would be foolish to pretend that all the older industries of the north of England expanded or even recovered equally with the new secondary industries, particularly concentrated in the suburbs of London. A great number of factories, especially in the textile trade, were suffering from a failure to modernize and rebuild. While some had modernized and turned over to electrical power, many had not, and tried to compete with overseas manufacturers with equipment hopelessly out of date. Thus scores of cotton mills in Lancashire were forced to close. The iron and steel industry, whose production fell in 1931 to 5,200,000 tons, slowly recovered and then expanded until by 1937 it was producing some 13,000,000 tons. But the recovery was uneven. Tremendous new plants were erected, as at Corby in Northamptonshire, but in Wales and elsewhere a number of plants were shut down. As the industry became more and more highly centralized, so a number of old or inefficient plants were simply bought out and closed. New plants might open several hundred miles away, but this was little consolation to the family thrown on the dole.

In coal-mining the owners steadily resisted more than a minimum of government interference. They had to agree to a Coal Mines Act in 1930, which set up a central council with quotas of production for each district, and in 1938 they were to be obliged to agree at long last to nationalization of royalties, since heavy rearmament was making the miners' co-operation a necessity. But between these dates the owners had it mostly their way, great inefficiency in many old mines continuing. Production fell to 207,000,000 tons in 1933 but rose to 241,000,000 tons in 1937.

The industry which recovered least from the depression was ship-building. The 1920's had seen a boom, as the losses of the 1914–1918 war were made good, but by the end of the decade this had been achieved. Now, at a time when the volume of world trade was shrinking, foreign merchant marines were relying less and less on British yards for their new ships. In 1920 the tonnage launched was the record of 2,000,000 tons; in 1933 it was to be 133,000 tons. In 1930 the ship-building companies formed themselves into a company, the National Shipbuilders' Security. They planned to buy up

Jarrow marchers nearing Bedford, October 1936

shipyards and close many, thus trimming the industry to its new shape. In four years this company reduced the potential of British ship-building to a maximum of 1,400,000 tons. This sounded very neat, but in the case of at least one town, Jarrow, which was almost entirely dependent on one firm, Palmers (now liquidated), it meant that in 1935 72·9% of its insured population was unemployed. Gradually new industry was to come to this most famous of all the depressed areas: a steelworks, engineering and ship-breaking, and by 1939 it was recovering. But it had suffered from a crude and ruthless version of 'private enterprise.' It was the employees of the ship-building industry who provided the majority of the hunger marchers who, in the mid-thirties, came south to London. These in their turn contributed to the expansion of Communism, a characteristic of the decade. One way in which the government tried to aid the industry was by a British Shipping Assistance Act in 1935, by which subsidies could be granted to tramp shipping and government loans made available on a 'scrap-and-build' scheme. The most publicized of such loans was that to the Cunard and White Star companies, now merging, in order to complete the hull of No. 534, which was duly launched as the *Queen Mary*. Its aim was to regain the blue ribbon for the north Atlantic and in 1938 it succeeded.

Planned economy and depressed areas

The economist J. M. Keynes dominated economic thought in the 1930's if not yet economic policy or practice. His books, especially the *Treatise on Money* (1930) and the *General Theory of Employment, Interest and Money* (1936), effected a revolution in the popular attitude to economics. It was no longer the 'dismal science' but suddenly became, in the popular mind, the magic key by which nations could at last free themselves from blind forces against which up to now they had been helpless. Keynes had four basic ideas:

1. The control of policies influencing credit and investment should not be in private hands, but in those of the government.

2. Low interest rates should be the rule when employment falls off, to encourage expansion.

3. Investment should in such times be stimulated by a programme of public works.

4. The more equal the distribution of income, the greater will be the ability to consume and thus the greater will be employment.

All this meant government planning; yet the Conservative Party was pledged to private enterprise. The Labour Party increasingly believed in a planned economy and nationalization of basic industries and Keynes's ideas reinforced these beliefs. Unfortunately the National government was in many ways held back by its large Conservative majority in the House of Commons. For example, the depressed areas such as industrial Scotland and South Wales had provoked the government in 1934 to appoint unpaid commissioners with powers to initiate and aid measures for 'economic development and social improvement of the depressed areas'. But Parliament would provide them with no more than £2,000,000 spending money, which was entirely inadequate and provoked Lloyd George to ridicule the scheme as 'Conscience Money' to keep the Keynsian advocates of planning at bay. Yet gradually the idea of such government aid and interference was accepted until after the war it was to be policy common to both political parties.

At the same time some nationalization of industry crept in. Before the war Lloyd George had set up the Port of London Authority. The 1920's had seen the setting up of the B.B.C. The 1930's saw the emergence of B.O.A.C., out of the failure of heavily subsidized but competing private airways companies. At the same time the London Passenger Transport Board was formed, with a monopoly for all passenger traffic within the area of greater London, directed by a board appointed not (as with B.O.A.C.) by the minister, but by five independent trustees. Such empirical examples of nationalization were attacked by many critics, but by the country as a whole they were seen to be sensible and inevitable.

Unemployment Act 1934

The 10% cuts in benefits were restored in 1934, although the Means Test lasted until after the war began. A Consolidating Act was passed in 1934 which set up the Unemployment Assistance Board which, with a staff of 6000, was to have offices all over the country, relieving the Labour Exchanges. It would be responsible for all the able-bodied unemployed. The Act widened eligibility for relief and eased the Means Test, but it was unpopular, since its new scales, to be operated from 1935, were to be uniform throughout the country, whereas, before, these had been subject to local conditions and cost of living. There were protests, some Communist-inspired, against this uniformity, and the government delayed its introduction until November 1936 as a result of this pressure.

Statute of Westminster and India

In Chapter 18 the important decisions and acts passed during the 1930's concerning the Empire are discussed at greater length. In November 1931 the new Parliament passed the Statute of Westminster, which recognized what had been decided at the Imperial Conference of 1926. The four white Dominions became independent countries, appointing their own Ambassadors and High Commissioners and with nothing to tie them to Britain but the common link of the crown and common citizenship. Probably very few indeed foresaw how quickly the Asian and African colonies would effect their own transfer from Empire to Commonwealth. Only for India was it grudgingly accepted that this must soon take place, although Churchill feared the communal passions of Hindu and Moslem and warned the government that they 'would tear each other to pieces, men, women and children with their fingers'. For this reason he deplored any further move to hand India over to her own leaders, but from 1931 to 1935 continual negotiations did in fact go on, with Lord Irwin (later Lord Halifax) on one side and Gandhi on the other. They were to result in the India Act of 1935 which is discussed in a later chapter.

Jubilee and government changes

In May 1935 King George V had been King for twenty-five years and it was decided to celebrate by a Silver Jubilee. The cynics saw this as a cheap pre-election stunt by the government to gain popularity. In the event it proved how remarkably popular the King and Queen had made the monarchy during their reign. Victoria in her later years had been a popular figure, but partly only because she had lived for so long. Edward VII never won the deep affection of his people (his reign was possibly too short), but George V did. They never knew the details of his private life; its meticulous attention to official business and the reading of documents. They never knew how often he had interfered to reduce political passion (from the first days of his reign over the Parliament crisis), and to exploit to its full extent his right 'to be informed, to encourage and to warn'. But they had sensed his concern for the welfare of the country. Jubilee enthusiasm, particularly in the working-class suburbs, for this rather trim little man, who liked dressing up in uniform, and for his forbidding but kind and warm-hearted wife, was very remarkable. The techniques of press photography and the King's annual Christmas broadcast had helped to bring the personality of the monarchs into the homes of people in a way not previously possible.

The Jubilee was followed in June by a government reshuffle. MacDonald, whose health continued to decline, changed places with Baldwin. Samuel Hoare replaced Sir John Simon as Foreign Secretary. It was a Conservative government, although still calling itself National and containing three National Labour ministers: Ramsay MacDonald as Lord President, his son Malcolm as Colonial Secretary and the faithful J. H. Thomas as Dominions Secretary. Sir John Simon for the National Liberals moved to the Home Office. On 14 November 1935 came the last general election before the war.

11

The National government 1935–1939 and rearmament

Baldwin, Chamberlain and Eden

Stanley Baldwin, who was Prime Minister from 1935 to 1937, is said to have been remarkably indolent, especially about foreign affairs. But this does not mean that the National government in these years was not interested in them. Neville Chamberlain, although still Chancellor of the Exchequer, had strong views; so also did Anthony Eden, Minister without Portfolio for League of Nations Affairs in 1935 and then Foreign Secretary for three years 1935–1938. Unfortunately, however, the views of these two clashed. Eden was strongly devoted to the cause of the League of Nations and to the traditional methods of diplomacy; Chamberlain was convinced that the League was dead. He believed in 'personal diplomacy' between heads of states and that it was possible to achieve European stability by a combination of rearmament and the 'making of agreements freely concluded' with the dictators, to limit what could not be prevented. This latter policy was named appeasement, which for some years a majority of the country preferred to the risk of war. The clash of personality between Chamberlain and Eden was to lead to the latter's resignation in 1938.

Pacifism and the Peace Pledge

The years 1930–1936 saw a remarkable development in pacifist ideals, the reasons for which are many. The horrors of modern air warfare and the possible destruction of civilization was a factor; so was a spate of war-books, which revealed the bestiality and uselessness of the 1914–1918 war. After ten years or more it had become possible to look at it from various points of view: American and German, as well as British. Within the Anglican Church a strong feeling flourished for a while, led by Canon Dick Sheppard, that war for any reason was anti-Christian and that the idea of a 'just war', even against atrocities and aggression, was a contradiction. There was a correspondingly strong feeling among many nonconformists and in the Labour Party George Lansbury, the ageing leader, was devoted to this belief. Out of all this grew several movements. One was the Peace Pledge Union, which by 1936 had over 100,000 members. Another was the National Declaration Committee, which organized a great Peace Ballot through house-to-house canvassing. It raised the massive vote of 11,500,000 in favour of the League of Nations and against unilateral agreements, rearmament and the private manufacture and sale of arms. Faced with this feeling, Baldwin in 1934 and 1935 seemed to be playing for time.

General election 1935

The National government, now almost entirely a Conservative Party government, had two appendages: the Liberal Nationals and National Labour. Against it stood the Labour Party, led by Lansbury, and the Liberal Party, led still by Samuel, with Lloyd George and his family forming their small independent Liberal Party. At the general election in November the latter stood strongly for the Council of Action for Peace and Reconstruction, another movement dedicated to peace. The Conservative Party allegedly stood for support of the League of Nations and for the application of sanctions against Italy, if she continued her aggression in Abyssinia. They and their supporters won a massive victory, gaining 428 seats. The Liberal Party won only 17 seats, while Labour obtained 154 seats, a considerable improvement on 1931. The Government had won a vote of confidence, or perhaps a vote of no-confidence in the Labour Party. Ramsay MacDonald was personally defeated by Emmanuel Shinwell of Labour and a safe seat had to be found for him until he finally left the government, through ill-health, in 1937.

The government had decided before the election that great rearmament was necessary, having issued a short but crucial White Paper on 4 March 1935. How far they concealed this from the electorate in order to win the election and postponed it until safely re-elected, has been disputed. Churchill has attacked them for having 'lost the years which the locusts have eaten' and Baldwin claimed that they had had no mandate for extensive rearmament before 1935; but he did not in fact obtain this at the election since it had been fought on the platform of sanctions and the League of Nations. However, safely in the saddle for another five years, the government began to gear the country to the more intensive rearmament programme later described.

Hoare–Laval pact

Having won the election partly on the promise to uphold the League, the government found itself putting less and less trust in that organization. Sanctions against Italy, who had invaded Abyssinia during 1935 (see Chapter 12), were utterly ineffective, largely because the powers, especially France under Pierre Laval, were unwilling that they should be anything else. The government wanted to retain the friendship of France which was determined on a settlement between Italy and Abyssinia. Hence the December Hoare-Laval proposals (see again Chapter 12), which caused such an outcry. These proposed that much of Abyssinia be ceded to Italy outright and the remainder be made into a 'zone of economic expansion and settlement reserved to Italy'. In return Abyssinia would receive a corridor to the sea: what *The Times* called a mere 'corridor for camels'. The proposals were the first of a series that this government was to make. They were to be followed by similar ones for Palestine (see Chapter 19) and Czechoslovakia (see Chapter 12). On this first occasion Baldwin was forced by public opinion to ask Hoare to resign, his place being taken by Anthony Eden. During 1936 Abyssinia was to be occupied, the Rhineland reoccupied and the government to become firmly wedded to its dual policy of appeasement and rearmament.

The Labour Party takes stock

If the National government, dominated by the Conservative Party, had some contradictions in its policies, the Labour Party was no more united in its aims, especially over foreign affairs. The party was now increasingly recognized as the official opposition group, the Liberals having dwindled away. Also during the 1930's it became increasingly respectable and acceptable to the middle classes, some distinguished members of the party being offered and finding themselves able to accept knighthoods and other honours. Especially did the trade-union section of the party become more conservative. The differences in the party during the thirties tended to be between the moderate and conservative trade unionists and Parliamentary leaders, as opposed to more doctrinaire and socialist groups, often centred in the universities. The driving force from the left came from the Socialist League, founded in 1932, and containing such men as Stafford Cripps, Harold Laski and Sir Charles Trevelyan. The party conferences of 1932, 1933 and 1934 debated many proposals, which came from this League, on the future of the party. A pamphlet was published for the moderates, *For Socialism and Peace*, which extended the list of industries recommended for nationalization: the Socialist League would have preferred the more extreme policy as published in its pamphlet *Forward to Socialism*. What split the party further was the question of pacifism. In 1935, with the Abyssinian crisis, Britain was faced by the risk of war, through the full application of sanctions, as an alternative to simply watching an act of naked aggression. The Labour Party divided along three main lines: the convinced Christian pacifism of the leader George Lansbury; the socialist pacifism of the Socialist League, which attacked even the

League of Nations as merely the tool of the capitalist system; and the third and largest group led by the trade unions, who unequivocably supported any action against Italian aggression. The leader of the last group was Ernest Bevin. Soon after the great 1935 party debate at Brighton, when these three views openly clashed, Lansbury resigned from the leadership of the party and his place was taken by Clement Attlee: a moderate, an intellectual skilled in debate and committee and one who would support the idea of the necessity of war under certain circumstances. It was the Spanish Civil War (begun in 1936, see Chapter 12) which was to help win many of the socialist pacifists in the party over to a similar view. The spectacle of a democratic republican government being smashed to pieces by a military group, supported by German and Italian troops and arms, was to have a profound effect on left-wing opinion. At the same time it was to bring Labour, Conservative and Liberal together on to a series of platforms up and down the country and on to a series of committees: for Spanish Medical Aid, for Spanish Relief and for the Basque Children, among others.

Edward VIII and the abdication

While great international events were taking place in Abyssinia, Spain and Germany, in London during the last months of 1936 occurred the abdication of Edward VIII. He had been very popular as Prince of Wales, spending much of his time, in his own words, 'getting to know the people of nearly every country of the world, under all conditions and circumstances'. George V had died on 20 January 1936, after a brief illness, and Edward had succeeded at forty-one and still a bachelor. During the summer of 1936 he spent some weeks on a Mediterranean cruise with, among others, a Mrs Ernest Simpson, the wife of a London stockbroker. She was an American and the divorced wife of an American naval officer. Throughout the autumn of 1936 the press of the world, but especially America, speculated on the possibility of the King marrying Mrs Simpson. The British press was persuaded to keep absolutely quiet even when in

October Mrs Simpson received a divorce from her husband. The British cabinet and the Archbishop of Canterbury were opposed to the King marrying her. Edward was determined on the marriage, if need be at the cost of ceasing to be King, an office that entails supreme governorship of the Church of England, which does not recognize divorce. On 2 December the news of the clash between King and cabinet leaked into the British press. The editor of *The Times* next day spoke strongly against the King allowing 'his private inclination' to clash with his public duties. A party of 'King's friends' appeared, led by Winston Churchill, who pleaded for Parliament to be allowed to discuss the matter, but on 11 December the King made up his mind. He chose to marry 'the woman I love' and broadcast to the nation explaining his motives for abdication. His next younger brother succeeded him, as George VI. Edward became Duke of Windsor and left the country to spend most of the rest of his life in exile. The crisis had far fewer repercussions than might have been expected. All the Dominions accepted what had been done except the Irish Free State, which took this opportunity to break yet further away from England.

The establishment of Eire

In Chapter 6 were outlined the events of the Irish Civil War and the establishment of the Irish Free State, with Cosgrave, a moderate, as the first Prime Minister. His government fell in 1932 and he was replaced by the more extreme republican, De Valera, under whom there began a slow process of breakaway from the United Kingdom. First there were insults to the Governor-General, who, as the crown's representative, was housed in a suburban villa and excluded from all government occasions. Meanwhile land annuities (interest and principal repayments for land purchase) under the land Acts of the period 1870–1903 were to be withheld from the British government. Next the right of appeal to the Privy Council was abolished and an Aliens Act made all who were not Free State citizens aliens. In December 1936 came the abdication. The Irish Parliament or Dail took the opportunity of passing two acts removing the King from the Constitution, while retaining the Irish crown as a theoretical 'organ' for use in diplomatic and other affairs. In December 1937 the Free State adopted its Gaelic name Saorstat Eireann, or Eire: a sovereign independent democratic state, governed by an elected President, an elected Dail, and a Senate, elected by the Dail. Eire did not yet formally contract out of the Commonwealth, but she was to remain neutral in 1939 and in 1949 was to become the Republic of Ireland (see Chapter 18).

Baldwin and MacDonald resign

In May 1937 came the coronation of the new King, George VI, and of his wife Elizabeth. He had never expected the succession and had all his life been overshadowed by his elder brother. As Duke of York he had taken a great interest in social conditions and had supported attempts to mix in an annual camp upper-class boys from public schools with lower-class boys from industry. For years he had been fighting, increasingly successfully, a speech impediment. His coronation was a popular event and the new King and Queen were to become as well loved as any English monarchs had been for several centuries. Within a few weeks of the coronation Baldwin resigned as Prime Minister and became Earl Baldwin, his reputation having already begun to fall. In the 1920's he had won and maintained a reputation for 'sincerity and honesty', for which the electorate were willing to forgive him much. But since the 1935 election there had been a growing feeling that this was not justified. From being one of Britain's best-loved figures he became by 1945 one of her most distrusted and disliked. During the war he lived quietly in retirement in Worcestershire, but became locally very unpopular. His successor as Prime Minister of what still called itself a National government was Neville Chamberlain. Ramsay MacDonald left the government at this time and died in November 1937 on a cruise to South America. Winston Churchill remained excluded from office.

A David Low cartoon at the time of the 1935 election. Baldwin won the election but his popularity began to decline soon afterwards

Eden's resignation from office

We have mentioned already the opposing nature of the views of the new Prime Minister, an autocrat of increasingly shorter temper, and of his Foreign Secretary Anthony Eden, at that time respected throughout the world as an advocate of the League of Nations. Chamberlain quite sincerely believed that the only hope for Europe lay in Britain's coming to terms with the three strong men: Hitler, Mussolini and Franco. He did not abandon this belief until March 1939, if then, while Eden by 1937 had come to believe it unsound, if not immoral. Hence it was not really surprising that in February 1938 Eden felt bound to resign from office over the question of closer links being established with Mussolini's government. The resignation was regarded by many at home and abroad as a victory for the dictator nations and a humiliation for the democracies, since Eden had been the target for powerful German and Italian attacks. Lord Halifax became Foreign Secretary, but the Prime Minister largely ignored the whole machinery of the Foreign

Office in this disastrous period of personal diplomacy 1938–1939 which will be discussed in the next chapter.

Social legislation 1933–1939

At home the National government obviously had to concentrate mainly on the problem of unemployment. In the last chapter we noted that the total declined after 1933; although in 1938 it still stood at 1·81 million, yet some important social legislation had taken place during the decade.

The important Unemployment Act of 1934, which among other things extended relief to unemployed youths of fourteen to sixteen, has already been mentioned. Agricultural workers were brought into the scheme in 1936 and domestic servants in 1938.

1933 had seen the passing of the Children and Young Persons Act, which extended the Act of 1908 with reference to questions of cruelty to children and to the powers of Juvenile Courts. This 1933 Act (to be amended further in 1952) has been described as 'a landmark in the history of child protection', obviously an important aspect of any Welfare State.

In 1934 the Milk Act made it possible for school-children to obtain a third of a pint of milk each day for a halfpenny, or free if necessary. By 1939 about half the children in the country's schools were receiving this. The 1944 Education Act was going to extend this by improving facilities, and the milk was to be free to all after the Family Allowances Act of 1945.

In 1936 a comprehensive Public Health Act was passed, consolidating the regulations of preceding acts. 1935 and 1936 saw the introduction of two new housing Acts by the Minister of Health, Sir E. Hilton Young. They gave further powers to local authorities to clear slums; to provide or assist in the provision of community centres; and to oblige all authorities to make plans to end overcrowding, which was to become a legal offence. Unfortunately in 1938, with rearmament pressure, the subsidy to local authorities for slum clearance was to be reduced. But some progress had been made towards the idea of total town-planning, as it was to emerge during and after the war.

Lastly we might notice the Factory Act of 1937, which summed up and extended the legislation of the previous century since the first important landmark in 1833. This remains the principal Act protecting all industrial workers. It extends protection to workers in ship-building yards, docks, building sites, film studios, laundries, various charitable institutions such as hospitals, as well as in ordinary factories and workshops. It covers personnel such as van-boys and office-boys as well as machine operators. It covers all matters of safety, cleanliness, light, space, temperature, sanitation and fire-precautions. It is a very complex and highly important piece of social legislation which has had to receive only minor amendments in the years since it was passed.

Rearmament

For the year 1932–1933 Britain spent £103·7 million on armaments: the lowest figure since the war. In the same year there began an International Conference on Disarmament, which finally collapsed in 1934. But also in 1932 the British government ordered a survey to be made of the 'worst deficiences' in the country's armaments. In 1933 Churchill began his series of warnings against the dangers of German air attack and of the inadequacy of Britain's air defences. From 1934 onwards he reiterated his warnings against 'the crash of bombs exploding in London'. At the same time the government increased its first-line air strength immediately from 850 to 890 planes, and aimed at 1304 within five years. Labour still at this time strongly opposed rearmament on the grounds that it would worsen international relations, and the pacifist movement reached its height in the years 1935–1936 for the variety of reasons already indicated.

In March 1936 the National government, after winning the general election the previous autumn, stepped up its rearmament programme. The Territorial Army was to be reconditioned and re-equipped. The Regular Army was to be modernized, although horse cavalry still had pride of place over mechanization and traditionalists (or what some called the 'bow-and-arrow brigade') still dominated the army. The name of Captain Liddell Hart, who throughout the period fought for modernization and mechanization, was still execrated in the War Office. Only with the appointment of Hore-Belisha in 1937 as the new War Minister were some of his ideas to make very slow headway.

At sea two new battleships and one aircraft-carrier (whose new paramountcy was not really to be grasped by any navy until the middle of the next war) were to be laid down. Existing ships were to be modernized and eleven cruisers laid down.

The air-force expansion programme was again (March 1936) stepped up, the target for first-line planes being raised to 1750, with a total of 8000 planes to be built within the next three years. A big recruiting and training scheme was to be launched to produce the personnel to fly them. A new office was created, the Minister for Co-ordination of Defence; Sir Thomas Inskip being the first holder. The 1935–1936 armaments expenditure figure was £137,000,000; that for 1936–1937 £186,000,000. To finance the estimated requirement for 1937–1938 of £190,000,000 Chamberlain wanted a National Defence Contribution on business profits, but he was forced by the City to abandon the scheme. A few months later he became Prime Minister, appointing Leslie Hore-Belisha as Secretary for War. For the air force new types of aircraft began now to appear: Wellington, Hampden and Blenheim bombers; Hurricane and Spitfire fighters, the latter being the last and finest creation of the talented aeronautical engineer R. J. Mitchell.

In April 1938, after Austria had been reunited with Germany, yet another scheme was approved for stepping up rearmament. The R.A.F. was to acquire 12,000 planes in two years and many new factories were to be laid down. For the army, mechanization was to be speeded up, as well as

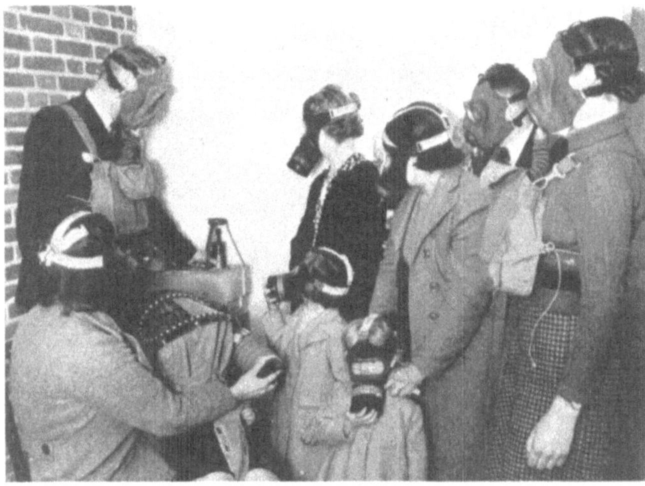

Gas-masks being fitted and issued to everyone as part of the preparation for war

anti-aircraft defence. Slowly the idea was accepted of the possibility of the army having to be sent out of Britain once again as an expeditionary force. For the navy, expenditure was stepped up from £42,000,000 to £63,000,000 for the year, the expansion programme being accelerated.

In 1937 a Civil Defence Act was passed and in the years just before the war, especially after Munich in September 1938 (see Chapter 12), its programme accelerated, every citizen receiving a gas-mask (see Chapter 15). Steel air-raid shelters were erected in back gardens and public shelters in parks; A.R.P. (air-raid precaution) wardens were recruited; and intensive training was given in first-aid. In the year 1938–1939 radar stations for detecting aircraft were built all round the coast. Undoubtedly Britain was far more prepared for war when it came in 1939 than a year before when it had threatened.

12

Foreign affairs 1930–1939

Fascism and Communism

In Europe party feelings were far more bitter than in Britain between the wars. The Communist Party was strong and ruthless. Its appeal to a defeated nation, such as Germany, was considerable. In reaction to the Communists appeared extreme groups on the right, of which the Fascist Party in Italy, which gained power in 1922, and the Nazi Party in Germany, formed in 1923, are the most notorious examples. Large land-owners, militarists, many industrialists, and to a certain extent the Catholic Church, all believed that Fascist regimes, often headed by a dictator, were preferable to the Communist dictatorship of the proletariat, with its anti-God propaganda. By 1939, not only Germany and Italy but Spain, Poland, Hungary, Bulgaria, Roumania, Yugoslavia, Albania and Greece were under regimes more or less dictatorial and backed by at least some of these forces. In nearly all of these countries among the peasantry and factory workers there were strongly organized Communist cells. Everywhere police methods deteriorated and torture and imprisonment for political offences were increasingly used. The methods of the German Nazi Party were only worse in degree, not in kind, than those used through much of Europe. Fascism and Communism both sought by strong government to restore economic stability and national welfare. Both appealed most in times of mass unemployment and thus it was after 1929 that danger from them was greatest. In 1938 France, Czechoslovakia and Switzerland survived as democratic republics; Belgium, Holland and the Scandinavian countries remained constitutional monarchies. However, the France of the Third Republic had become notoriously corrupt. She was prepared to defend her frontiers and had the biggest army in Europe manning the Maginot Line, but she was less and less prepared to consider action beyond this point and thus counted less and less in European diplomacy.

Germany and the Nazis; Russia and Communism

Up to the economic collapse of 1929 it seemed as though Western Europe was recovering stability and prosperity, while the U.S.S.R. was preoccupied with her own problems and Five-year Plan. Unfortunately in Germany people who had been told for years that all their troubles were due to Versailles wrongly attributed the unemployment of 1930–1932 to that as well. In fact they were not connected, but the result was the same: a strengthened nationalism and among all sections of the middle class a determination to keep out the Communist danger. Statesmen both in and out of Germany in 1932 were convinced that her economy must be stabilized, since they feared that the collapse of Germany would mean chaos and Communism for all Western Europe. Thus the coming to power of Hitler and his party was at first welcomed by many both inside and outside Germany, since it was by no means apparent at first that his methods were to be so much worse than those of many other political leaders in the post-war world. Although anti-semitism was always part of the Nazi platform, it was only to become violent in the second half of the thirties and in the forties. German-speaking people who were not part of the new German Reich—those in Czechoslovakia, Austria, Poland and elsewhere—began to be affected by the tide of enthusiasm which followed the success of Hitler's government. Whether the pressure for their incorporation into a greater Germany (an idea at least a century old) came more from them or from Hitler himself is in dispute. But certainly they exerted pressure.

The Russia of the Revolution passed from the hands of Lenin in 1922 when he had a stroke. He died in 1924 and a triumvirate, Stalin, Zinoviev and Trotsky, succeeded him. Gradually Stalin gained supreme control. Trotsky was outlawed and Zinoviev dismissed from the leadership of the Comintern and from the party. Stalin in 1928 inaugurated his first Five-year Plan by which a new class of scientist and technician was to be created; new towns were to be built and industries developed; and the land was to be brought under collective farms. The peasants had originally welcomed the Revolution, as it drove out the hated landlords. Now they themselves were ruthlessly forced to hand their land over to collective farm units. Many thousands were killed or sent to forced-labour camps in Siberia, where much of the new Russia was being created. The worst years of forcible collectivization were from 1928–1930. Since then, although the process has gone on, it has been more gradual.

Hitler's Nazi Party and Stalin's Communists both used similar methods, particularly to maintain party discipline: torture, drugs and elaborate interrogations, as described in Arthur Koestler's novel *Darkness at Noon.* Both, in the 1930's, were purged: the Nazis in 1934 and the Communists between 1936 and 1938. In Russia many thousands were shot. But still it is possible that in both Germany and Russia the regimes were more popular than those which had gone before. Certainly Stalin's Russia was less corrupt and for the masses more prosperous than that of the Czars. Social services, education and general standards of living were many times superior for the great mass of the people. Russians were enthusiastic and optimistic now, which they had not been during the last years of the Czarist regime.

Germany and Russia made a pact of mutual friendship at Rapallo in 1922. In 1924 MacDonald wished to ease the international situation by re-establishing diplomatic relations and trade connections with both countries, but he was thwarted and the 'Zinoviev letter' exploited in the 1924 election. Germany, on the other hand, from 1925 until 1929 under Stresemann, was accepted again into the European fold. In the 1930's Stalin made strong efforts to win international friendships; he was anxious about the growing power of Japan in the East. He achieved admission to the League of Nations in 1934 and in 1935 obtained pacts of mutual assistance with France and Czechoslovakia. Possibly if France had really trusted Russia and believed in the sincerity of her promises the German question might have been held in check. Unfortunately none of the great powers trusted one another. Britain undermined the Stresa Pact (see below) by a bilateral naval agreement with Germany in 1935. Italy would have no dealings with Communist Russia. France trusted neither Britain, Italy nor Russia. In January 1935 a plebiscite in the industrial Saar Valley, whose inhabitants are mostly Roman Catholics, brought a 90% vote for reunion with Germany in what was undoubtedly a free election. This shows the strength of reviving German nationalism.

Stresa and the Anglo–German naval pact

Early in 1935 there had been talks between Britain, France and Italy against the German menace, of which MacDonald said he was apprehensive. Italy was still determined against Germany absorbing Austria. On 11 April MacDonald led the British delegation to Lake Maggiore in Italy, where at Stresa a pact of mutual friendship was made with France and Italy. The latter, however, was warned unofficially by the British delegation that if she were to invade Abyssinia this pact would be invalidated. There followed a curious action on the part of the British government. On 3 June von Ribbentrop, German plenipotentiary for foreign affairs, came to London with proposals that Germany should limit her navy to 35% of the British navy, but that she should have a submarine tonnage equal to that of the British Empire. MacDonald had personally negotiated at Stresa, but the Foreign Secretary, Samuel Hoare, negotiated in London. The German proposals were accepted, although they were a repudiation of Versailles. The British defence was that they only recognized what was becoming a *fait accompli* after the collapse of the Disarmament Conference of 1932–1934. But France and Italy regarded themselves as double-crossed and Anthony Eden was sent to restore confidence in the Stresa Front. He may have done so, but the Anglo-German pact certainly weakened Britain's moral position when she came to try to put pressure on Italy over Abyssinia.

Abyssinia

The question of Abyssinia was central to the problems of the middle years of the 1930's. She had been admitted to the League of Nations in 1923, in spite of British protests that she was too barbarous a country to join such a civilized community. Since then she had received a certain amount of American investment, but had remained extremely under-developed. It seems that by 1934 Mussolini had decided to conquer her and thus 're-create the Roman Empire'. It is not known what were the full British reactions to his proposals, which he probably outlined at Stresa, but in November 1935 the National government won a general election on the platform of support for the League of Nations and through it of collective security by the application of sanctions against Italy if she continued her pressure against Abyssinia. In July Eden had offered Abyssinia access to the sea via British Somaliland in return for giving Italy some of her territory, but Mussolini had rejected this scheme since he wanted the glory of war, and in the autumn of 1935 he had attacked. The League applied economic sanctions against Italy, although not seriously, and Mussolini's armies met with little resistance. A strong group in the Foreign Office, worried about Germany, wished at all costs to retain Italian friendship. Thus the Eden scheme was revived in December 1935, only this time it was more generous to Italy, who had conquered much of Abyssinia during the intervening months. The scheme was mysteriously 'leaked' in Paris to the French press and British public opinion strongly objected to this 'Hoare-Laval pact'. The governments of Britain and France were denounced for their cynical sale of an ally, the scheme was abandoned and Sir Samuel Hoare left the government. By May 1936 the Abyssinian Emperor Haile Selassie had left his country and Mussolini proclaimed his new empire. Fifty-two nations in the League, excluding Germany, which had left in 1934, had combined and denounced Italian aggression, and the only result had been that instead of the Hoare-Laval scheme by which Haile Selassie would have retained half his kingdom, he had lost it all. Italy left the League, which had proved itself so inept, in December 1937. Popular opinion in Britain was more hostile to Italy as a result of all this, and was to become even more so with the Spanish Civil War. But diplomatically the Foreign Office still worked hard to keep Italy within the British orbit and to prevent any irrevocable union with Germany.

The Rhineland

It will be remembered that the Rhineland had been occupied after the First World War and then in 1925 demilitarized by the Treaty of Locarno, which had sought to appease public

Rhineland reoccupied. German troops leaving Aachen

feeling in Europe against the Versailles Treaty. In 1936 Hitler, acutely conscious of Italy's success in Abyssinia, and claiming, rightly or wrongly, that the Franco-Russian pact (1935) invalidated Locarno, ordered his army to reoccupy this key district. Since the disarmament conference of 1932 had collapsed, Germany had been rebuilding her army, actually with British approval, since, as *The Times* wrote, there would be 'more reason to fear for Germany than to fear Germany', unless her government was allowed some means of exerting armed force. By 1936 this new army was hardly trained and it certainly was not issued with ammunition when it marched into the Rhineland. A plebiscite revealed 98·8% support for what the Führer had ordered: the Fatherland was reclaiming its children and they were happy it should be so. The Allies could scarcely have prevented the reoccupation, unless the French army had moved in against a hostile but unarmed population and held it by force. But by her military occupation Germany ended the devices of security set up by the Treaties of Versailles and Locarno.

In Winston Churchill's phrase there was now a 'loaded pause' of two years before Hitler made his next move. During it he rearmed, being less prepared in 1936, we now know, than Churchill at the time imagined. According to A. J. P. Taylor, Hitler, having destroyed the post-war settlement, was 'at a loss what to do next, even if he had the power to do it'. One thing that he did do was to lend technicians and some equipment to General Franco for his Spanish military revolution. Mussolini was to give far more; so much indeed as seriously to weaken Italy's fighting power.

Spain

Spain in the First World War had managed to remain neutral under King Alphonso XIII. She had exhausted herself in the nineteenth century by civil wars and the loss of the remnants of her empire to the U.S.A. in 1898. She was economically backward and scarcely industrialized Madrid, Barcelona and Bilbao being almost her only industrial cities. During the 1920's she had a right-wing government under the strong hand of General Primo de Rivera, who fell from power in 1930, unable to survive the economic problems of that year. The King abdicated and a coalition government was formed, genuinely democratic but also very weak. In a predominantly Catholic country there were many anti-clericals who would use any methods, legal or otherwise, to weaken the power of the Church. In opposition on the right wing was the Falange Party, steadily gaining in strength. To counteract its power, the government depended increasingly on trade-union support from the cities, although even after the rebellion started it was reluctant to give the trade unions the arms they demanded until it was too late. On 17 July 1936 a group of senior army officers seized power in Melilla in Spanish Morocco. Their example was followed according to plan all over Morocco and the mainland. General Franco flew to Morocco (in a hired British aeroplane) from the Canary Islands. The Falangist and Carlist (monarchist) parties were in the plot and everywhere gave their support. There was much sympathy from the Roman Catholic Church against which the Republican government had been increasingly antagonistic.

Franco would quickly have gained control of the whole country but for the resistance of the Madrid government. It is false to assume that the rebellion was at first either staffed or planned by the Germans and Italians; the dictators intervened only after the revolution was well under way. On the other hand it seems possible that the legitimate government might have triumphed if it alone, and not the rebels, had been allowed to acquire arms abroad. For within ten days of the revolt starting Soviet Russia was sending help to the Republic. France at first thought of sending aid too, but was talked out of it by Britain, who, claiming to act in the interests of general peace, argued that if France did not aid the Republic, Italy and Germany might not help the rebels. A Non-intervention Committee was set up in London, which all the great powers attended, making solemn promises. Italy and Germany at once proceeded to break theirs and Soviet Russia announced that she would keep hers only so long as Italy and Germany kept theirs. Thus Soviet aid continued and it kept the Republic going for two years. When war began the Spanish government was far from Communist, but by 1938 the Communist Party had full control, since Russia was the only source of effective

Franco's troops manhandling guns near Burgos

Republican aid. A Fascist regime, financially indebted to the West, was thought by many to be a preferable alternative, and this was what emerged after over two years of horror: atrocities and counter-atrocities. Franco was recognized by Britain in 1939. Having won, he did not tie himself to the Fascist dictators and he did not attack British Gibraltar. He created a one-party state, militarist, but probably no more corrupt than its predecessors and supported by the Catholic

Church, which has done something to soften its more ruthless intransigence.

Effects of the war

Internationally Franco's victory did nothing to alter the balance of power. But diplomatically and in British politics its effect was profound. It drove a new wedge of distrust between Russia and France and Britain. The latter two wanted the war to end, even if this meant a Franco victory. In Moscow statesmen concluded that Britain was indifferent to democracy and would never therefore fight for it in Europe. On the other side, for many in Britain, Soviet intervention in Spain seemed the thin end of the wedge which might lead to Communism becoming established throughout Europe. Better to live at peace with the dictators than this; thus the Foreign Office throughout 1937, 1938 and 1939 continued to make efforts to settle its differences with Mussolini, and to advocate the recognition of Franco's regime.

By 1938 many if not most of the left-wing enthusiasts for the Republic had been disillusioned in it, as writers and journalists returned from Spain with evidence of the extent to which the once democratic republic had fallen into the grip of the Communist Party. The war was clearly no longer a fight for democracy, but this did not prevent the Left from being increasingly war-minded towards the German and Italian regimes. Churchill and the Labour Party came together in the last years of peace to work against appeasement, and this meant that when war finally came in 1939 Britain could enter it far more united about the morality of fighting than ever she could have been three years earlier. Basically it was Spain which was responsible for this.

The annexation of Austria

In July 1934 the Austrian Nazi Party had made a bid for power. They had murdered the Austrian Chancellor Dollfuss and committed various acts of barbarism in Vienna. They had hoped for active support from Hitler, but he had felt in no position to give this, since Mussolini was exerting strong pressure on him not to intervene. Kurt von Schuschnigg replaced Dollfuss and under Mussolini's protection he restored order. By 1938 the situation was very different. Hitler and Mussolini had proclaimed Germany and Italy linked as 'The Axis' in October 1936 and again in November 1937. Mussolini had conquered Abyssinia and Chamberlain was anxious to recognize this conquest. At the same time he was urging both dictators to accept an agreement for the evacuation of foreign troops from Spain, which they said they were willing to do, since the war was in its last stages: massed bombing attacks being aimed at the Republic's last stronghold of Barcelona.

In November 1937 Hitler had talked of the possibility of overthrowing Austria and Czechoslovakia, either simultaneously or in succession. On 19 November he had met Lord Halifax at Berchtesgaden, Hitler's mountain retreat. Halifax had praised Germany 'as the bulwark of Europe against Bolshevism'. In December Eden had told Ribbentrop that 'people in England recognized that a closer connexion between Germany and Austria would have to come about sometime'. In Austria Nazi agitation had continued. Hitler did not fear Anglo-French opposition, but he did not encourage revolution in Austria, hoping for 'an evolutionary solution'. Schuschnigg could get no offers of help against his internal problems from Italy or the Western powers and in January 1938 he uncovered an Austrian Nazi plot to seize power. He asked for an interview with Hitler and on 12 February he arrived at Berchtesgaden. Hitler at this moment seized his opportunity and insisted that Seyss-Inquart, later a Nazi and already in sympathy with extreme nationalist views, be made Minister of the Interior and in charge of the police. There was some bullying by Hitler at this meeting, but Schuschnigg gained what he wanted: condemnation of Austrian Nazis and agreement that they could if necessary be forcibly evicted and sent to Germany. There was to be co-ordination over foreign and economic affairs and both Hitler and Schuschnigg seemed satisfied.

Suddenly, on 9 March 1938, against advice from Mussolini, Schuschnigg decided to hold a plebiscite in Austria, within three days, as to whether Austria should remain independent of Germany. His reason for this decision remains obscure. Hitler at once realized that he must act or run the risk of humiliation and he demanded that the plebiscite be cancelled. Schuschnigg appealed to Italy, Britain and France, but got no comfort. He therefore agreed not to hold the plebiscite, but this was not now enough: his resignation was demanded. Seyss-Inquart was made Chancellor on the threat of German invasion, but Germany still invaded. Its army rolled into Austria; 70% of its vehicles, we are told, breaking down between the frontier and Vienna. Suddenly, at Linz, where he had gone to school, Hitler announced that Austria was to be incorporated with Germany, and Seyss-Inquart, Chancellor for a day, was ordered to issue a law accordingly. He did so, and on 10 April 1938 99·08% voted in favour of this. Chamberlain's comment was that he was shocked, since Austria was a member of the League of Nations. Austria was the centre of the communication system of south-east Europe. From there Germany could move into the whole Balkan peninsula, as so many had feared she might since the days of Bismarck. On 16 April Britain and Italy completed a pact of friendship, which was to have singularly little effect.

Czechoslovakia

Chamberlain still believed that in spite of the annexation of Austria, some *modus vivendi* with the dictator powers was essential for peace. Politicians have always argued that ends justify means and there is no clearer example of this than Chamberlain's attitude to Czechoslovakia, which he sacrificed because he believed this to be necessary for world peace. Czechoslovakia was a well-governed country with strong defences, some twenty-one regular divisions under arms, fifteen reserve divisions and pacts of mutual assistance with France and Russia. She had a powerful set of frontier defences.

Russia sought a four-power conference to prevent further German aggression, but Chamberlain ignored the Russian suggestion, thus, in the opinion of some, making his gravest blunder. Instead he began a policy of driving a wedge between France and Czechoslovakia, since he was determined that the Western powers should under no circumstances be dragged into war if Hitler did decide to annex all or part of Czechoslovakia. Hitler set himself a time-table: the German minority (some 3,100,000 Sudeten Germans, as they were called) must be united to the German Reich by 1 October 1938. By 4 September Benes, the President of Czechoslovakia, had granted the Sudetens full autonomy of local government, but in London *The Times* urged more: that he must be prepared to abandon the strategic and highly fortified frontiers in order that an undoubted wrong (i.e. the exclusion of the Sudetens from Germany) might be righted. Chamberlain believed that the alternatives to Czechoslovakian dismemberment were either world war or complete reliance on Soviet Russia, and he was unwilling to risk either. He decided therefore to fly to Germany to interview Hitler, and set off on 15 September, without his Foreign Secretary, Lord Halifax. He returned convinced of the necessity of handing over to Germany all areas where the population was more than 50% German, wrecking the Czech defence system. He called this a solution 'which would not bring about a European war, and therefore a solution which would not automatically compel France to take action in accordance with her obligation'. There remained the matter of persuading France and Czechoslavakia. In France Daladier and Bonnet, the new Prime Minister and Foreign Secretary, won slender but adequate support for Chamberlain's plan. On 21 September the British and French ministers in Prague told Benes that he must give in, and after twenty-four hours he reluctantly agreed. Next day Chamberlain returned to Germany and joyfully told Hitler at Godesberg that he had won support for his plan. Germany, however, had raised the stakes, and now demanded immediate German occupation of all

German-speaking areas. After a protest from Chamberlain, Hitler agreed to extend his time-limit by a week, to his original 1 October, and Chamberlain set about persuading France and the Czechs that the new ultimatum (known as the Godesberg Memorandum) must be accepted. He found opposition. In the cabinet his Foreign Secretary at first demanded its rejection. The French government took heart and rejected it unanimously, and so of course did the Czechs. Public opinion in Britain grew restive, and even newspapers who supported the government, such as *The Times* and the *Telegraph*, thought the time had come to make a stand, but Chamberlain was not convinced. He still abhorred the idea of war, and behind the scenes he resumed the work of winning over the French and the Czechs. Hitler telegraphed him on 27 September: 'Would not he continue to use his good offices to bring the Czechs to reason?' He immediately agreed and contacted Mussolini in Italy and Daladier in France. Next day Hitler invited the statesmen to visit him at Munich.

The Munich Conference accepted Hitler's demands made in the Godesberg Memorandum. Czechoslovakia's representatives were not present, but after the conference was over Chamberlain and Daladier called them in and told them that they must agree to give in. The Czech minister in London, Jan Masaryk, commented: 'If you have sacrificed my nation to preserve the peace of the world, I will be the first to applaud you, but if not, gentlemen, God help your souls.' Czechoslovakia lost her richest provinces; her defence system was shattered; her treaties with France and Russia were forfeited. Within six months far larger areas, including Prague, were to be occupied by Germany, while Poland also was to take a picking. In Russia Stalin commented: 'One might think that the districts of Czechoslovakia were yielded to Germany as the prize for her undertaking to launch war on the Soviet Union.' Yet Chamberlain, a tired rather lonely figure, still believed that he had won 'peace for our time'. He genuinely loathed war. 'The path which leads to appeasement is long and bristles

A David Low cartoon at the time of the Munich crisis. Britain (Chamberlain) and France (Daladier) ignored all offers from Stalin to help solve the Czechoslovak crisis in 1938

with obstacles,' he said in the House of Commons; yet he was convinced that it was the right path. A majority both in Parliament and in the country still agreed.

Events leading to war

Early in 1939 Chamberlain and Halifax visited Rome in the hope of cementing Anglo-Italian friendship as a balance to the German-Italian Axis. In February 1939 Chamberlain granted recognition to General Franco's Fascist government in Spain, having four days before vigorously denied in Parliament all possibility of such action. On 10 March the Prime Minister told the press that in his opinion 'Europe was settling down to a period of tranquillity' and the Lord Privy Seal, Sir Samuel Hoare, on the same day looked forward to a new age when the three dictators and the two

Western prime ministers would bring to Europe not only peace but standards of living raised to heights never before thought possible. Five days later Czechoslovakia was invaded, Prague occupied and the province of Bohemia-Moravia declared a German protectorate. Chamberlain in his heart must have expected this. Certainly he showed no violent reaction. It was his Foreign Secretary Lord Halifax who at this point seems to have talked him into a new policy. Public opinion was swinging away from the policy of appeasement and the Prime Minister must make a stand. Thus Chamberlain was persuaded to rewrite a speech prepared for delivery in his native Birmingham. This speech marks a turning-point. He defended the Munich Agreement, but if Hitler was attempting to dominate the world by force 'then he must realize that this nation . . . would take part to the uttermost of its powers in resisting such a challenge'.

At last he had made a stand. But it was a reluctant one and he again rejected a Russian proposal to call a conference of Central European powers, Britain and France, to discuss means of countering aggression.

The Versailles Treaty had granted Poland a corridor of land between East and West Prussia. It had also made the port of Danzig a free city, which was now demanding restoration to Germany. This would mean a readjustment of the corridor. Poland appealed for help and Chamberlain now did for her what he had refused to do for Czechoslovakia, which he had described in a broadcast as 'a far-away country' with a quarrel 'between people of whom we know nothing'. This time he promised that Poland would 'receive all the support in the power of His Majesty's Government' if her independence was in any way threatened. Lloyd George pointed out that in fact this was a hollow promise for 'If war occurred tomorrow you could not send a single battalion to Poland. . . . I cannot understand why, before committing ourselves to this tremendous enterprise, we did not secure beforehand the adhesion of Russia. . . . We have undertaken a frightful gamble.' The rest of the summer was to be spent in fitful negotiations between Britain and

Russia, but it is difficult to know how serious they were on the British side (see Chapter 14). If Russia joined Germany there were chances of regaining those parts of Poland lost in 1921. If she supported the Allies she might be left to fight the Germans in the east as she had been in 1914, since Britain had hardly any army and France would not send hers far from her Maginot Line.

On 26 April the government introduced conscription for all men aged twenty to twenty-one for six months' compulsory military training. It was the first time such a measure had been introduced in peace-time and a great break with tradition, but war was now too near for any other policy. In the same month, April 1939, Mussolini occupied Albania, then ruled by a dictator, Ahmed Zog, and Albania became an Italian puppet kingdom.

That war finally broke out in Poland on 1 September was possibly inevitable once Russia decided on a German pact of mutual non-aggression. This was signed (see Chapter 14) on 23 August and the British and French missions left Moscow on the 25th empty-handed. The day before, Parliament had passed an Emergency Powers Bill supported by all parties and such statesmen as Churchill and Eden, both still out of office. Chamberlain tried for the last time to persuade Hitler to negotiate over Poland; this time he assured him that Britain meant to fulfil her obligations. On 1 September the German army invaded Poland and for three days the British government tried frantic last-minute consultations. Then on Sunday, 3 September, at 11 a.m., a state of war was declared by Chamberlain to exist between Britain and Germany, since satisfactory guarantees had not been received. Chamberlain's comment was that 'everything that I have worked for, everything that I have believed in during my public life, has crashed in ruins'. He was to live another year, but he was a man unsuited to organization for war and when once the disasters of 1940 began he was persuaded to resign.

This account may seem unfair to Neville Chamberlain, and probably, even after twenty years, it is not possible to be objective in assessing the events leading to war. Chamberlain had had to face some tremendous problems. Public opinion in Britain in the mid-thirties was strongly pacifist as we have seen. British rearmament would not approach parity with Germany before about 1940. France was extremely weak: politically unstable and militarily unprepared in spite of a large army. Fourthly there was a deep and profound mistrust of Soviet Russia through most sections of the country. This was by no means peculiar to the 'Men of Munich', in the way later commentators liked to imagine. Churchill and Lloyd George, in advising a pact with Russia, were still in a very small minority, perhaps made smaller by Russia's recent equivocal behaviour in Spain. Above all, Chamberlain was a man of peace, who, while perhaps using means which we might question, hoped desperately until the last minute to achieve that end.

13

The thirties: a survey

Just as the 1920's are popularly but mistakenly remembered as a 'gay decade', in a similar way the 1930's are remembered as a 'grim decade': unemployment, hunger marches, violence and war. Such a memory is reasonable, yet for many in Britain it was again a time of rising living standards and greater middle-class security.

J. B. Priestley's four Englands

In the 1840's Disraeli had described an England divided into two nations, rich and poor. In the 1930's J. B. Priestley thought he could detect four Englands. There was the old England of the cathedral towns and southern counties. Second, and in terms of population by far the largest, there was the England of the nineteenth-century industrial revolution in the north, a country seared in the 1930's by silent blast-furnaces and unsightly slag-heaps and 'thousands of rows of little houses all alike'. Thirdly there was what he called the twentieth-century post-war England of the bustling Home Counties: 'filling stations and factories that look like exhibition buildings'; 'giant cinemas and dance-halls and cafés, bungalows with tiny garages, cocktail bars, Woolworths, motor-coaches, wireless, hiking, factory-girls looking like actresses, greyhound racing and dirt-tracks, swimming pools, and everything given away for cigarette coupons'. Finally he found a fourth England: that of the dole. This last was concentrated in certain areas: Scotland, South Wales, Tyneside, Teeside, Lancashire and a few areas in the Midlands. Miners, ship-builders and cotton operatives were the worst hit of the 2,000,000 to 3,000,000 unemployed in the early years of the decade.

The dole

The Means Test was degrading and scarcely conducive to thrift; the unemployed were kept alive, but at well below the minimum estimated standard for good health. There was little agitation among those who queued at the Labour Exchanges, possibly because plain-clothes men were keeping a sharp watch, but more likely because it was the wives rather than the husbands who suffered most. Meanwhile the attempts of the government to provide some form of occupation or even to keep the men fit were largely ineffectual. In fact very little relief work was provided, unless by private organizations. Some prosperous towns and counties from the south 'adopted' hard-hit areas elsewhere: Surrey taking on the worst town of all, Jarrow; Bath, the Cornish town of Redruth. There is no doubt that one of the worst effects on the morale of the depression areas was simply that the men involved *did* become so apathetic and reconciled to their fate. Far from showing signs of revolution, they just 'settled down to living on the dole'. As George Orwell showed, they cut down on necessities and concentrated on luxuries: 'small bets on the pools, threepennyworth of chips or a two-penny ice-cream'.

Income differences

Meanwhile the number of persons with very high incomes continued to fall. By 1937 some £250,000,000 was being redistributed each year by taxation from the rich to the poor through social welfare. Even an unemployed worker with a family in the 1930's was better off than an unskilled labourer in 1913, and to this extent the vision of the thirties as a decade of great social suffering is incomplete. The suffering was there, but in material terms it was probably less than for the Victorian 'submerged tenth', whose living standard had been so abysmal.

Gaps in welfare

Still there were gaps in the scheme of social welfare. Wives and mothers were not provided for in the scheme of National Insurance and there was no system of family allowances, except for those in receipt of national insurance payments. In education free grammar-school places had still to be won by a scholarship, and the expansion schemes were the victims of the economy campaign 1931–1934, as were teachers' salaries. In 1938 only 1·14% of children in England and Wales received state secondary education. For the middle classes who did not qualify for the health scheme, hospital costs could be alarming. Of the 3029 hospitals in the country 1013 were entirely voluntary and kept going by charges and subscriptions; in 1935 London had 133 flag days for hospitals and charitable institutions dependent on voluntary aid.

Housing

As already mentioned, the low bank-rate made money available for housing and one of the main ways that the economy recovered after 1931 was by the boom in building. Of the 4,000,000 houses built between the wars, about 2,500,000 were built by private enterprise without subsidy. Yet local authorities did much towards clearing slums during the decade and the pattern set in the 1920's continued. The Labour government of 1929 had great plans under the Wheatley Act for increasing the subsidies paid to housing and under this Act some 500,000 houses had been built before the subsidy was abolished in 1933 as an economy. In 1935 a new Housing Act was passed under which some 266,851 slum houses were demolished and replaced, it being estimated that there were still 1,000,000 houses unfit to be lived in. The type of house built remained much as in the 1920's and private speculators were under very few restrictions. Many buildings of historic importance were demolished and thousands of acres of land lost to agriculture without any overall plan, the Liberal pleas of the twenties for stricter town-planning going largely unheeded. For the middle-class home, variations of the 'Tudor style' were still the most popular, although there were occasional examples of good neo-Georgian architecture. 'Modern' architecture for public or private buildings remained of a low standard compared with America or the continent, although there were some examples of good functional architecture, for example some of the London Underground Tube stations.

Domestic habits

All classes continued to gain by the increase of labour-saving devices for washing, cleaning and cooking. Stainless-steel cutlery became universal and silver-plated ware very common. In cooking, processed foods came more and more to replace such operations as making blancmange, custard, caramel and even pastry and cakes. Breakfast foods of all kinds became the fashion, although cornflakes date from the 1880's. Traders delivered free of charge and shopping by telephone became a middle-class habit. Shops were cleaner and neater and cellophane wrapping was widely used. The first chain stores began to develop: Littlewoods, financed from profits from football pools (highly popular in the decade, an average of 6,000,000 people a week filling in a coupon); and Woolworths, whose store served nothing over the price of 6*d*. Every new housing estate quickly received a Woolworths and shops from the other big chains, for example Boots, International Stores and Mac Fisheries.

Meals

Subtle class distinctions remained as to what one ate, at what time of the day one ate it and what one called the meal. All called their first meal breakfast. But this would vary from an elaborate three-course meal of cereal or porridge, fried eggs, bacon or kidney, toast and coffee, to a hasty plate of porridge or cereal and tea.

The midday meal was dinner for some, luncheon for others and just plain lunch for the rest. Many industrial workers and agricultural workers had sandwiches and a flask of tea, but an increasing number of children (about 250,000) had a hot meal provided at school at a subsidized cost. In the afternoon suburban homes had 'afternoon tea' at four o'clock; the gentry had tea at five o'clock; most working-class families had Tea at about six o'clock, consisting of bread-and-margarine, tinned fish or meat, jam or fish-paste, and tea. Possibly there might be another cup of tea and a biscuit before going to bed. Upper-middle-class families, who ate lunch, had dinner between 7.30 and 8 p.m.: a two- or three-course meal, served by the resident maid. A large number of quite modest families still kept one resident servant in this decade of low wages and high unemployment.

There were fashions in diet; vitamins had been taken up in the 1920's, and slimming was periodically the fashion in both decades among the middle classes. Yet a survey carried out in 1936 revealed that only 30% of the population could be considered to be receiving a completely full diet, although the consumption of fruit had increased by 88% on 1910, of vegetables 64%, of butter and margarine 50%, of eggs 46%,

A picnic lunch for middle-class ladies on Derby Day, 1936

of meat 6% and of potatoes 1%. As a result of this survey, a Physical Training Act was passed in 1937 and a campaign started to 'get fit'.

Fashion

It was a decade of 'crazes', which came and went: for the games of monopoly, and yo-yo; for nudist camps; for hiking (the Youth Hostel Association was founded in 1930). In interior decoration there was a beginning of the revival of the Victorian. The Paris fashion house of Dior dictated the lengths of ladies' skirts and English housewives and shop-girls felt obliged to comply by buying the mass-produced off-the-peg clothes of the department stores. Rayon or artificial silk became a fashionable material, but the era of the new fabrics, such as nylon and terylene, was not yet. Sun-bathing became a cult and bathing costumes increasingly briefer. In men's clothes there was less change. Oxford bags disappeared and Englishmen remained very conservative in what they wore. There was rather more colour in their sports clothes, but city suits made few concessions either to climate or to pleas for greater informality. Altogether the changes in fashion in this decade were nothing like as startling as in the 1920's, being little more than advertisers' gimmicks to keep up sales. Those between 1918 and 1928, at least for the women, had reflected profound social changes.

The press

The press remained largely what it had been in the 1920's with some important changes. Lords Rothermere, Beaverbrook, Camrose and Kemsley now owned most of the national daily press and in the early 1930's a battle raged between them to achieve the 2,000,000 circulation figure. The methods used were house-to-house bribery on an unprecedented scale. First, readers were offered various insurance schemes; next they were enticed with offers of 'fountain pens, silk stockings, cameras, ladies' underwear, tea-sets, flannel trousers, kettles, mincing machines, mackintoshes, wrist watches, boots and shoes and mangles', all for signing a form undertaking to become a registered reader, brought round by an obliging member of the unemployed class. The *Express* reached the 2,000,000 reader figure first and then revealed that it had cost 8*s* 3*d* per reader to do so. This was in July 1933; after this the racket declined. Presentation, use of photography and type all greatly improved during the decade; but in no case when a newspaper proved dramatically wrong in any of its predictions did its sales at all decline. By the end of the decade the four giants were the *Daily Express*, the *Daily Mail*, the *Daily Herald* and the *Daily Mirror*. The *Daily News*, which absorbed the *Daily Chronicle* in 1930, became the *News Chronicle*, the only Liberal paper, but its sales did not compete with the four giants. The *Morning Post* was bought by the *Daily Telegraph* in 1937 and numerous provincial papers died as London extended its monopoly. *The Times*, under its editor Geoffrey Dawson, ended its position as an unprejudiced 'Fourth Estate of the Realm' and indulged in some very one-sided presentations and suppressions of news. The *Manchester Guardian*, under G. P. Scott, who died in 1932, had become a national newspaper, although it was not to be printed in London until 1961.

Broadcasting and the arts

There were no outstanding developments in broadcasting. The pattern of B.B.C. programmes as laid down in the 1920's was developed, London and the regional stations providing daily programmes. Commercially sponsored radio came from Radio Luxembourg, which was highly popular on Sundays when the B.B.C. ban on light music was in operation. Outside broadcasts improved, although no commentaries were allowed in Westminster Abbey for the coronation of George VI. George V began his series of Christmas Day broadcasts in 1932 and the tradition has lasted since. The B.B.C. regions all boasted a symphony orchestra and the quality of musical performance and of programmes steadily improved during the decade. In 1936 B.B.C. Television was begun at Alexandra Palace.

Some remarkable films were made during the decade, but unfortunately seldom shown on the popular circuits. The French cinema rose in prestige, while that of Germany sank after 1933. From Hollywood's hundreds survive a few fine films such as those of Chaplin and the Marx Brothers. It is easy to condemn low artistic standards, but the cinema of the 1930's gave immense pleasure. Why else, as the critic Roger Manvell wrote, would 'queues stand in the rain to buy three hours of warmth, comfort and star-solace for lives spent in factories and counting-houses or shopping in dismal little streets?' Every town now boasted two or three vast theatres, with their chromium, plush carpets, usherettes and ice-cream. Three visits a week were quite common in this age before mass-television. Few would have predicted in 1939 how short was to be the life of most of these buildings. Coloured films arrived, but of disappointing quality.

In the live theatre first nights remained fashionable but there were not many exciting new ventures. In 1935 T. S. Eliot wrote *Murder in the Cathedral* for Canterbury Cathedral. The poets, Auden, Isherwood, Stephen Spender and others, took up the search for a new verse drama. For the West End J. B. Priestley emerged as a writer of conventional plays with a fine command of language.

The Sadler's Wells Opera Company did much to popularize opera in English and its ballet company continued to increase its popularity. Drury Lane Theatre ran such musicals as Ivor Novello's *Dancing Years* and at Covent Garden Opera House some notable opera performances were given, but rather more artistically satisfying were those at the enlarged country house of Mr John Christie at Glyndebourne. Here, under two men of theatrical and musical genius, Carl Ebert and Fritz Busch, new standards of operatic production were established.

In the visual arts London caught up with the Europe of the 1920's. Dadaism (a nihilist movement in the arts begun in Zürich in 1916 and popular in Paris in the twenties) arrived; so did Surrealism. The International Surrealist Exhibition of 1936 was attended by 20,000 people. Salvador

Dali, who was the most fashionable of its exhibitors, attended wearing a diving-suit decorated like a Christmas tree, with a motor-car radiator cap on top of the helmet and hands of plasticine stuck on the body of the suit. But few accepted the movement at the time. It was described as 'fake revolution'; 'obscene or unintelligible'. 'They stand for violence and neurotic unreason', said J. B. Priestley. A retrospective exhibition of the German surrealist artist Max Ernst in 1961 escaped all such adverse criticism.

Max Ernst's surrealist *Elephant and the Celebes* painted in 1921 and exhibited in London, 1961

In literature a number of new poets emerged. Apart from W. H. Auden already mentioned, there were Cecil Day Lewis, Stephen Spender, Louis MacNeice and Robert Graves. For a while many of these were actively concerned with politics. They were idealists, usually on the Left, although all of upper-middle-class origin. Perhaps Roy Campbell was the greatest of the right-wing poets. Those of the Left felt that they must join forces 'with the millions of workers who have nothing to lose but their chains'. In this way the 1930's was a far more politically conscious decade than had been the 1920's, although possibly less of its literature may stand the test of time. Among the new novelists, Graham Greene, who published *Brighton Rock* in 1938, is perhaps one whose work will survive, and George Orwell is another. He fought in the Spanish Civil War, publishing *Homage to Catalonia* as a result, and also wrote powerful if political studies, such as *The Road to Wigan Pier*, published in 1937.

Transport

The 1930's saw no new or revolutionary changes in transport, but the steady growth of motor transport helped to bring the city even further out into the country. Many new roads were built and many more widened. Few country towns survived intact without at least some red-brick or stone-faced department store or bank replacing older traditional shops. The traffic problem began to choke more and more towns, the most notorious example being Oxford, as it was turned by the motor industry from a university town into an industrial centre with a university lodged within. The number of private cars rose from about 1,000,000 in 1930 to nearly 2,000,000 in 1939.

Scientific discovery

In the world of nuclear physics the 1930's in England were really exciting. In 1932 Lord Rutherford said: 'We are living in the heroic age of physics', and this feeling continued. Sir Charles Snow has called 1932 the 'most spectacular year in the history of science', when the 'neutron had been discovered and the existence of the positive electron proved'.

The Cavendish Laboratory at Cambridge was the centre of the most important research in the world and the excitement of its discoveries led to great optimism. Snow has said that 'it was difficult to find a scientist who did not believe that the scientific-technical-industrial revolution, accelerating under his eyes, was not doing incomparably more good than harm'. At the same time they were not complacent. A very high proportion of the leading physicists of the time took an active part in politics. Possibly there was less nationalism and more international co-operation among scientists than ever before or since. Peter Kapitz, one of Rutherford's favourite pupils from Russia, went continually backwards and forwards from Leningrad to Cambridge. There was an air of intellectual triumph among the scientists of the time, and, to quote Snow again, 'because England had just gone through its greatest age of physics . . . the English scientists were by and large more effective than those of any other country throughout the war with Hitler'.

The work of Alexander Fleming, bacteriologist at St Mary's Hospital from 1924 to 1948 and discoverer of penicillin in 1928, led to a wholly new development in medicine, which was to have particularly important effects during the war. In another field Frank Whittle worked throughout the decade on his jet-propulsion ideas. He eventually persuaded the Air Ministry to support him (1936) and his work led to great developments in aeronautics during and after the war. These are just two of many key advances in science and technology during the decade.

Agriculture

Farming in the 1930's saw something of a recovery. Education in agriculture developed at the universities (particularly Reading), agricultural colleges and farm institutes, and important work was done in such experimental stations as Rothamsted and Woburn. It was becoming increasingly clear that the agricultural industry was a highly complex affair, depending upon extensive scientific research. Its recovery would result in the expansion of a number of interlocked industries, for example agricultural fertilizers and farm machinery. But this could not be obtained without great care and some government cost. Gradually it was being realized that the whole of agriculture must be subsidized. In 1931 an Agricultural Land Utilization Act was passed, which, among other things, gave the Ministry of Agriculture power to acquire land and to create demonstration farms. 1932 was the year of the Ottawa Conference and British farmers were given some protection by a Wheat Act which provided a standard price for farmers of 10*s* per cwt for millable wheat, and by an agreement regulating importation of chilled meat. But this proved inadequate and so in 1934 a subsidy was introduced for livestock which was put on a permanent basis by the Livestock Industry Act of 1937. Marketing of produce was made easier by the Agricultural Marketing Acts of 1931 and 1933, Marketing Boards for hops, potatoes, milk and pigs being set up. The Agriculture Act of 1937 granted assistance to farmers who were seeking to increase the fertility of their land, which in many cases had been overworked and was in desperate need of manures and draining, both requiring considerable capital. Thus in an era of world surplus British farming gained protection and began its journey along the road to recovery which was to be stimulated by the Second World War.

Fascism and Communism

There is no doubt that many schoolboys and undergraduates were convinced in the 1930's that there was something rotten in the state of Britain. Hunger marches from Jarrow and long queues at the Labour Exchanges were their evidence. A few turned to the Roman Catholic faith, the only Church which continued to make converts during the decade. Others turned to the right-wing British Union of Fascists, which was founded by Sir Oswald Mosley in 1932 and whose membership rose to 20,000 in 1934. In June of that year at a mass meeting at Olympia violence was used against hecklers and the police took no action. *The Times* newspaper at first showed sympathy for the movement, but gradually this declined. Still in 1936, the police in East End Fascist demonstrations seemed more eager to protect Fascists than their Communist and Jewish opponents. The movement at first appealed to many of the aristocracy and

Fascists saluting during Sir Oswald Mosley's speech, May Day demonstration, October 1938

upper-middle classes, but after 1934 their support slowly faded. There were increasingly fewer intellectuals who turned that way. Far more turned to the Left, which in the 1930's was probably more vocal, if not more powerful, than it had ever been before.

Not all 'The Left' were necessarily members of the Communist Party, nor of the Labour Party, which many now regarded as a stuffy and old-fashioned organ of the trade unions. At the same time by 1935 the U.S.S.R. was becoming rather more respectable, especially after the publication of *Soviet Communism, a new civilization?* by Sidney and Beatrice Webb. The circulation of the *Daily Worker* went up steadily and, as its middle-class readership expanded, it acquired a weekly book page and reviews of the arts. In 1936 was founded the Left Book Club, which issued a book a month to subscribers, all written from a socialist point of view; and between 1935 and 1937 nearly 1,000,000 Communist pamphlets were sold in Britain.

Towards the end of the thirties there began something of a process of disillusionment among many intellectuals, possibly partly as a result of their experiences over Spain. We have noted already that this helped to end the movement for pacifism, but many reacted by a cry of 'a curse on both your houses'. They emigrated to the U.S.A., still a centre of isolationist feeling. Among these were Aldous Huxley, W. H. Auden and Christopher Isherwood. As Europe seemed by many to be on the brink of self-destruction, America appeared as the last refuge for the culture of the West.

PART FOUR

The Second World War

1939–1945

14

The origins and early stages of war

The outbreak of war 1939

As with the 1914–1918 war, there is controversy over the reason for the outbreak of war in 1939. A. J. P. Taylor has argued (*The Origins of the Second World War*) that Hitler never really wanted to have to fight the Western powers at all and that war broke out in the West through diplomatic miscalculations on both sides. Hitler had planned ever since 1923 to advance one day into Eastern Europe, which would almost certainly mean eventual war with Russia, and he was encouraged by the weakness of France and the earlier appeasement policy of Britain over Czechoslovakia to believe that he could get what he wanted in Poland without war. This thesis is not accepted by many historians, but what does seem to be accepted is that by no means all the pressure for German annexation of traditional German lands (the Rhineland, Austria, Bohemia, Poland) came from Berlin. Very strong local Nazi parties and nationalist pressures were at work, far less under the thumb of Hitler than was perhaps once thought. Certainly, too, the vision of the unification of all the German peoples into one vast state was a frightening one for British and French statesmen. In this sense it can be said that Britain went to war in 1939 to prevent a further upset in the balance of power in Europe, as she had done in August 1914.

During and after the war the idea was current that Britain was fighting the governmental system of the Nazis. This was only true in a limited sense. The traditional British policy is one of non-intervention against internal policies of regimes —an exception being in 1918, with intervention in Russia. Nazi methods in Germany, against Communists, against Jews and against any enemies of the regime, were more bestial than anything Europe had yet seen. But Britain did not go to war against Nazi anti-semitism and internal

From 1935 onwards, bestialities against the Jews were encouraged by the Nazi Party, culminating in the extermination policy of Eichmann during the war

political methods, even though public feeling in Britain against Nazi atrocities was a powerful factor in bringing her to the point of war, as it helped to continue the process of halting the pacifist movement and uniting all parties in their desire to fight.

In 1939 the Nazi Reich was an expansionist, but destructive and violent force, rearming at a rate considerably higher than any Western country, even if not at as high a rate as some thought at the time. Her generals had very early appreciated the potential of the aeroplane and of armoured and mechanized forces. They thought in terms of aggression, whereas the French army (still the biggest numerically in Europe) thought in terms of defence. It sat behind the impregnable Maginot Line, which stretched around France's north-eastern frontier, but stopped at Luxembourg. The British army, even after war was declared, had hardly accustomed itself to the idea of mechanized fighting and nobody had a very clear idea where it could fight. Poland was inaccessible except by air, and to move an army entirely by air was not to be attempted until the German air invasion of Crete in 1941.

Poland

Czechoslovakia had been a fairly stable and effective democracy, allowing a free press and Parliamentary elections. She was a multi-racial country, carved out of the old Habsburg Empire, with German, Polish and Magyar minorities. In 1938 the French had been unwilling to fight for her; Russia would not act alone; Britain had believed that no Czech government could ever hold down her dissatisfied Sudeten Germans and that her own preparations for war were inadequate. On 12 March 1938 Lord Halifax had admitted that if pressure should come from Germany 'quite frankly . . . our plans, both for offence and defence, are not sufficiently advanced'. Therefore it was necessary to make concessions and thus had Czechoslovakia been carved up.

What was the regime in Poland which a year later Britain went to save? It would be idle to pretend that it was democratic. Modern Poland had come into being as a result of the treaties of Versailles and Riga. She was landlocked except for a corridor between the two Prussias (see p. 236). The hero of the new state had been General Pilsudski, who had commanded the victorious troops against the Red Army in 1920. In 1926 he had seized power as Prime Minister and he was effective dictator of Poland until his death in 1935. He and his fellow officers sought to restore the lost glory of medieval Poland, a Catholic land whose wealth had lain in vast agricultural estates, and whose landowners had had absolute power over their armies of peasant serfs. In 1934 Pilsudski and his Foreign Minister, Colonel Beck, had made a pact of mutual non-aggression with Germany. Hitler assumed that a military dictatorship, backed by the land-owning class, would become a willing satellite of Germany, opposed as it was to Russian Communism. The Polish government, however, sought to increase its power and prestige by playing off against one another the four great powers of France, Britain, Germany and Russia, and thus to maintain Poland's independence. But they lacked the power. The Polish army was never a force to stand comparison even with that of Czechoslovakia. It never mustered more than 250 antiquated aeroplanes and one tank battalion.

Britain, France and Italy all considered that Danzig, like the Sudetenland, ought to be restored to Germany. They were convinced that this could be done by diplomatic means and none regarded it as worth fighting over. Poland and France had been allied since 1925; Italy and Germany were united by pacts of 1936, 1937 and 22 May 1939; Britain had committed herself to Poland in March 1939. Hitler believed that Britain and France would force Poland to hand over Danzig, as they had obliged Czechoslovakia to hand over the Sudetenland. In fact by refusing to negotiate until the last minute the Polish government found itself at war on 1 September. Britain, after two days of unsuccessful diplomatic action, found herself equally involved against Germany. The French, sitting in the Maginot Line, likewise proclaimed a state of war. Hitler had miscalculated over Britain, if not over France. But if Britain had gone to war to save the balance of power in Europe she had not done so to save a corrupt and militarist regime in Poland. The question then arises whether, had Britain and France successfully negotiated with Moscow during the summer of 1939, war in September could have been avoided.

Russo-German pact

Once Germany had secured her eastern frontier with Russia in August, she was clearly going all out for Danzig and the corridor. On 3 April Churchill had argued in Parliament that to fulfil promises made to Poland, military alliance with Russia was essential. 'The worst folly . . . would be to chill and drive away any natural co-operation which Soviet Russia in her own deep interests feels it necessary to afford.' Lloyd George had said: 'If we are going in without the help of Russia we are walking into a trap.' The Franco-British negotiations with Russia were based on proposals of the U.S.S.R. of 17 April that France, Britain and the U.S.S.R. should offer military aid to any Eastern European state, from the Baltic to the Black Sea, which was the victim of aggression. Britain was reluctant to guarantee aid to Russia if Germany should choose to attack her via the Baltic but was anxious to see the Baltic states of Latvia, Estonia, Lithuania and Finland preserved. By July negotiations were languishing, although a British and French military mission was dispatched by sea to arrive in Russia at the end of the month. By this time the Kremlin was also having trade talks with Germany and Molotov had replaced Litvinov (a pro-Western diplomat) as Foreign Commissar. Early in August German feelers detected a response towards developing these talks into something more, but this was after Britain and France had been negotiating since April, so that the charge of Russian duplicity here seems hardly fair. Molotov feared Japan and accused Germany of encouraging her and even on 4 August it still seemed that Stalin wanted a Western alliance if he could get one. But on 14 August the British and French negotiators again got bogged down on the question of what they would be prepared to do, and accept, in the event of war between Russia and Germany. It seems that this issue had remained the central stumbling-block through the whole negotiations, while Poland had throughout objected to Russian assistance, since she feared Russia's aims and internal Communist revolution. Also on 14 August

Ribbentrop in Berlin approached Moscow for the opening of political negotiations, and Molotov agreed on the 19th. Next day a commercial treaty between Russia and Germany was signed and on 21 August the Allied missions adjourned, unable to make promises. On the same day Ribbentrop was invited to Moscow; he went on 23 August and signed an agreement. On the same day the Poles at last agreed to a formula that collaboration between Poland and the U.S.S.R. was not excluded in the event of German aggression, but it was too late. The British and French had already packed their bags and on 28 August the British stated that while an Anglo-German agreement would be welcomed they could not desert Poland.

Early Nazi successes

From this brief account it seems that Britain and France may have to bear some of the blame for the Russian decision to ally with Germany, although even if Russia had made a pact with Britain and France this need not have prevented war breaking out. It seems agreed that Germany was determined on eventual war; Hitler, if not his staff, was prepared to fight the Western powers, if diplomacy failed, and war in fact began when German troops crossed the Polish frontier on 1 September 1939.

On 17 September Russian troops marched west and within a month Poland ceased to exist. Germany and Russia now had a common frontier once again and Communist and Nazi regimes were installed in the respective Polish provinces. No other significant military campaigns occurred that year. A British expeditionary force was sent to France under Lord Gort and they took up their old positions on the west of the Allied line, but the French army made no attempt to attack Germany while her army was in Poland. France had an unassailable defence position; good but over-deployed mechanized units; but practically no air strength. The German generals felt that war had come too early and they did their best to restrain Hitler, but in the spring of 1940 he attacked Norway and Denmark, wishing to gain

Crowds wait for news in September 1939. In spite of the grins they are deeply disturbed. Compare p. 82

control of the Baltic entrance and to be able to import supplies of Swedish iron-ore without interference. Britain sent an expeditionary force to try to help Norway, troops being landed along the coast as far north as Narvik. But they had no air support and were soon obliged to withdraw. A number of German naval vessels had been sunk, but that was the total British achievement. The apparent failure of the Allies led to a violent attack on the government, which Churchill and Eden had joined at the outbreak of war.

By now the situation was extremely grave, since the German army had attacked Holland and Belgium, whose efforts at neutrality were brushed aside. A large hole was punched in the French line through Luxembourg and south-east Belgium, where the French frontier was practically undefended. The British were cut off from their French allies and retreated into the north-west corner of France. Here they were rescued from Dunkirk. Some 338,000 men (British and French) were brought back from France, in every kind of vessel, across an abnormally calm sea. They had lost all their equipment and much of their morale, regarding themselves as defeated. At home in Britain they were welcomed as heroes, but it would be some time before they were fit and equipped again for active service. One hundred and seventy-nine German and twenty-nine British aircraft were shot down during the operation. Meanwhile the German army turned against the French, who were bewildered and outwitted, rather than out-fought. In June Churchill made great efforts to keep France in the war, offering mutual citizenship and union of the two countries. But there was little wish to fight; indeed, there were many right-wing Frenchmen who thought France had been dragged into war by the inept Chamberlain and Daladier, and who welcomed the right-wing government which Pétain now set up in Vichy. Many Frenchmen, on the other hand, fought on, some coming to London to join De Gaulle's Free French movement.

If we are looking for evidence that Hitler had not specifically planned to fight Britain it appears in his next moves. He lacked both a proper fleet and sufficient air superiority to invade the country. Through the late summer of 1940 the Battle of Britain raged; it marked his attempt to gain sufficient mastery of the sky to feel in a position to mount an invasion. Only now did he, like Napoleon before him, order the building of a fleet of landing-craft. But air superiority was needed and this he failed to establish. From 8 August until October, reaching a climax about 15 September, waves of bombers escorted by Messerschmitt fighters were sent across the Channel and 1733 were shot down, the pilots either dying or being interned. Spitfire and Hurricane fighters, built in the years just before the war and slightly superior in design to the earlier-designed Messerschmitts, were responsible. Never before 'in the field of human conflict was so much owed by so many to so few'. Airfields, port installations and London were the main targets. By October the invasion season was past and Hitler switched to night-raids, using incendiary and high-explosive bombs on London and other great cities: Bristol, Plymouth, Southampton, Coventry, Liverpool. The City of London was gutted by fire on 29 December 1940 and on 10 May 1941 so was the House of Commons. Only gradually did fire-watching and fire precautions become more effective. Some 5000 people a month died during the winter 1940–1941 from air-raids. School-children, who had been evacuated in 1939 and returned, were now re-evacuated into country areas. Anti-aircraft guns, which purposely made a great deal

A remarkable photograph of a falling building during a London air-raid, 1941. Compare p. 95

of noise to raise morale, were at first not very effective. Gradually however, by means of radar and night-fighters, increased numbers of bombers were brought down. The government made the important decision that aircraft production must concentrate on bombers suitable for retaliation on German cities. This policy has been attacked as having deprived more important arms, the navy and the army, of tactical aircraft and of having used up greater resources than it destroyed. Certainly it neither broke

German morale nor prevented German war production and possibly it served only to stimulate both. But in the lonely year of 1941 it was considered by Churchill the best contribution to winning the war that Britain could make at the time, although it was to cost Britain many thousands of highly trained air-crews. It was intended by some to make an Allied invasion unnecessary. This was over-optimistic, but it helped to make the invasion of 1944 successful. Meanwhile in 1941 air-raids on Britain died down until towards the end of the war. Germany had made her fateful decision to attack Russia.

Italian contribution and North Africa

In the summer of 1940 Italy had entered the war, hoping to acquire Tunisia and parts of the Riviera coast from France. She was unlucky. Vichy France, by making peace, technically preserved for France her overseas territories. In return she had had to allow most of France north of Vichy itself to be occupied by German troops, and French North African territories to come under German surveillance. Thus the Axis powers had virtual control of the whole North African coast from the Egyptian frontier, through Italian Libya, to Spanish Morocco, which was scarcely unprejudiced in its neutrality. In this way the old threat to Middle East oil and to British India arose again. Britain managed to keep open the Mediterranean by defeating the Italian navy at Taranto (November 1940) and Cape Matapan (March 1941) and troops and supplies were being shipped to Egypt from Britain even before the threat of German invasion had completely ended. Italian East Africa and Abyssinia were occupied by British troops during the winter of 1940–1941 when General Wavell also drove across North Africa from Egypt to Benghazi and beyond. Great hauls of Italian prisoners were taken and the British position seemed secure, but the Germans now decided to occupy the whole Balkan peninsula, including Crete (May 1941), and to send German reinforcements to Africa under General Rommel. British reinforcements were sent to Greece and withdrawn again to Crete. By the end of May 1941 they had to withdraw from there, after the first large-scale glider and paratroop operation carried out by the Germans. Denuded Libya was lost to General Rommel and the Mediterranean almost closed by the establishment of air-bases in Sicily, forcing nearly all supplies to travel via the long Cape route. In April 1941 Britain had occupied the vital oil supplier Iraq and in June and July Syria and Lebanon were taken over from Vichy France. But by then the pressure was relaxing, for Hitler had invaded Russia.

Lend–Lease

Thus the European war of 1939 began in 1941 to enlarge into the world war of 1941–1945. From the New World the U.S.A. committed herself to helping Britain, which for a year, June 1940–June 1941, had stood alone. American intervention had almost certainly won the war of 1914–1918 for the Allies, but afterwards the Western Giant had withdrawn again into isolation. Neither President F. D. Roosevelt nor the American people had at first felt any desire to enter the war of 1939. They had shown strong moral disapproval over Munich and 'the betrayal' of democratic Czechoslovakia, but without offering to boost Western diplomacy. The first reaction of Congress to the new war was an act forbidding American shipping to enter any belligerent port. But this could gravely affect the American economy, and so a Cash and Carry Bill was passed in 1940 by which belligerents wanting American goods should pay for them and carry them off, the German merchant navy being effectively prevented from doing this by the British royal navy. Gradually American opinion swung behind Britain. There was a real fear that Germany, now master of Western Europe, would threaten American interests and in the autumn of 1940 Congress granted fifty destroyers to the British Navy in return for aircraft and naval bases in the British West Indies. Meanwhile President Roosevelt decided to make an unprecedented bid (since made impossible by a Constitutional amendment) to stand

The situation in November 1941—November 1942

for a third term as President. He had personally come to want far greater aid for Britain. He was elected in the autumn of 1940 and in January 1941 he introduced to Congress his scheme of Lend-Lease. Britain had exhausted her credits in the first year of war and could no longer pay cash. Therefore the President was empowered to order the manufacture of any arms thought necessary for the defence of America and to 'sell, transfer, exchange, lease, lend or otherwise dispose of' them. In April 1941 American shipping was allowed to carry equipment to the Red Sea and East Africa, greatly helping the British forces who were dependent on the long haul round the Cape for survival.

Battle of the Atlantic

Meanwhile unrestrained submarine warfare by German U-boats and the use of magnetic mines had been going on since the war began. The British were unable to use the ports of Southern Ireland, while Germany had the use of Brest and Lorient in Brittany as U-boat bases. Aircraft greatly helped Britain in the struggle, as they became increasingly available. Destroyers and fast corvettes, with depth-charges and radar equipment, were the main weapon against U-boat attack. All shipping moved in convoy. Refugee governments from occupied Europe still for the most part had control over their navies, which thus helped to augment British shipping engaged in the struggle. The lone Q-ship of the First World War did not reappear, but armed merchantmen did, such as the *Jervis Bay*, which was sunk while protecting a convoy in November 1940. In other ways the struggle was very similar to the earlier one. A few surface engagements took place, for example those against the *Graf von Spee* in November 1940 in the River Plate and against the *Bismarck* in May 1941. British losses to U-boats reached a peak in October 1940 with 400,000 tons and they totalled something over 3,500,000 tons during this year, which was by far the worst. After that, with American aid, they declined a little; but throughout the war the Battle of the Atlantic went on.

15

Enlargement into world struggle

Germany v. Russia

By June 1941 Hitler had virtual control over the whole of Western Europe from the Baltic to the Mediterranean. Yet he had not subdued Britain; he had not won the vital oil-fields of the Middle East; he had made no serious effort to break through to India, as Napoleon was probably trying to do in 1798. But if he had learnt from Napoleon's earlier mistake, then he certainly did not learn from his worse mistake of 1812. Against the strongest military advice he decided that his longed-for moment of challenge to Russian Communism had come. This was what he had been dreaming about since 1923 and he decided to act. On 22 June 1941 British listeners to the B.B.C. heard that they were no longer alone. Hitler had invaded Russia, with the help of Balkan and Finnish troops, and Winston Churchill had offered Stalin all co-operation and help possible. The excuse given was failure to supply raw materials promised in the pact of 1939 and at first all went well for the Germans. Great numbers of prisoners were taken but there were also attacks from peasant partisans and a scorched-earth policy. Hitler, always a gambler, staked everything on a quick victory. But his mechanized army was overstrained and the rate of mechanical breakdowns was phenomenal. The suburbs of Leningrad and Moscow were reached by December, but the Red Army was still intact and at once the factor of weather intervened, again following the earlier Napoleonic pattern. Possibly Hitler had been misled by the Red Army's performance in its Finnish War of 1939–1940, and he failed to realize that already by 1939 Soviet Russia was second only to the U.S.A. as an industrial power. Or perhaps it was precisely because he had realized this that he had decided that it was a case of 'now or never'. It was to be proved by December 1941 that it would be never.

Japan v. America

On 7 December 1941 the Japanese navy attacked the American naval base at Pearl Harbour in Hawaii, 8 battleships, 3 cruisers, and 3 destroyers being damaged or destroyed. The United States at once declared war on Japan, who was already allied to Germany and Italy. These two replied by declaring war on the United States, and thus the struggle of 1939–1941 had become world-wide. Britain's part from now on would be increasingly subsidiary. The European colonial powers in the Far East (Britain, Free France and Holland) were now challenged by Japan, this first Asian country to achieve economic parity with themselves. They were unprepared and a rapid collapse of European power in the Far East followed. The Americans too, who since 1898 had been governing the

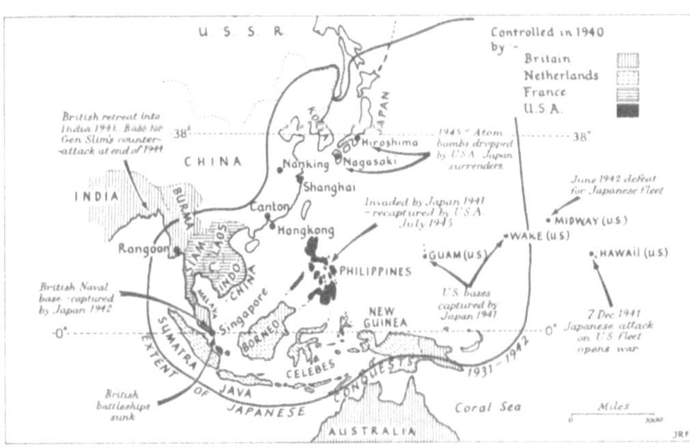

The Far East

Philippines until such time as the Filipinos proved fit to govern themselves, were equally unprepared. The Japanese swept into French Indo-China, British Malaya, Singapore, Burma, the American Philippines and the Dutch East Indies. The British under General Alexander skilfully retreated through Burma into India, which became a base for counter-attack. Politically educated Indians were strongly neutralist, many having to be imprisoned, including Gandhi and Nehru (see Chapter 18).

Heavy naval defeats were at first incurred by the Allies, Britain losing the battleship *Prince of Wales* and the battle-cruiser *Repulse*, sunk by shore-based aircraft. Only in the spring of 1942 did the American navy muster its strength to deliver counter-blows. The battles of the Coral Sea and Midway Island were great Allied victories, won entirely by aircraft. They mark the end of the battleship era. Japan, by losing six aircraft-carriers, was very greatly weakened and the day approached when the slow reconquest of the Pacific could begin.

Reaction of the coloured peoples

Probably the most important event of the post-war years will prove to be not the cold war between Russia and her Western Allies, but the emergence of the coloured peoples and of the non-European nations: China, India and Pakistan, Malaya, Indonesia, the Arab states and the many new African countries. Despite all the forecasts of the European administrators, who were driven out by Japan in 1942, these peoples have proved themselves capable of self-government and determined to resist what they imagine to be European imperialism. There seems no doubt that it was the temporary hegemony of Japan in the Far East which is most responsible for this situation. In order to stretch her resources Britain tapped her empire for man-power: African troops were used against the Italians in East Africa and from 1942 several divisions were raised from both East and West Africa and taken to India, where they joined Indian units for service in Burma. Such troops, able to march long distances in jungle and tropical conditions, would obviously be well suited to Burmese conditions. Thus to hold off the Japanese Britain relied upon Indian, Gurkha and African divisions, until Europeans could be released from North Africa and Europe. In the later reconquest of Burma in 1944–1945 these forces still played a vital role. The experiences of moving from one's paddy-field or bush-village into army camps; of seeing Europeans of types other than the hand-picked civil servant or district officer; of receiving technical training and education; of fighting and dying alongside Europeans in conditions of equality: such experiences contributed a great deal to the phenomenal growth of political consciousness. Such men would be reluctant to return to their native villages and they would certainly be reluctant to return to European rule. At the same time, once European control was removed, ancient rivalries and antagonisms might re-emerge, for example the tension between Hindu and Moslem in India.

Allied counter–attack in Europe

1942 saw the Allied position in Europe as still very weak and in the Middle East Australian troops had been withdrawn to defend their own country against Japan. Tobruk, an Allied position successfully held for eight months during 1941 behind the enemy line in Libya and maintained from the sea, was captured in June 1942 by the Germans. General Rommel was not stopped until El Alamein, only seventy miles from Alexandria. In Russia, Hitler had some three-quarters of his fighting forces engaged, and General von Paulus's army put enormous pressure on the south-east sector of the front, advancing from the Dneiper to the Donetz, and on to the Volga, where it was held at Stalingrad, which was reached in October and battered for two terrible months. On 19 November the Russians launched a counter-offensive, encircling and wiping out von Paulus's 6th Army. A German retreat was ordered to prevent further losses. Stalin's 'winter offensive' under Marshals Zhukov, Malinovsky, Konev and Petrov drove the German line back beyond the Donetz.

The Russians had been putting very strong pressure on Britain and America to launch a Second Front in Europe. A series of commando raids was, in fact, made, the most famous being the disastrous Dieppe Raid in August 1942, from which invaluable experience was gained at great cost. Bomber Command steadily attacked German industry, with increasing accuracy, but at tremendous and controversial cost. Plans were laid for an invasion in 1944. To have attempted one before would have been to court disaster. But Stalin remained suspicious that his Western Allies were deliberately allowing Russia and Germany to destroy each other, and this suspicion may well have affected his post-war diplomacy.

In October 1942 the British launched their offensive in Egypt under Generals Alexander and Montgomery, which carried them forward for the third time along the North African coast. For the British, the Battle of El Alamein remains one of their great achievements in the war. On 8 November, under General Eisenhower, a combined force of American, British and Free French forces landed

The Mediterranean

in Morocco and Algeria. They began an advance eastward to link up with the British 8th Army advancing from Libya. By January Montgomery had reached Tripoli. By May 1943 some quarter of a million German and Italian troops had surrendered and the rest were withdrawn. The war in Africa was ended and the besieged island of Malta relieved.

In America a Combined Chiefs of Staff had been set up in Washington to co-ordinate planning. Its American members somewhat reluctantly agreed to the British proposal to concentrate on defeating Germany before Japan. Churchill, directing the war for Britain from his bunker under the Admiralty, set off on numerous air-trips to confer with his opposite numbers. He was not always successful. His plan for attacking Italy and detaching her from the Axis was accepted, but failed in execution due to delay in high places. His plan for a Balkan invasion to link up with the Russians, and at the same time prevent the latter from absorbing this area, was rejected.

In July 1943 British and American troops landed in Sicily. This caused a revolution in Rome, as Churchill had foreseen, Mussolini being overthrown and a government set up by Marshal Badoglio. The Allied advance, however, was very slow. They did not land on the mainland, at Salerno, until September, when Badoglio made peace. But this was of little use, since the German army now moved in and the Allied armies, badly equipped for mountain warfare in an Italian winter, made slow progress.

Allied supplies continued to reach Russia from Iran, via the Persian Gulf, and by sea from Murmansk and Archangel. With the reopening of the Mediterranean they could be delivered via the Dardanelles (as they never could be in the First World War). Turkey had remained neutral, but gradually found herself leaning towards the Allies.

Through the summer of 1943 the Russian counter-offensive continued. Leningrad, which had been besieged since 1941, was relieved. The whole German line, pivoting on the Baltic, was pushed back, until by December 1943 it was beyond the Dnieper. Russian equipment (from factories beyond the Urals), Russian manpower and Allied equipment produced an overwhelming superiority against the Germans. Nineteen-forty-four was to see the final offensives, both East and West, which led to victory. In November 1943 Churchill, Roosevelt, and Stalin met together at Teheran for the first time to plan the coming Second Front landings.

Normandy landings and victory in Europe

Allied troops were landed on the Normandy coast on 6 June 1944. Within six days 326,000 men had been put ashore. An artificial harbour of prefabricated concrete sections was sunk into position (Mulberry), and oil piped across the Channel by an underwater pipeline (Pluto). General Eisenhower was Supreme Allied Commander. Montgomery directed the early stages of the battle, but as the troops deployed, he was joined by two American generals, Bradley and Patton. The French Resistance or Maquis forces, who had been increasingly well organized and supplied by parachute, everywhere co-operated. After losing the Battle of the Falaise Gap, the Germans began a rapid withdrawal, having lost their 5th and 7th Panzer armies. On

Normandy Landings, June 1944. Compare p. 89

24 August a Free French Force under General Leclerc reached Paris, which surrendered the next day. General Alexander was now advancing rapidly up Italy, Rome and Florence having been captured. On the Eastern Front the Russians were again attacking.

As the Allies advanced through Europe they captured the launching-pads of the V1 and V2 missiles. The former ('doodle bugs' or pilotless bombers) started raiding London on 13 June 1944, a week after the Normandy landings. The

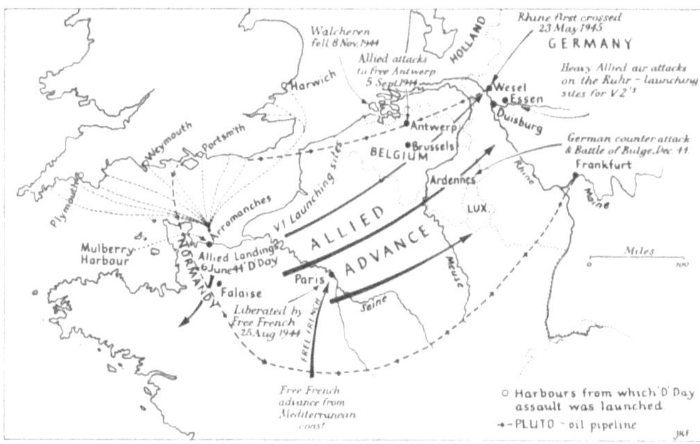

War in the West 1944–1945

V2 rockets started in September. The V1s could be shot down or intercepted by barrage-balloons and anyway by the winter most of their launching-pads had been captured. But the V2 missiles, launched from the Ruhr and prototypes of all later rocket development, could not be stopped until after the Allies had crossed the Rhine early in 1945. About 1230 V2 rockets fell on London before this could happen: a harrowing experience in the hour of victory.

An attempt by a group of German generals in July 1944 to assassinate Hitler had failed, scorching his trousers and paralysing his arm. He had had the generals executed and the war had gone on. German troops had evacuated France by the autumn, but Montgomery failed to persuade Eisenhower to let him drive a solid wedge into the German line. Instead, the policy of uniform advance was insisted upon. In December 1944 Hitler ordered a last counter-attack in the Ardennes district and the 'Battle of the Bulge' followed, until the Western Allies resumed their advance in February 1945. By this time the Russian army was once again advancing through Poland, as it had done in 1939, setting up a puppet Communist government at Lublin.

A second Big Three conference was held in February 1945, at Yalta in the Crimea. Plans were laid for a conference at San Francisco, from which was to come the United Nations. Germany was to be fought until unconditional surrender, and the Russians demanded that reparations should then be exacted. It was agreed that Germany be divided into four zones and occupied, Churchill insisting that France join the Western occupying powers. Berlin should also be divided into four zones, although within the Russian-occupied area. Russia should regain her Polish provinces lost at Riga, and Poland be compensated with German lands. The Polish government in London was to have to fight the new Communist government at Lublin in 'free elections': needless to say, it was going to lose. Probably the average Polish peasant in 1945 preferred the prospect of Communist collectivization of land to a return of the old landlord regime and possibly he still does after nearly twenty years.

Meanwhile Germany steadily collapsed as the Allied armies broke in. By 25 April 1945 the Russians had surrounded Berlin and Hitler had committed suicide on 20 April. On 2 May German troops on the north Italian front surrendered and on 4 May Montgomery received the surrender of the armies in north-west Germany, Holland and Denmark. On 7 May Admiral Doenitz surrendered Germany to General Eisenhower. The war in Europe was over and in August 1945 the conference at Potsdam sought to settle the problems it had raised.

The atom bomb and the war in Asia

By the end of 1943 the Allies were fully on the offensive in the Far East. New Guinea had been recaptured and the Americans began closing in on Japan, island by island. At the end of 1944 General Slim took the offensive in Burma under Lord Louis Mountbatten, now British Supreme Commander in South-East Asia. The 14th Army advanced from Mandalay to Rangoon in the early months of 1945, capturing the port on 3 May. By July 1945 the Americans had reconquered all the Philippines. Preparations were now made to invade and capture Malaya, from where possibly an overland campaign might have been staged through Siam and Indo-China. None of this proved necessary because of the decision by President Truman (President Roosevelt had died suddenly in April 1945) to drop the first atomic bombs at Hiroshima and Nagasaki. The argument in favour of this action was that it prevented loss of lives of countless Allied troops, who would have had to battle their way inch by inch against fanatical Japanese.

It carried the argument of total war to its logical conclusion. Early in the war the British had been genuinely shocked at German bombing of civilians, in towns or as refugees. Such a moral attitude had gradually been abandoned as impractical and Bomber Command had been hammering away at German cities for years, flattening Berlin. In 1945 had come the Allied raid on refugee-packed Dresden, and now came the horror not only of 200,000 casualties, but of the deliberately inflicted radiation which would affect not only the living inhabitants but their unborn children (for a moving account of this see *Children of the Ashes* by R. Jungk).

It seems certain in retrospect that Japan would in fact have capitulated, if full details of the probable effects of the bombs had been released, without the bombs having to be dropped. For it is now known that strong forces were at work in Japan urging the Emperor to seek peace. Of course this was not known at the time and very powerful anti-Japanese propaganda had made the argument for mass-destruction of these 'Asian fiends' acceptable to many who would possibly have resisted its use against Europeans.

The Americans under General MacArthur quickly occupied Japan, where a powerful pacifist movement soon began. In a remarkably short time she was to become the chief American bastion against Communism in the Far East.

The Communist triumph in China

A textbook on Britain is perhaps unjustified in following up events in the Far East any further. Yet unless we do so we will not understand the history of the post-war years. Throughout the Far Eastern war the Allies had been supporting a movement in China called the Kuomintang, which had arisen in the 1920's led by Chiang Kai-shek. Originally it had been a Communist-trained and -inspired movement, but had broken with Mao Tse-tung and Chou En-lai in 1927, receiving aid instead from those Western powers interested in China. During the 1930's it had won for itself the control of southern China and was recognized by the Western powers as the legal government of China. It fought both the Communists—who retreated into the far north-west, setting up headquarters at Yenan—and the Japanese, advancing from Manchuria. When America and the Western powers were at war with Japan huge quantities of supplies were flown into China to aid the Kuomintang. Unfortunately, many of these supplies were ill-chosen, while corruption swallowed a very high proportion of the rest. But still Chiang Kai-shek was regarded as one of the victorious leaders, whose representative took his place in the United Nations when that was founded.

In November 1945 the American General Wedemeyer reported to Washington that Chiang Kai-shek would be unable to consolidate his authority in China without first securing 'a satisfactory settlement with the Communists, the assistance of foreign administrators and technicians, and political, economic and social reforms through honest, competent civilian officials'. These were not to be found and gradually the control of his 'National' government withered away. The major problems were transport, currency and agriculture. Although the worst ravages of famine were checked by 1946, these three problems remained unsolved. In June 1946 General Marshall achieved a truce between the Communists and Chiang Kai-shek, whose government was increasingly autocratic. But the following January Marshall asked to be recalled to Washington, as he could see no solution to a situation again rapidly deteriorating. The National government began its final retreat, which was to end in the island of Formosa (liberated in 1945 from the Japanese, who had held it since 1895). Here, with American aid on a vast scale, it managed to establish itself. In October 1949 the Communist People's Republic of China was proclaimed, Russia providing economic aid in return for raw materials, American dollars and tea. China had acquired the strongest government it had had since the Manchu dynasty in the eighteenth century. What Professor Latourette has described as 'a social experiment which for magnitude was without parallel anywhere on the globe' now began.

Britain recognized the Communist government in 1950, but inevitably her position in the Far East has been affected. Shanghai, in which Britain had over £100,000,000 invested before the war, had fallen to the Japanese in 1938, when many of these assets were liquidated. In 1945 the European firms returned to the city, but in 1949 it was attacked by the Communists and in 1950, after heavy bombing, it was captured and its trade has much declined. Britain's other Chinese city, however, the island of Hong Kong, has been left untouched and flourishes as the chief point of contact between China and the rest of the world. But the success of Chinese Communism was gravely to affect Malaya and other Far Eastern countries where Britain had interests (see Chapter 18).

The United Nations

In 1942 the governments of all the countries fighting either Germany or Japan or both (at that time twenty-six) signed the United Nations Declaration, by which they promised not to seek a separate peace and to abide by the terms of the Atlantic Charter (see Appendix II) which Churchill and Roosevelt had signed in mid-Atlantic in August 1941, putting forward their aim that all men everywhere be able to live out their lives in freedom from fear and from want. This was the essential aim of the 'democratic nations'. The Charter eschewed 'territorial aggrandizement' and the 'use of force' in international relations. In 1943, following the Teheran meeting between Stalin, Roosevelt, Churchill and Chiang Kai-shek, came the Moscow Declaration, proposing a new international organization to replace the League of Nations. This came into being after the conferences at Dumbarton Oaks (1944) and San Francisco (1945), the League handing over to it its financial assets. Fifty nations signed its Charter in San Francisco in June 1945. Its aims were similar to those of the League, but this time a balance was struck between the great and the small nations. There would be a General Assembly, meeting once a year, to which all member nations were to belong. There would also be a Security Council of five permanent members (U.S.A., U.S.S.R., Britain, France and National China) and six non-permanent members elected from the Assembly, each with one vote. The five 'Major powers' would have a power of veto, which in fact was to paralyse the United Nations, once the Cold War began, on many important occasions. The United Nations was to encourage the creation of various agencies to deal with particular problems, some of which were to make vital contributions to the post-war world, as have U.N.E.S.C.O., U.N.I.C.E.F., U.N.F.A.O. and others.

16

The war at home

Government changes 1939

At 11.15 a.m. on Sunday 3 September Mr Chamberlain had announced that a 'state of war' existed between Britain and Germany. All the British Dominions, with the exception of Eire, soon followed Britain's declaration, although South Africa, under her Prime Minister Herzog, was somewhat reluctant (see Chapter 18). A War Cabinet of nine was set up: Chamberlain, Simon, Halifax, Hoare, Lord Chatfield, the ex-cabinet Secretary Lord Hankey, and the three service ministers Hore-Belisha (army), Kingsley Wood (air) and Churchill (navy). The Admiralty signalled to the fleet: 'Winston is back'; he had returned to the office he held in August 1914. Eden also returned to the government as Dominions Secretary.

Government controls and organization

Evacuation of mothers and children from major cities began as soon as war was declared. Even before this, on 24 August, Parliament had passed the important Emergency Powers Act which gave wide powers to a government in a 'time of emergency', for defence purposes. These included conscription of men up to the age of forty if needed; the suspension of habeas corpus; and the granting of internment powers and the power to commandeer any property, factory or industrial establishment needed for government purposes. A series of defence regulations was issued under the terms of this act, including Regulation 18B, under which persons allegedly in sympathy with the enemy could be imprisoned without trial. Inevitably many suffered under this, including some refugees. Sir Oswald Mosley was arrested and interned until 1943. In January 1940 food rationing began and at once agriculture was given high priority. 'Grow More Food' was a government slogan and families were encouraged to dig up their lawns for vegetables, keep chickens and save kitchen waste for pigs. Food subsidies were introduced, to keep the cost of essential basic foods relatively low. The Ministry of Agriculture and Fisheries could draw on the experience of the last years of the First World War. Similar county organizations were set up with similar compulsory powers and agriculture became a reserved occupation (i.e. those working on the land were not eligible for the armed services). Prisoners of war and land girls helped the labour force and camps for schoolboys were formed each year to help bring in the harvest. Milk production also had priority, since the high consumption of butter, milk and cheese, which had developed between the wars, had been largely dependent on imported Commonwealth and Danish produce. The latter was no longer obtainable after June 1940 and the former involved hazardous risks. Many new ministries were created, for example the Ministries of Supply, Economic Warfare, Information, Food, Shipping and Aircraft Production. Income tax was at once raised to 7*s* 6*d* in the pound (it was to reach 10*s* before the war ended), and a heavy Excess Profits Tax was introduced, which would fairly effectively prevent a repetition of the very great profiteering which had been a feature of the First World War. Identity cards were issued to all civilians. One ministry, that of Labour, acquired almost complete control over the available manpower of the country, in accordance with plans laid down in the 1930's, and on 8 September 1939 it became the Ministry of Labour and National Service (see below).

Churchill forms his government

Chamberlain had sounded the Labour and Liberal parties in September 1939, but they had rejected any suggestion of a Coalition. By April 1940 his government was under attack for its failures in Norway during these early months, which were nicknamed the 'phoney war'. Chamberlain called for a vote of confidence and Lloyd George led the attack: the Prime Minister having appealed for sacrifice should set an example, 'because there is nothing which can contribute more to victory in this war than that he should sacrifice the seals of Office'. The government majority fell to eighty-one. Labour still refused to serve in a government led by Chamberlain, who then suggested that Lord Halifax be asked to form a Coalition government. The latter refused and Churchill was summoned to Buckingham Palace at 6 p.m. on 10 May. He promised to submit five names to the King before midnight, as the core of his War Cabinet. Attlee and Greenwood agreed to serve with Chamberlain and Halifax. Churchill went to bed at 3 a.m. (his usual hour), he tells us, 'conscious of a profound sense of relief. At last I had the authority to give directions over the whole scene. I felt as if I was walking with destiny and that all my past life had been but a preparation for this hour and this trial. . . . Though impatient for the morning I slept soundly.'

Churchill as Prime Minister

The career of this remarkable man had reached its high point. He had first come to important office in 1908, as a young Liberal, an enthusiastic ally of Lloyd George and his successor at the Board of Trade. He had been one of the most powerful politicians of the First World War and in Lloyd George's Coalition government 1918–1922. He had been in Baldwin's government 1924–1929 as an uneasy recruit to the Conservatives and had then had ten years out of office. He was to become Prime Minister for the last time in 1951, at the close of our period. He had made a profound study of war: having written the classic life of his ancestor, the first Duke of Marlborough, and having brooded for long on the mistakes of the First World War. He had the confidence not only of the public in Britain and America (his mother was an American), but also of the service chiefs, in a way which neither Asquith nor Lloyd George ever did in the First World War. Undoubtedly mistakes were made in planning. He has been accused of not following through sufficiently far the decisions made at the top and compared unfavourably here with Lloyd George. Obviously once Britain ceased to stand alone there were inevitable tensions with both America and Russia. Yet in spite of all this what *The Times* said of Churchill in 1945 can still be accepted:

'With a deep knowledge of military history, he committed his country to the pursuit of its traditional strategy to maintain the Empire's lines of communications round the globe, to contain the enemy within the ring of sea-power, and to challenge him on land at the extreme limits of his dominion until his strength should begin to exhaust itself. Thus would time be won to mobilize the reserves of the imperial commonwealth and to range in the line for the decisive stroke, the forces of all other nations that would rally to the standard of liberty.'

There has been a flow of memoirs since the end of the war, which have revealed some of Churchill's unconventional methods: for example conserving his energies by dictating telegrams from his bed, incredibly short sleeping hours, vast consumption of cigars. But none of these publications has seriously challenged his remarkable achievement as 'architect of victory'. Roosevelt had the vision, as Wilson had done in 1917, of liberating the peoples of the world, and winning for them their human rights. Churchill had the strategic ideas on how this could be achieved.

Coalition Government 1940

His War Cabinet was small: himself as Prime Minister and Minister of Defence; Chamberlain as Lord President of the

Council; Halifax as Foreign Secretary; Attlee as Lord Privy Seal and Deputy Leader of the House of Commons; and Greenwood as Minister without Portfolio. Churchill's colleagues who had opposed appeasement, Eden, Amery, Duff Cooper and Lord Cranborne, were all given office. Offers were made to Lloyd George, but he declined them. Other members of this government were the trade-union leader Ernest Bevin as Minister of Labour and National Service; the Liberal leader Sir Archibald Sinclair as Air Minister and Lord Beaverbrook as Minister for Aircraft Production.

On 30 September Chamberlain resigned through ill-health, having worked absolutely loyally with Churchill and done much to win for him the affection of the Conservative Party back-benchers, who up to now had never enthused about him. On 9 October these same back-benchers elected Churchill the leader of the Conservative Party, while Chamberlain died on 9 November. He was replaced in the War Cabinet by Sir John Anderson, an ex-civil servant.

Home Guard, A.R.P. and the National Fire Service

By now Britain stood alone and was undergoing the nightly bomber attacks which had driven many of the children into the country again. In May 1940 the Local Defence Volunteers had been formed, the precedent being 1803 and Napoleon's threat of invasion. Its name was changed by Churchill to the Home Guard in July. Few men who were not conscripted, nor committed to Civil Defence, failed to join their local unit. At first they were theoretically equipped with steel helmet, rifle and an arm-band to wear with civilian clothes, but often only the arm-band was available. Pikes, shot-guns, pigeon-revolvers, sabres and trophies from the First World War were all mustered. With German invasion hourly expected, concrete road-blocks were assiduously manned (even when there was a perfectly good unminded alternative route through fields); camouflage-nets and paint were liberally spread

L.D.V. troops inspected, July 1940. Each man has a gas-mask and arm-band, but as yet no rifle

around the countryside; much sleep was lost as units stood-to through the night. The odd German airman was captured, escaping by parachute, and there were numerous false alarms. Possibly if the invasion had come such defences would have proved of little use. But the formation of local units throughout the countryside greatly strengthened morale. It was thus a brilliant stroke of psychological warfare, whatever its military results might have been in 1940, if the enemy had landed.

Gradually Home Guard equipment became available, and the force was turned into a formidable reserve. Battle-dress uniform, rifles, mortars, grenades were all issued and boys serving in their local units received valuable pre-military training. Even anti-aircraft units were to be manned by the Home Guard in 1943, thus releasing full-time units for service abroad. By then there were 1000 battalions and over 2,000,000 members of this unpaid voluntary force, which came to an end on 1 November 1944.

Civil Defence plans against air-raids were not effectively made until 1937, following the beginning of mass-bombing in the Spanish Civil War, when an Air-Raid Precautions

Act was passed by Parliament. A system of air-raid sirens was instituted, total blackout was to be enforced, a corps of air-raid wardens was to be formed, a cheap gas-mask issued to all citizens and some half-hearted provision of air-raid shelters made. When the bombing of 1940–1941 came the latter proved inadequate and Londoners took to the Tube stations in thousands. In the suburbs back-garden (Anderson) shelters were erected and regularly slept in throughout that winter by those families who were not evacuated.

An Auxiliary Fire Service had been created by the Air-Raid Precautions Act and many volunteers trained on a part-time basis. The air-raids of 1940–1941 were fought by both Auxiliary and Regular Fire Brigades, but in August 1941 all local Fire Brigades, Auxiliary and Regular, were united to form the National Fire Service, which had far greater mobility for fighting air-raids in different parts of the country. Into this N.F.S. conscripts were drafted for their national service and to it goes the credit of having successfully fought those air-raids launched from 1941 to the end of the war.

Government centralization and industrial production

Meanwhile the process of government centralization and industrial direction inevitably increased during the war. Until American Lend-Lease began in March 1941 the manufacture of goods for export had to be continued to help pay for 'cash and carry' goods bought in America. With Lend-Lease, industry could be further geared to war production only. A purchase tax was introduced in 1940; at first a flat-rate tax, it was later modified by Sir Kingsley Wood, luxuries being taxed 33⅓% and necessities at a lower rate. There was a strict quota scheme for allocating materials, which resulted in 'utility' standards for furniture and other goods. In 1941 clothes rationing was begun and a 'points' scheme was introduced for many foods not yet rationed. One was allocated so many points per month; how one spent them was no concern of the Food Ministry officials. In 1942 a Ministry of Fuel was created to control the coal industry. Direction of miners was enforced, and by the end of the war there was conscription into the mines by ballot of 'Bevin Boys'. The Ministry of Labour had two tasks: the allocation of available men as they were called up into the three fighting services and the much more difficult problem of allocation of labour into industry: aircraft production, armaments, engineering, ship-building, precision instruments, etc. A Production Council of the War Cabinet had been set up in 1940, of which the Minister of Labour was a member, but this did not prevent the development of numerous problems; particularly between the Ministries of Labour and Aircraft Production. In 1942, following strong Parliamentary criticism, a Ministry of Production was created to take over the work of the Council and co-ordinate priorities. Many factories were built in remote country areas, where workers were housed in hostels. It was to help raise their morale that the Ministry of Labour sought the help of C.E.M.A. (see below) and E.N.S.A. This latter, the Entertainments National Service Association, was formed in June 1940 for the entertainment of both troops and factory workers, providing plays and variety programmes all over the world. By the end of 1940 over 8600 performances had been given to factory audiences. In the First World War there had been little done to cater for the welfare of workers beyond the passing of drinking regulations under D.O.R.A. (see Chapter 5). Now the responsibility of the state for the social welfare of its workers was accepted and incidentally convictions for drunkenness between 1938 and 1945 actually fell by 50%.

Factory hostels were for both men and women, for the war demanded not only all available men but the women as well. At first they contributed voluntarily: Civil Defence, Auxiliary Services (A.T.S., W.A.A.F., W.R.N.S.), hospitals, Land Army, factories. But in March 1941 compulsory registration of women became necessary. Those who wanted could volunteer for the services, the rest could be drafted by the Ministry of Labour to centres of acute labour shortage. In December 1941 unmarried women and childless widows could be drafted into the services as well.

Thus did Britain (whose industry in the months following Dunkirk willingly worked a seventy-hour week, so strong was the national determination to survive at that time) become the most highly mobilized nation ever engaged in war. At the same time there were far fewer labour troubles than in the First World War, due to a number of factors. The war itself was more generally accepted as justified. The Home Secretary, Herbert Morrison, and the Minister of Labour, Ernest Bevin, were both popular and respected members of the Labour Party. After Russia joined the war in 1941 those trade unionists who were members of the Communist Party gave their utmost support. In addition there were the better social amenities: E.N.S.A. and C.E.M.A. concerts; factory canteens and hostels; nursery schools; social and athletic clubs; rest rooms; and at the bench the B.B.C.'s 'Music while you Work' (the B.B.C. introduced the Light Programme and ended its ban on Sunday jazz). As new factories were built, greatly improved lighting, heating, canteens and amenities were insisted upon. A Ministry of Labour order increased considerably the degree of medical supervision in factories. Between the wars the Institute of Labour Management had been encouraging firms to send staffs for proper managerial training. This advice was now increasingly followed, while industrial psychologists and welfare workers were widely employed. All these factors contributed to the success of Britain's war effort.

By June 1944, out of every nine of the potential labour force, two were in the armed forces and three engaged in war production, leaving the balance for all administrative, banking and commercial work. Yet in spite of what has been said, from 1942 onwards there was a rising tide of radical feeling in the country. This was stimulated by the publication in December 1942 by Sir William Beveridge of a report recommending a free National Health Scheme for the whole country, the enlargement and consolidation of existing unemployment, sickness and old-age benefits, the introduction of children's allowances and the creation of a Ministry of Social Security. The Labour Party at once adopted the Report and a left-wing group among Conservatives, led by R. A. Butler, the Minister of Education, also approved.

Social legislation

It was an alliance of this 'Tory Reform' group with Labour which helped to bring about a number of important pieces of social legislation during the last two years of the war. For example, in 1943 Ernest Bevin introduced a Catering Bill for state regulation of wages in the catering industry, for long one of the most notoriously exploited sections of the labour market. The Town and Country Planning Act of 1944, based on two reports of 1942, was greatly to increase the powers of both local and central government in order to prevent the same kind of indiscriminate waste of land which had been a feature of speculative building between the wars. A third example was the vital Education Act of 1944, which sought to give secondary education to all. Grammar-school fees in state schools would be abolished, although direct-grant schools would continue with a proportion of fee-paying pupils. Secondary modern schools would be created for children failing to gain entry to an academic grammar school. It was hoped that these schools would provide 'education for living' by exploiting the natural aptitudes of the pupils without their being regarded as 'poor relations' of the grammar schools. An examination at eleven-plus from the primary schools would determine a child's aptitudes, and on this would be chosen his school. It was hoped that the school-leaving age would rise soon after the war to sixteen, but it would be raised at once to fifteen for all, with part-time education up to eighteen. The Act has been attacked by many since. Some feel that by making a distinction between academic and other forms of secondary education it helped to perpetuate class divisions. Others feel that it did not go far enough in enabling the very best children to be creamed off and given very special treatment. But undoubtedly it revolutionized English education. Many remarkable secondary modern schools came into being, as well as some which were no more than pale and ineffectual imitations of grammar schools. The quality of maintained grammar-school education steadily rose until it bore comparison with that of the fee-paying public schools. The demand for university places continued to rise and for the most part was to be met, by steady expansion, during the 1950's. Gradually any student gaining a university place would come to receive a grant from his County Education Committee to help finance him.

Another important piece of social legislation was the Family Allowances Act introduced into Parliament in 1945 as a result of the Beveridge recommendations. By it allowances were to be paid to the second and all other children 'for the benefit of the family as a whole', until the age of sixteen or the beginning of full-time employment. The age was to be raised to eighteen in 1956 to cover children staying at school beyond 'O' Level. Originally the amount paid was 5*s* per week. It was to be raised to 8*s* in 1952 and for the third and subsequent children to 10*s* in 1956. The allowance was not to be a subsistence one and a family in greater need would have to apply for other assistance, to be provided after 1948 by the National Assistance Board.

Other social legislation in war-time

Many people imagined in 1939 that the war would curtail social services. Instead the state found itself having to extend its help in various directions: to servicemen's families destituted by war casualties; to expectant mothers whose husbands were overseas; to children below school age whose mothers were employed; to the old whose families were just not available to assist them. The strain of evacuation, bombed housing, separation and mobilization of women threatened many families. But alongside this there was a new social awareness, particularly strongly felt during

Evacuees awaiting transport from London, September 1939

1940. To survive the crisis of that year great steps had to be and were taken. Between 1939 and 1941 some 3,000,000 mothers and children were evacuated into rural areas and many of these were found to be hopelessly ill equipped in clothes, shoes and necessities. These revelations produced a sharp awakening of the public conscience when so high a percentage of the nation's children were found to be so badly handicapped by poverty. In the month of Dunkirk *The Times* was speaking of the universal right 'to work and to live'; to ensure this right it was prepared to see far greater 'social and economic planning' in terms of 'social and economic equality'. Thus in that summer of 1940 were introduced a number of measures: supplementary pensions for old-age pensioners in need and unable to make ends meet on their ordinary pension; the broadening of the scope of school meals and the milk service, so that by 1945

1,650,000 subsidized dinners were eaten against 130,000 in 1939, and almost all the children received milk against about 50% in 1939; a National Milk Scheme of subsidized milk for mothers and children for whom milk would cost 2*d* a pint as against 4½*d*. This was to be followed in December 1941 by the Vitamin Welfare Scheme of orange juice, cod-liver oil and vitamin tablets for expectant mothers and babies. All these schemes were to survive the war.

In October 1940 the Means Test was abolished for National Insurance. It had long been regarded as a class barrier, but from now on social services were to be free of social discrimination; they were to be available to all.

At the end of the First World War Parliament had passed a Maternity and Child Welfare Act, giving local authorities power to set up nurseries and infant-welfare clinics. But between the wars a bad gap had remained for children's health between birth and school age. Only during the war was this to be more efficiently filled by wider application of the 1918 Act: more nursery schools for working mothers; universal clinics; more health visitors. The result has been a great improvement in the health of the nation.

A special problem revealed by the war was that of tuberculosis, which was increasing rapidly. The government, in need of protecting the war effort, found itself obliged to protect 'individuals harmful to the community, by providing an allowance'. In April 1943 therefore a Tuberculosis Allowance Scheme was introduced of 39*s* per week for a married man. Yet it was a scheme severely criticized, since it applied only to those 'with a good chance of recovery' and not to chronic cases. Mass radiography also began to be used against a disease 'killing 25,000 persons a year in their prime'. The allowance scheme was to end in July 1948 to be replaced by the National Assistance and National Health schemes.

The arts in war-time

A Ministry of Information had been formed in 1939 and considerable importance was attached to propaganda, a number of artists and writers being recruited for this purpose. But the first effect of the war was to threaten all the arts. All London's theatres closed except two: the Windmill, with its leg-shows, and the Unity Theatre, where a political play called *Match-Girls* was presented. Picture galleries closed, art treasures were moved to be stored under the Welsh mountains and amateur work in all the arts at first suffered.

There were many unemployed artists and many people who had already left home to be housed in hostels and camps all over the country. With this in view there occurred an historic telephone conversation in December 1939 between Lord de la Warr, President of the Board of Education, and the secretary of the Pilgrim Trust, Dr Thomas Jones. De la Warr asked for a £5000 grant towards encouragement of the arts. He was immediately offered £25,000 by the Trust. The Treasury agreed to double any grant made and thus was born the Council for the Encouragement of Music and the Arts which, as announced in Parliament on 12 June 1945, was to become the Arts Council of Great Britain. J. M. Keynes, who became the Chairman, said: 'The day is not far off when the Economic Problem will take the back seat, where it belongs, and the arena of the heart and head will be occupied or reoccupied by our real problems, the problems of life and human relations, of creation and behaviour and religion.' This was a profession of faith and it marks a further step towards the building of a Welfare State, when government comes to regard such things as its responsibility.

The air-raid-shelter crowds had quickly generated spontaneous concert parties. Soon C.E.M.A. moved in and began to provide professional entertainment, and not only in London Tube shelters but also in village halls, works canteens, churches, art galleries and workshops throughout the provinces. Within a year C.E.M.A. was giving 400 concerts a month and in 1944 it gave 6140 concerts which varied from symphony orchestra to solo violin, with few concessions to what was thought of as popular taste. It

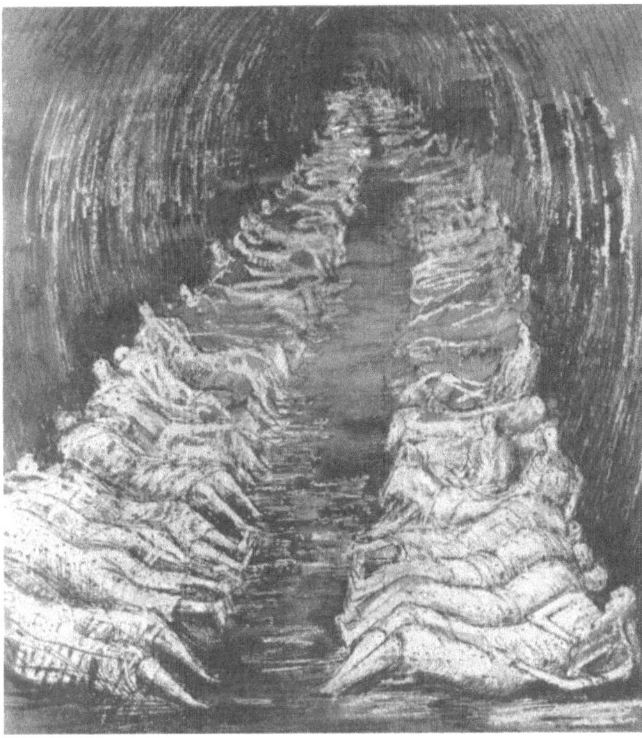

Tube Shelter Perspective. In 1940–1941 Henry Moore painted a number of shelter scenes of which this is one. Something of the horror of modern war is portrayed by these endless supine figures

is true that the audiences were largely captive and other entertainment was scarce, yet the size and enthusiasm of these audiences surprised all. Suddenly it was Bach, Beethoven, Sibelius and Byrd who were found to be the popular composers. Scott Goddard wrote: 'What is going on today in camps and factories has begun one of the greatest popularizing movements of our times,' and all those who took part in these concerts seem to have been equally enthusiastic. In London the B.B.C. Promenade Concerts were resumed in 1942 in the Albert Hall, the Queen's Hall having been blitzed.

C.E.M.A. now had directorates of music, art and drama. For the latter, at a time when few people were on wheels, the policy was to bring the 'theatre on wheels' to the people. In the year 1942–1943 there were seven companies touring with the works of Shaw, Goldsmith, Ibsen and Shakespeare, the most popular play in the factory hostels being Ibsen's *Hedda Gabler*. The Old Vic and Sadler's Wells had moved to Burnley in 1939. From there and from Liverpool they also organized tours, joining C.E.M.A. in 1943.

One of the most remarkable things about the arts in the 1940's was the sudden popularity of ballet. New ballets, breaking away from classical dance and much more akin to early pantomime, were extraordinarily popular. Sadler's Wells, the Ballet Rambert and the Kurt Joos Ballet were all on constant tour.

In the visual arts C.E.M.A. mounted travelling exhibitions of any original works available, including contemporary work; an important example was the 1942 exhibition of Henry Moore, John Piper and Graham Sutherland. It also commissioned lithographs which, with good reproductions, were displayed in canteens, British Restaurants (subsidized restaurants run by Borough Councils), hostels and schools. After the war the Arts Council's main preoccupation was to be in staging art exhibitions in London and the provinces, such as the Picasso-Matisse exhibition 1945–1946, visited enthusiastically by 350,000 people and a triumph for modern art. Possibly the greatest English painter to emerge in the decade was Graham Sutherland, and the remarkable thing is the extent to which he was appreciated at the time. He was to be commissioned for designs in Coventry's rebuilt cathedral.

Throughout the war, in spite of paper shortages, the demand for books of all kinds greatly increased. There was a keen and critical reading public for contemporary writing among many with too much time to spare: fire-watching or sitting in guard-rooms and barracks. Two magazines,

Horizon edited by Cyril Connolly and *New Writing* edited by John Lehmann, were highly successful, while the Penguin venture of 6*d* paperbacks, launched in 1936, continued to publish a number of new works as well as established classics. Established poets of the 1930's, such as Cecil Day Lewis, David Gascoyne, Louis MacNeice and Stephen Spender, continued to write, and so too did Dylan Thomas. But even so there were curiously few new writers in the war, either poets or novelists, whose work was to prove good enough to last. In 1943 the Arts Theatre arranged a play competition. There were 500 entries, but the winner was a very slight and flimsy piece. Exciting new writing was to emerge, especially for the theatre, but only after the war.

The fall of the government and the 1945 election

In 1942 a committee on reconstruction had reported to the government and in 1943 Churchill had appointed Lord Woolton Minister of Reconstruction. The government published in 1944 a Treasury White Paper, showing the influence of Keynes, now one of its officials, and pledging itself to a policy of full employment. In 1945 the Family Allowances Act was passed. But the public apparently felt that this was not enough. Two by-elections in 1944 went against the government and early in 1945 there was talk of a general election. The Conservatives relied on the prestige of Churchill, 'the architect of victory'. But the electorate remembered the Conservative-dominated National governments and condemned them for their failure to solve the social problems of the 1930's. Whether this is just is irrelevant. Public opinion in 1945 was obviously convinced that the thirties had been a bad time for Britain and that the governments of the day could have done more than they did. The Labour Party put forward its programme in a manifesto *Let us face the Future* and won 393 seats, giving them a large majority over all the rest of the House: 213 Conservatives, 12 Liberals, 3 Independent Labour Party, 2 Communists, 2 Irish Nationalists and 14 Independents.

Churchill's prestige had proved insufficient to win the first general election for ten years, even in the hour of victory. The new Parliament met in August and victorious Labour M.P.s sang 'The Red Flag'. For the first time the Labour Party had an overall majority—how would they use it in this hour of victory?

PART FIVE

Britain and the post-war world

17

Home affairs 1945-1951

Labour Party programme

The election programme for the Labour Party had appeared in April 1945. It contained recommendations for greater social and economic security; plans for further restriction of the powers of the House of Lords; promises to nationalize the Bank of England, fuel and power, inland transport, iron and steel; proposals for agriculture, housing, education, recreation, health and social insurance; and recommendations for the supervision of monopolies and cartels.

It summed up much of what the party had been advocating in the 1930's, but in some ways it showed a failure to move with the times. Its section on foreign affairs was perhaps unduly optimistic and showed little grasp of the realities of power politics. Many in the party rather naively believed that nationalization in itself could cure social and economic problems, often of the greatest complexity.

Mr Attlee's cabinet

The election was held on 5 July and the results were published on 26 July. Although the war with Japan continued, Mr Attlee abandoned the principle of the small War Cabinet for a larger cabinet of twenty members, with an inner group of senior ministers co-ordinating particular spheres of government: Herbert Morrison was to be Lord President of the Council; Ernest Bevin, Foreign Secretary;

Danebury School, London. The 1944 Education Act called for thousands of new schools. Educational theory and practice had changed much since 1906. Compare p. 39

Hugh Dalton, Chancellor of the Exchequer; Sir Stafford Cripps, President of the Board of Trade; Aneurin Bevan, Minister of Health. Attlee himself was at first Minister of Defence.

Atomic bombs were dropped on Japan on 6 August and 9 August, on which day Japan agreed to cease fighting. On 2 September American Lend-Lease was ended, although only on 12 September did Japan formally surrender. The greatest war yet seen was ended, but so was American economic aid to Britain.

Problems of peace

This was a tremendous blow to Britain's economy. She had at once to grapple with her vast debts (over £3,000,000,000) at a time when her industry would need all the capital it could get in order to turn over to peace-time production and when nearly all her overseas assets had been liquidated by the war. Britain's natural markets were her empire and Europe. The economy of the former had been profoundly altered by the war; for example industry had greatly expanded in Canada and Australia, which were now intent on seeking protection. On the other hand, Europe was in ruins. J. M. Keynes (now Lord Keynes) was sent to Washington in the autumn of 1945, where he fought for some kind of U.S. financial aid. In the end he accepted a loan of £3,750,000,000 with an obligation not to discriminate against U.S. trade and a promise that 'convertibility' would be restored within a year, i.e. free exchange between sterling currencies and any others.

With this behind her, Britain saw a year of remarkable recovery, 1945–1946, although there remained some problems for the government. One of these was demobilization, which in fact proceeded very smoothly during the next three years on a basis of preference for age and length of service. Much bomb damage had to be repaired, some 5,000,000 houses having been destroyed or damaged. If the 1944 Act was to be implemented thousands of schools had to be built at a time of acute shortages. Food was still very scarce in Britain, while parts of Europe were threatened with famine. Indeed, rationing was to continue throughout the period (bread was rationed for the first time and with potatoes was not derationed until 1948; clothes and shoes in 1949; milk and soap in 1950; and sugar and tea in 1952). Lastly from 1946 onwards there was the problem of United Europe. For four years until 1950 the government was to toy with the developing projects for European unity (see Chapter 19). Finally in 1950 it was to be decided by the Treasury and the Chancellor of the Exchequer to keep Britain out: 'she must avoid any commitment, political or economic, which might damage, directly or indirectly, the sterling area and the network of trading and monetary policies built upon it'. Sir Stafford Cripps was to say: 'In our view participation in a political federation, limited to Western Europe, is not compatible either with our

Commonwealth ties or obligations as a member of the wider Atlantic community or as a world power.'

The crisis of 1947

The winter of 1946–1947 was extremely severe. Raw materials were in short supply, while industry was expanding. The coal-mines were suspended between war-time control and nationalization, which came into effect on 1 January 1947. All these factors meant that increased demands for power just could not be met and by January 1947 many industrial areas were near collapse. Heavy electricity cuts were imposed and the government was attacked for lack of foresight, the Cabinet coming near to break-up on methods to tackle the fuel crisis. It survived, but with some important shifts of power—becoming more firmly grouped under Foreign Secretary, Chancellor of the Exchequer and Lord President. The crisis in the winter was one of production. It became a financial one through the summer of 1947 as the deadline imposed by the Americans for convertibility approached, which was on 15 July. For a week there were no adverse effects, but in mid-August £237,000,000 sterling were withdrawn from London in six days. Convertibility had to be abandoned and the country had to face the worst financial crisis since 1931. A programme of national austerity was the only solution, together with strict import controls and currency regulations; a special budget was to be introduced in November 1947. When he came to do this Hugh Dalton mentioned a detail to a journalist as he entered the House of Commons. This was technically a breach of confidence and he felt bound to resign, when Sir Stafford Cripps took over. His policy was that full employment and expanding productivity must continue, but there must be strict planning and control of essential raw materials. Strong anti-inflationary measures must be imposed through wage restraint and high taxation. Many trade unionists felt that this latter policy was incompatible with Cripps's professed socialism. But Cripps was a Christian Socialist, who tried always to put his religion before all other considerations. His socialism reflected his Christianity and he believed that 'neither capitalism nor socialism is more than a means through which men can achieve some far greater destiny'. He had strong prejudices, especially against the foreign financiers, who made profits out of Britain's current financial troubles, but he also was a firm patriot and saw the economy as a whole and not in terms of out-dated class divisions.

The year 1948 saw an economic recovery, but in 1949 there was a recession in the U.S.A. which led to fewer imports by America of British and Commonwealth goods. This in its turn brought a new cycle of economic troubles in London. It was decided to devalue the £ from $4·03 to $2·80. This, together with the Cold War, the Berlin crisis and the Korean War (see Chapter 18), led to financial recovery. America began to rearm and to stockpile, so that Commonwealth raw materials, for example Malayan tin and Australian wool, fetched high prices and the sterling area gained. In 1950, in spite of the Korean War, the economy was recovering and the volume of exports in that year was 177% that of 1946. But 1951 was to see another swing back. There then began a serious decline in industrial expansion as German and Japanese competition arose. The general election result in 1951 in favour of the Conservatives was not to be of any noticeable help to the economy and unemployment figures were to reach their highest since the war in 1952. Balance of payments crises were to continue throughout the 1950's.

Nationalization

A firm part of the Labour platform since 1918 had been the need for nationalization of many industries. In 1945, with a solid majority, this was at last possible. In some cases nationalization was just the logical conclusion of a process; in others it was highly contentious:

(i) *The Bank of England.* The Labour Party had for long convinced itself, rightly or wrongly, that this institution had 'wrecked the Labour government of 1931' and it believed it essential that it 'be made answerable to us, the people', by nationalization. In October 1945 a nationalization Bill became law. Stockholders were to receive very fair compensation: for £100 stock £400 compensation would be paid. The composition of the Court of Directors as appointed by the government turned out to be very similar to that previously co-opted from prominent City figures. Nevertheless, in a last resort a government could now feel that it had the whip-hand in economic policy. Or, as others argued, Treasury officials would in future have one less brake on their policies.

(ii) *Coal-mining*. In 1946 the coal industry was nationalized and placed under the National Coal Board. This was the logical conclusion to a long story. In 1944 the Reid Committee of experts had reported on the industry. They had noted a shortage of capital; too many uneconomic concerns (this was war-time when the mines were being operated by the government); and a failure to modernize techniques. They considered that numerous separate units could be far more economically run if grouped together, for example in the South Wales valleys.

When the war ended, war-time subsidies to uneconomic units were maintained while the Coal Nationalization Bill was drawn up and presented to Parliament in December 1945. The Coal Board would consist of nine members. It would have two advisory councils, one representing consumers and the other distributors. It would be able to borrow up to £150,000,000 in the first five years for modernization. Mines employing less than fifty men underground would not be included, but their owners would become licensees of the Board. Over 800 companies were thus nationalized and the Board acquired in addition: coke-ovens, plants for benzol, tar-distilling and sulphuric acid, brick-works and much property. The total assets were valued at £164,660,000.

But the industry was far from healthy and presented some

grave problems: on the human side to produce sufficient incentives and to raise morale; on the technical side to make less accessible seams productive. In 1885 the average coal output had been 319 tons per man per week. In 1938 it was 309; in 1948 only 272. By 1950 another fuel crisis was to loom as coal production failed to expand with the rest of industry. But nevertheless the N.C.B., planning ahead, was to produce an industry which is far healthier in terms of labour relations, wages and technical efficiency than was that of 1939.

(iii) *Transport.* Air transport was rapidly expanding after 1945. Just before the war B.O.A.C. had come into existence: an amalgamation of Imperial Airways and British Airways. In 1944 a Ministry of Civil Aviation had been created. In 1946 two new corporations were formed: British European Airways and British South American Airways, although the latter was soon incorporated into B.O.A.C.

For inland transport it was the aim of the government to have a similar, if more complicated, nationalized system. Therefore in 1947 the British Transport Commission was created to which were transferred railways, road passenger transport, long-distance road-haulage services, together with railway hotels, docks, canals and other properties. Road operators using a radius under twenty-five miles were to remain in private ownership. The merit of the scheme would seem to be that an essential section of the transport system in great need of vast capital investment, i.e. the railways (government-controlled and run almost to a stand-still during the war), would gain from the quick profits made on road haulage. There were strong technical arguments for bringing the railways under the Commission, which the Conservative Party accepted. However, it pledged itself, if elected, to repeal those parts of the statute concerning road haulage. It was not to do this entirely, retaining the British Road Services, but it was to allow so much scope for private enterprise in its denationalization Bill of 1952 as to precipitate between road- and rail-haulage a struggle which the latter seemed likely to lose, before the Beeching plan.

(iv) *Electricity and Gas.* The Electricity Act of 1947 and the Gas Act of 1948 produced the British Electricity Authority, with subsidiary Area Electricity Boards, and the British Gas Council with Area Gas Boards. In fact both electricity and gas had for long been under considerable Parliamentary control and competition in these industries had been restricted by Parliament before the war. Thus the so-called nationalization of these industries was largely administrative: centralization and reorganization.

(v) *Iron and Steel.* The iron and steel industry had contributed some 35% of the unemployed in the years 1931–1935. After 1932 tariffs had protected the industry from overseas competition, while the Iron and Steel Federation of Employers had given the industry security and reduced competition by price agreements. A few new plants, for example at Corby and Ebbw Vale, had been built between the wars, but most companies had failed to invest sufficiently in modernization, research or replacement. On the other hand, in 1945, relations between the Federation of Employers and the industry's trade union, the Iron and Steel Confederation, were very good. The industry had greatly expanded production during the years of rearmament and the war.

In 1945 both Dalton and Bevan were determined on the nationalization of the industry, while other members of the cabinet felt less strongly. In 1947 Mr Wilmot, the Minister of Supply, set up an Iron and Steel Board to supervise the industry. The Federation accepted this, but there was strong pressure from the rank and file of the Labour Party for full nationalization. Mr Wilmot was replaced by Mr Strauss and a decision was made to press ahead with full nationalization. Some ninety-six iron and steel companies, out of the 2000 supervised by the Iron and Steel Board, were to be affected, concerns producing less than 5000 tons per annum escaping. The function of the Iron and Steel Corporation would be not to direct day-to-day production but to procure adequate supplies of raw materials and to produce the right quality steels as required, i.e. to combine the function of the pre-war Iron and Steel Federation with that of the Iron and Steel Board of 1947.

The industry certainly had a poor record between the wars for failing to plan ahead, invest in research and seek new markets. But how far this legislation was more than party politics, more than fighting the battles of the thirties in the changed conditions of the forties, it is difficult to say. The Bill was bitterly attacked. The President of the Iron and Steel Federation called it a grieviously prejudicial policy and in Parliament it became law only after being postponed by the Lords until February 1951. The Conservative Party pledged itself to reverse the bill. This it was to do in 1953, while retaining the Iron and Steel Board, on which sat trade-union representatives, to oversee capital investment and fix prices. In an industry as complex as this, inevitably a large degree of government control is needed. But it seems far from certain that total nationalization is the answer.

Agriculture The 1930's had seen some recovery in agriculture. The Agricultural Marketing Acts had produced marketing systems for milk, pigs, bacon, potatoes and hops. Production of milk had risen from 1,270,000,000 gallons in 1933 to 1,330,000,000 in 1938. During the war the Ministry of Food had said what was wanted, and the Ministry of Agriculture had tried to produce it, by a mixture of compulsion and subsidies. It had made available P.O.W. labour, tractors, fertilizers and draining schemes and the problem in 1945 was how far to dismantle the war-time machinery. By the Agriculture Act 1947, which had the support of both sides of the House, the government sought a compromise. It undertook to maintain some continuity over prices and quantities of commodities to be marketed. First, annually in February the minister would meet the farming community and work out with the farmers needs and prices for the year. The farmer could then work to a known target, since the prices of such things as cereals, stock, milk and eggs were guaranteed, subsidized by the government where necessary. Secondly, the Act laid down rules for good husbandry and estate management. County Committees were to be retained, with powers to protect tenants against eviction. At the same time the minister reserved the power to order, through a County Committee, after twelve months, dispossession from land being allowed to waste. An Agricultural Land Tribunal would hear appeals. The central cog in each county would be the County Agricultural Executive Committee of twelve men, all themselves farmers. Farming was not altogether feather-bedded by the Act, as its critics have maintained. But it became possible once more to make a living out of farming while at the same time standards of output steadily rose.

Town and country planning To say that town and country planning had not existed at all before the war is not strictly accurate. The first town and country planning Act dates from 1909, but it was entirely permissive. The Garden City movement (Letchworth, 1905, and Welwyn Garden City, 1920) had given architects the chance to plan towns as a whole: schools, shops, factories, as well as housing. But these were private ventures, and had not been followed up since. Instead had come the characteristic 'ribbon development' of between the wars. The Town Planning Act of 1943 had given the duty of making a development plan for its own area to each local authority and had set up a Ministry of Town and Country planning. But it was the Town and Country Planning Act of 1944 which increased the powers of both local and central government sufficiently for it to become really effective. In 1946 a New Towns Act was passed by which completely new towns, as against dormitory suburbs, were to be created. These would be local-government owned, the land being bought by compulsory purchase. Examples are Crawley, Stevenage, Harlow and Basildon; in a sense they are a logical development of the Garden City movement earlier. In 1947 a new Town and Country Planning Act was passed which was revolutionary in its attitude to compensation. Really large-scale planning had

A new town: Crawley

too often been held up by prohibitive compensation costs. These were now to be realistically tied to the difference in value of the land, developed and undeveloped. At the same time all private development, for example conversion of a house into flats and even the erection of a garage in the garden, was to be subject to planning permission.

Housing The problem of housing, as against planning for development, was a responsibility of the Ministry of Health until 1951, when it was to be handed to the Ministry of Housing and Local Government. Aneurin Bevan, as Minister of Health, had to tackle the problem of 5,000,000 bomb-damaged houses, together with great increases in demand for houses from young married couples with young war-time families. There were two housing Acts, 1946 and 1949. Bevan was faced by acute shortages and decided to concentrate on the building of council houses for rent. All private building would have to have a licence, which in the early post-war years could only be obtained if there was a surplus in the area of labour and materials. The ministry subsidized housing costs and tried to keep these down by standardization. By 1949 1,000,000 subsidized houses had been built and most war-damaged houses repaired, but the costs continued to rise. A house costing £380 in 1938 was costing nearly £1600 in 1949. Bevan made great efforts to reduce this, but without much success. His policy was attacked as favouring the working class. Yet certainly, given the shortages of materials, a firm control over speculative building was necessary if those most in need of housing were to be provided for. Britain produced more housing in the first five years after the war than any other European country.

Constitutional changes There were a number of constitutional changes made during the time of this government. In 1948 a Representation of the People Act abolished university votes and also additional votes possessed by some business men in connection with their business address. It improved the arrangements for registration and made one of the periodic adjustments of constituencies relative to population changes. Such adjustments are always alleged by the opposition party to be in favour of the government party. In 1947 a Bill to amend the Parliament Act of 1911 (to be retrospective to 1945) was introduced into the Commons. It became law in December 1949 under the 1911 Act. It reduced the delaying power of the House of Lords from three sessions to two. This was partly an expedient to enable the Iron and Steel Bill to pass more quickly, but no attempt has been made since to reverse it. Another constitutional change referred to in Chapter 6 was the repeal in 1946 of the Trades Disputes Act of 1927.

National Insurance Act 1946 This Act, introduced by James Griffiths the Minister for National Insurance, was based on the Beveridge Report. It repealed all previous legislation

Stepney. Slum clearance schemes after 1945 were in some ways made easier by bomb damage. The L.C.C. now built up rather than out, providing flats for London's still rising population

and sought both to expand the original scheme of 1911 and to bring the entire population into the new scheme. Compulsory payments by all employed or self-employed persons would contribute towards financing the National Health

Service, which was brought into being by an Act in the same year. In addition, the insurance scheme would provide various benefits, as had the earlier 1911 scheme: unemployment, sickness, maternity and widows' benefits; retirement pensions; family and guardians' allowances. Beveridge had wanted insurance rates for sickness and unemployment to be at subsistence level, but this they were never to be owing to the excessive estimated cost. Instead, anyone in further need of financial aid would have to apply for assistance; after 1948 from the National Assistance Board. Nevertheless a basic insurance payment was to be made to all, without a means test. It was realized that the cost of the scheme would quickly rise, partly owing to the rise in numbers of old-age pensioners.

National Health Service The National Health Service Bill of 1946 widened the medical scheme of 1911 to cover all members of the population, regardless of income. Since all were to contribute to National Insurance, all would be eligible for the National Health Service. Apart from the widening of doctors' panels to include all but a small minority of fee-paying patients, the main purpose of the Bill was the creation of a national hospital service by the nationalization of former municipal and voluntary hospitals.

An Emergency Medical Service had been set up in 1939 on the basis of plans prepared by the Ministry of Health on estimated casualties from air-raids. The ministry had taken over the cost of 'casualty beds' in the voluntary and municipal hospitals and by this means these establishments, nearly all in debt in 1939, became financially solvent by 1944 when the scheme was dismantled. Thus one of the many incentives for the setting up of the National Health Service was to use the war-time experience of a planned medical service to prevent the return of inadequate pre-war hospital finances.

In addition to the above, the service would provide free drugs on prescription, dental treatment, dentures and spectacles. Dentists as well as doctors would come into the scheme. Medical Practices Committees for England and Wales and for Scotland were to be set up to oversee the establishing of practices and to try to obtain even distribution of doctors through the country. A central advisory body, the Central Health Services Council, would be set up to advise the Minister of Health, with nine advisory committees attached to it, for example medical, dental and pharmaceutical. The School Health Service, responsible to the Minister of Education and built up since 1908, would continue to operate alongside the National Health Service.

The Bill was highly criticized on points of detail when introduced. Particular hospitals, especially teaching hospitals, were anxious to retain their identity and general practitioners feared that they would become no more than civil servants; there was talk at first of their boycotting the scheme. But as it finally emerged from various compromises the scheme managed to preserve completely the independence of the medical profession and since it came into operation it has had wide support from the profession. In 1961 there were only 600 doctors out of some 20,000 who had contracted completely out of the scheme, although many others continued to take some private patients. For those on their panel doctors receive so much per patient registered with them. Dentists are paid on a basis of treatment given and opticians on tests given. Consultants are paid a hospital salary, and one of the most important results of this has been the increase in specialist services available outside London. By far the largest part of the total cost of the scheme has been met from the start out of the Exchequer, only approximately 15% coming from National Insurance contributions. This cost, as we shall see in Chapter 20, was to continue to rise. But the Service was to give millions of people access to the kind of specialist medical care which they would never have been able to pay for as private patients. The general health of the nation has greatly benefited as a result.

National Assistance, Local Government and Legal Aid Acts

In 1948 the National Assistance Act was introduced jointly by Bevan and Griffiths. In 1929 the functions of the Poor Law Guardians had been placed directly under Local Government authorities. They were now transferred to new National Assistance Boards, which were a development of the Unemployment Assistance Boards of 1934, but able to handle all cases of hardship. A Central Board was to have 400 regional offices, to which anybody in need might apply: widows, old-age pensioners, the blind and invalids. Each case was to be judged on its merits. The Board was empowered to pay weekly subsistence rates, but also lump sums down in any emergency. In the first ten years of the Board's existence increasing care was to be taken over recruitment of officers, who must be tactful, discreet, firm and knowledgeable. In the year 1958 some 2,161,000 people were to apply for some kind of help.

A Local Government Act was also introduced in 1948 by Bevan, as a complement to the National Assistance Act, the two together finally winding up the old Poor Law System of 1834. This Act did more than this, however. It was a very complicated and highly technical measure concerned mainly with the financial relationship between local governments and the national government. It sought particularly to assist those areas where the income from local rates was low, owing to low population and/or predominantly low income-groups among rate-payers. It thus sought to keep the incomes of all County Councils and County Boroughs comparable. Much of the Act was also concerned with the granting of housing subsidies. In addition it gave local authorities the power to set up Citizens Advice Bureaux, which, before this, where they had existed, had been voluntary concerns. These have quickly gained the confidence of the public and make a large contribution in helping individuals through personal problems and disasters.

In 1949 a Legal Aid and Advice Act was passed. This made it possible for any citizen of 'slender means' to obtain legal aid from solicitor or barrister, 'wherever there is a sound case for litigation'. A person seeking such aid would have his means assessed by the National Assistance Board. Anyone in receipt of payments from that Board would automatically qualify for free aid. Others would bear part of the costs according to their means. Most of the cases concerned have been on behalf of tenants in disputes with landlords. Before this a complaint at least four centuries old had been that the poor man had seldom been able to afford to go to law, which was a prerogative of his 'betters'. The Act at least partially ended this grievance.

Elections and the defeat of Labour

In 1947 and 1950 two pamphlets had appeared, published by the left-wing of the Labour Party: *Keep Left* and *Keeping Left*, both highly critical of the government's foreign policy. The election in February 1950 was therefore fought by a Labour Party by no means agreed. It was fought by a Conservative Party contemptuous of continued shortages of food and raw materials, which they argued were the fault of too much 'planning', although in fact they were due as much to post-war economic problems. The government won a narrow victory. In the House of Commons the Labour Party held 315 seats; the Conservatives and allies 297; and the Liberals 9. A period of close divisions followed, with strict party discipline demanding constant attendance at the House of Commons.

Already a recession in America had led to an economic crisis in 1949 and devaluation of the pound. In 1950 the rise in cost of raw materials, although good for the sterling area as a whole, had led to a further rise in domestic prices. Then the Korean War, which broke out in July 1950, led to a split in the cabinet. In December 1950 Mr Gaitskell, the new Chancellor of the Exchequer, agreed to American demands for heavy defence expenditure and the budget in April 1951 introduced Health Service charges (50% charge on spectacles and dentures) and also raided the National Insurance Fund by reducing the latter's credit by £100,000,000. Aneurin Bevan, Harold Wilson and

John Freeman resigned, Bevan becoming the leader of a dissident group which published a left-wing pamphlet *Going our Way*.

In October 1950 Sir Stafford Cripps, one of the outstanding men of this government, had resigned through ill-health. In March 1951 Ernest Bevin also resigned for the same reason, while Attlee's health was at this time very indifferent. For these and other reasons he therefore decided in September 1951 to ask for a dissolution of Parliament. Although the Labour Party still polled the largest number of votes, it lost the election. The Conservatives and allies won 321 seats; Labour 295 and the Liberals 6. Winston Churchill, aged seventy-seven, became Prime Minister again.

Between 1945 and 1949 there had been a minor social revolution which, some felt, had not gone far enough. Certainly it was a cautious revolution, but because of this there was very little of the legislation involved which the Conservatives, now in office, wished to repeal. Great Britain had become a land of more equal opportunity than ever before and the greatest injustices and inequalities of fifty years before had been removed. What remained for the 1950's and 1960's to solve were the perennial problem of 'balance of payments' and the question of Britain's place in the world economy.

18

Empire into Commonwealth

The victory of the Allies in the Pacific in 1945 had decided that the American fleet would remain the dominant sea-power there. But 1941–1945 had so weakened the European colonial powers in Asia as to make their withdrawal inevitable. At the same time a rising tide of Asiatic nationalist feeling was determined to remain free of European control. This was to be made particularly plain at the Bandung Conference in Java in 1955 when some twenty-nine countries from Asia and Africa were to confer on problems of mutual concern. But by then these countries had nearly all gained their independence, mostly in the face of rising populations and often of reduced standards of living (inevitable with such a rise unless a vast programme of industrialization takes place, as in Communist China). This chapter will be devoted to those countries which were once part of the British Empire.

Before the war these could be divided into three main categories: British Dominions; the Empire of India; and the colonies of South-East Asia, Africa and the West Indies. The first had already by 1945 attained their independence; the second was very near to it; practically nobody foresaw the speed with which the third would obtain it.

The British Dominions

The 'Commonwealth' of self-governing Dominions is a term which was introduced at the end of the First World War to describe the countries of Australia, New Zealand,

Canada and South Africa, all of which had by 1910 attained more or less complete independence. In the case of Australia the six original colonies had become federated into the Commonwealth of Australia on 1 January 1901. By 1906 these British Dominions had complete independence to determine their own commercial policies as well as the conduct of their internal affairs. They had created a system of tariffs and Imperial Preference, which ran counter to the Free Trade policy of the English Liberals, and in 1911 an Imperial Conference in London discussed what rights and obligations the Dominions had in foreign policy, still conducted from London. It was agreed that they should at all times be consulted and kept informed. When Britain declared war against Germany she did so in the name of the British Empire. In South Africa there was a Boer revolt, but the majority concurred and South Africa played her part. Dominion troops fought at Gallipoli (Australians and New Zealanders), on the Western Front (Canadians at Vimy Ridge), in Africa and elsewhere. The four Dominions provided 1,000,000 troops and Dominion prime ministers in London met with British ministers in the Imperial War Cabinet (1917–1918), and Smuts, from South Africa, became a member of Lloyd George's War Cabinet.

At Versailles the four Dominions demanded and received separate representation, which they also received in the League of Nations. They no longer agreed automatically with all British decisions; for example, Canada disagreed with the United Kingdom over the handling of the Chanak crisis in 1922. In 1926 occurred a very important Imperial Conference in London which, under the chairmanship of Lord Balfour, defined the Dominion countries as 'autonomous communities within the British Empire, equal in status, in no way subordinate one to another in any aspect of their domestic or external affairs'. Springing from this conference came negotiations in detail, which led up to the Statute of Westminster passed by the Parliament at Westminister in 1931, which recognizes that no Dominion is bound by any 'earlier United Kingdom law' and that any

Dominion may if it wishes pass laws 'which might not be in line with United Kingdom law'. One year later this statute was put to the test at Ottawa, where hard bargaining ensued between Britain, now anxious for protection, and the Dominions, seeking guaranteed prices for their primary products exported to Britain but anxious to raise their tariffs against imported goods.

When Britain declared war in 1939 again all the Dominions followed: Canada a week later after a full debate in the Canadian Parliament and South Africa after much debate and a change of government. Dominion troops made contributions to the war all over the world: Canadians particularly distinguished themselves at Dieppe; South Africans gave great service in the various North African campaigns and Australian and New Zealand troops served in the Middle and Far East, campaigning in Malaya, New Guinea and Burma. An Empire Training Scheme trained thousands of air-crews in Canada, South Africa and Australia for service all over the world. Eire remained neutral, but many Irishmen served in British regiments and Irish agricultural produce helped to feed England through the war.

Since the war Canada, outside the sterling area, has been drawn further into the orbit of America, while retaining an independent view on numerous issues, such as the Suez campaign of 1956. Australia and New Zealand have negotiated separate treaties with the U.S.A., for example the Anzus pact of 1951. But there has been no noticeable change in sentiment except in South Africa, where a revival of Afrikaner nationalism has led by successive stages to a situation in which South Africa has felt it preferable (1961) to withdraw altogether from the Commonwealth. Emigration from Britain to Canada, New Zealand and Australia has continued steadily throughout the period. In the years following both wars it has been much encouraged. Since the Second World War Australia and Canada have been operating big schemes of assisted immigration not only of British citizens but also of Italian, Maltese, German and other European emigrants. The war increased Australia's productive capacity by some 400% and thus caused a labour shortage. At the same time it is widely accepted that either her vast unpopulated hinterland must be quickly filled by Europeans or the White Australia policy of excluding Asians be abandoned.

By 1948 the Ulster Unionists were if anything more firmly wedded economically to a tariff-free union with England than ever. In the Irish Free State, on the other hand, there were strong pressures for a total breach from the Commonwealth. The new Prime Minister, John A. Costello, agreed to break further away and an External Relations Act was passed proclaiming Ireland an Independent Republic from Easter Monday 1949. In theory this ended all connection; in practice there was little noticeable difference, questions relating to Ireland still being dealt with by the Commonwealth Relations Office and no effective barrier to migration between the two countries being set up. One incidental result, however, was the ending by Act of Parliament in 1949 of the old common British citizenship for the whole Commonwealth and its replacement by separate citizenships within the Commonwealth, for example Canadian or Australian.

India since 1906

Our second category was India, declared an Empire by Disraeli in 1876 and from 1898 to 1905 under the last of the great 'benevolent despot' viceroys, Lord Curzon. He had a considerable respect for Indian civilization, her arts and architecture; but very little for contemporary Indians. He decided, for administrative purposes, that Bengal should be divided, in spite of the fiercest opposition from the Bengalis, who regarded this as an insult to one of the most ancient provinces of India. Eastern Bengal had a majority of Mohammedans, and this division was to contribute to the later problem of Pakistan. Curzon resigned in 1905 and next year the Liberals came to office. John Morley became Secretary of State for India and Lord Minto was sent to be the new viceroy. They produced the Morley-Minto reforms of 1909, which opened the way for eventual self-government, although not intentionally. A few Indians of 'unimpeachable loyalty' were to be invited on to the viceroy's Legislative Council to advise; others were to be elected, by Hindu and Moslem electorates, on to advisory Provincial Councils. They were to have no powers, only, it was hoped, greater prestige. British control over the executive thus remained intact, and this was as far as an enlightened Liberal government could reasonably go. In 1911 the partition of Bengal was ended; a concession to Hindu pressure which produced great Mohammedan resentment.

About 2,000,000 Indians served in the First World War. Indian politicians at first supported the war, but as it dragged on they complained more and more bitterly of 'this European Civil War'. By 1916 the Indian National Congress (founded in 1885) was demanding an ambitious programme of Home Rule. At the same time an All-India Moslem League was founded which began agitation for partition. Lloyd George's government in 1917 decided that concessions must be made, and a report was drawn up in 1918 by Edwin Montague, the Secretary for India, and Lord Chelmsford, the Viceroy. This report was not adopted and carried through Parliament until the end of 1919, which was unfortunate, as great bitterness had arisen during the delay. These Montagu-Chelmsford Reforms created a Legislative Assembly, part nominated and part elected on a wide franchise, with the Viceroy retaining a veto. In the provinces there were to be provincial Assemblies which should take over all matters of social welfare, such as education and health, while leaving British officials complete control over the maintenance of public order. It was an advance, but it came only after the shooting at Amritsar, where a General Dyer had announced on 13 April 1919, after the murder of four Europeans, that for 'the safety of the British Community in India' it was necessary to 'strike terror into the whole of the Punjab'. He gave orders to his troops to fire at a hostile crowd, when 379 were killed and 1200 were wounded. The powerful Indian politician, Gandhi, became convinced that the British were being dishonest in their political promises and he began a fifteen-year campaign of passive resistance and non-co-operation.

The new Constitution came into force in 1920. Only a fraction of the largely illiterate population qualified for a vote and there was a determined body of 'obstructionists', who wanted to prevent the Constitution working at all. But during the 1920's much progress was made and the elected provincial assemblies did a great deal to improve working conditions in the factories and mines which were developing. In 1927 a Royal Commission was appointed under Sir John Simon.

It published its report in 1930. This recommended that in provincial government full control be extended to the Assemblies, subject only to the Governor's veto; and that the electorate be raised from 2½% to 10% of the population. The ultimate aim in India should be a federation of self-governing provinces, as in Australia, which should include the Indian states under independent princes. At the centre there would be a Federal Legislative Assembly elected by proportional representation (to safe-guard minorities) and an Executive Council, presided over by a Governor-General. Thus the principle of self-government was conceded only twenty-one years after the Liberals of 1909 had felt that they had gone as far as was possible. Three Round Table Conferences followed in London and the Government of India Act of 1935, in its 430 pages, sought to legislate on their proposals. The new Constitution was inaugurated in 1937, the Congress Party gaining control of seven of the eleven provinces, i.e. the Hindu provinces. A Mohammedan movement for partition, in the predominantly Moslem provinces (Punjab, Assam, Kashmir and Sind), soon appeared, and in 1940 the Moslem leader, Ali Jinnah, put forward his demand for partition and the creation of Pakistan.

The Federal government had not yet come into being by

1939 and therefore it was the Viceroy, Lord Linlithgow, who announced India to be at war. The leader of the Congress party, Mr Nehru, declared that India should not co-operate, and emergency powers had therefore to be invoked throughout the war years so that government could continue. When Japan threatened to invade India from Burma in 1941 a critical situation had arisen. Sir Stafford Cripps was sent to try to encourage co-operation, but he failed to persuade Gandhi and the extremists, who demanded that an Indian Defence Minister be appointed at once. Gandhi, Nehru and other leaders were imprisoned in August 1942, and riots took place, railways and telegraphs being cut. Most of the Congress leaders were imprisoned until 1945, while General Slim and Lord Mountbatten organized the recapture of Burma. Bad race riots now followed, not only against the British but between Hindu and Moslem. In February 1947 the Labour government promised that the British would leave India by June 1948. Lord Mountbatten became the last Viceroy and he decided that partition into Hindu and Moslem India would have to take place and that it should be in August 1947 and not June 1948. The plan was published on 3 June 1947, leaving just over two months in which to create two new Dominions. Boundary lines were drawn and millions of refugees flocked from one side or the other. Hundreds of thousands lost their lives. Mountbatten, the first Governor-General of the Dominion of India, urged the princes, who ruled the independent states, to join either India or Pakistan, which itself was made up of parts: West Pakistan on the North-West frontier of the continent of India, and East Pakistan, in what Lord Curzon had made into East Bengal. Most of the princes agreed. Hyderabad the biggest was compelled by force in September 1948.

The man who had done most to achieve independence was the Mahatma Gandhi. A devoted Hindu, he was opposed to religious fanaticism and believed that the new state must be secular and genuinely democratic. There is an ancient tradition of village democracy in India and this must be wedded to British Parliamentary democracy. Gandhi was assassinated by a Hindu fanatic on 30 January 1948, but his life's teachings have continued to exercise influence. Nehru became the first Prime Minister. He had never gone as far as Gandhi in condemning industrialization but he completely believed in the necessity of non-violence and it has been India's great contribution to the world since the

Mahatma Gandhi's funeral pyre on the banks of the Holy Jumna River, New Delhi

war, to show that democracy can work in an Asian country and that a neutral position is possible between the two great blocs of 'Communism' and 'The West'. In 1950 a new Constitution for India was proclaimed. She became a Republic within the Commonwealth. Pakistan, her poorer neighbour, has not proved so stable. After the assassination in 1951 of Ali Khan (Jinnah's close friend and successor) there has been a continual struggle for power. In 1958 came the establishment of a military dictatorship.

Burma

Burma had been annexed to British India by 1885. It was separated again in 1937. When the Japanese were driven out in 1944 the population was poverty-stricken, many villages having disappeared and the forest returned. The oil and teak industries were at a standstill; the rice-fields were overgrown; the hills and forests were infested with bandits or dacoits. A political leader, Aung San, who had at first collaborated with the Japanese but later deserted them, now emerged. He negotiated in London for independence, but was assassinated in September 1947. However, in 1948 a Burma Independence Act was passed at Westminster, by which Burma became a Republic, outside the British Commonwealth. Thankin Nu became the first Prime Minister, and his government set about trying to establish law and order. The murderers of Aung San and others were hanged. The frontier states were brought to recognize the Rangoon government and Karen nationalists as well as Communists were put down. British firms were encouraged to reinvest in the country and slowly prosperity has revived. The standing of Burmese politicians has also steadily risen, as men also determined to find a neutralist position in a world of power blocs.

Ceylon

This island, like India, has a racial problem: between descendants of Indian settlers, the Tamils in the west and east, and those of earlier inhabitants, the Sinhalese. Ceylon was acquired by the British from the Dutch in 1795, and in the nineteenth century became a wealthy colony of tea-plantations. It was successfully defended by the British navy against the Japanese, and Colombo became the headquarters of the South-East Asia Command for the reconquest of Burma and beyond. In 1943 full internal self-government was promised in return for co-operation in the fighting of the war. Before the end of the war this was not proving enough and the promise was raised to one of full Dominion status. This was granted by Parliament in 1947, and a new Constitution proclaimed in 1948. Until his death in 1952 Mr Senanayake successfully steered a middle course, allowing the British navy to retain bases and British firms to keep their assets. Since then strong left-wing movements have arisen, as well as racial agitation between Tamils and Sinhalese.

Malaya and Singapore

Between the wars this area experienced very striking advances. The rubber and tin industries greatly expanded, some £100,000,000 of British capital being invested in them by 1940. The area consisted of the Federated Malay States, under a British Resident General; the Unfederated States of Kedah and Johore; and the crown colony Straits Settlement, consisting of Penang, Malacca and Singapore. The last-named island continued to thrive throughout the period not only as a naval base but as one of the biggest commercial ports in the Far East. When the Japanese invaded Malaya from Siam there was no effective means of protection. Nobody had foreseen the possibility and Singapore itself easily fell, having no defences against attack from the mainland. As with Burma, the occupation ruined much of Malaya's wealth.

The hardest workers on the plantations and mines had often been the Chinese. These were now divided in their loyalties, some supporting Chiang Kai-shek, but many supporting Mao Tse-tung (see Chapter 16). Many of the latter, having learnt to resist the Japanese, were now determined to keep out the British after the war ended. There were numerous outbreaks of terrorism from Communist Chinese from 1945 onwards, and in 1948 a state of civil war developed between the British, allied with the Malays (to whom they promised self-government as soon as the emergency was over), and the Communist rebels operating from the jungle.

Immediately after the war the British government made the mistake (1946) of trying to force the pace of centralization. There was to be a Malayan Union, which would unite the whole peninsula, less Singapore. This would be ruled by a strong central government, reducing the powers of the traditional rulers of the states. The plan produced strong protests. A Malay party, the United Malay National Organization, dedicated itself to resisting the proposals, which were abandoned in 1948 and replaced by a Federal Plan, restoring the powers of the traditional rulers, while retaining for a while the colonial status of Penang, Malacca and Singapore.

In 1949 there was founded the Malayan Chinese Association in order to unite all those Chinese who, rejecting Communism, were anxious to co-operate with the government. Nevertheless the civil war was to go on, being particularly fierce between 1952 and 1954. In 1955 a New Alliance Party of Malay, Chinese and Indians was formed by Tunku Abdul Rahman, which won 51 out of 52 seats for the Federal Legislative Council, under a new constitution. They had promised a general amnesty to Communist terrorists and kept that promise, but it was rejected by the Communist leader Chin Peng. Complete independence of Malaya within the Commonwealth under a Federal Constitution finally came in August 1957 and the Communist threat has slowly declined, while Malayan prosperity has steadily returned. Singapore, which geographically belongs to Malaya, has remained separate so far (1963). Here internal self-government has been steadily extended since 1945 (David Marshall leading the government from 1945 to 1956), although Britain has tried to retain considerable control, owing to the port's strategic importance. At the time of writing it seems that Malaysia, a Federation of Malaya, Singapore, North Borneo and Sarawak, is likely soon to emerge.

Of Britain's other island colonies in the Far East, Hong Kong is by far the most important. It swarms with Chinese refugees and is grossly overpopulated. It is on the very edge of the Communist world, but as yet there are no signs of any change. It seems at present that there is no alternative to the status of crown colony. Nor is there any strong agitation among a largely refugee population which values the great efforts made for its social welfare by the colonial government.

The Labour government 1945–1951 had been faced primarily with colonial problems in the Far East. It is generally conceded now that its policy of concessions was wise. It avoided the kind of wars that developed in French Indo-China and the Dutch East Indies, where attempts were made to restore a pre-war situation. It enabled economic investment to continue and prevented the more violently nationalist and anti-European movements from gaining control. Three other areas now need to be considered: the eastern Mediterranean, tropical Africa and the Caribbean.

Egypt

At the end of the war Britain had successfully defended her oil supplies and the Suez Canal. She now had to adjust herself to new forces, particularly increased Arab Nationalism, which she had herself assisted during the First World War. In 1922 Britain agreed to recognize Egypt as an independent state, subject to a number of qualifications, the most important of which was the British right to maintain a garrison, for the protection of the Suez Canal and British interests, and to control the Sudan. In 1936 Britain agreed to withdraw her troops into the Canal Zone and made a treaty with Egypt for mutual protection. Under this treaty Britain was able to operate from Egypt during the war and fight the desert campaigns, but afterwards, in 1946, the Egyptian government asked for its revision. They appealed to the United Nations with no success and in 1951 declared they would no longer be bound by the 1936 treaty. The government of King Farouk, which said this, was, however, highly corrupt and the 1950's were to see the military overthrow of the Egyptian governing class and the establishment of a more left-wing regime led by Colonel Nasser. There was to be agreement with Britain over the Sudan and that country's independence, but also a quarrel over Suez, and in 1956 the tragedy of the Anglo-French Suez venture (see biography of A. Eden below).

Cyprus

The island of Cyprus was acquired by Disraeli from the Turks in 1878, as payment for diplomatic assistance against the Russians. For centuries it was a meeting place of cultures: European and Asiatic (the Crusaders used it as a base against the Turks, who themselves occupied it in 1570). It has a Greek-speaking majority, who had begun agitating for Enosis or reunion with Greece even before 1878. Between the wars the island was governed as a crown colony but unfortunately colonial administrators tended to treat the inhabitants in the same way as they did any other 'colonial people'. This for a proud people, whose civilization goes back to ancient Greece, was resented and in 1931 Government House at Nicosia was burnt down. The government replied by despatching troops and barring public meetings and nationalist newspapers. This situation continued throughout the war, but in 1946 the Labour government summoned a consultative assembly to discuss a new Constitution. Left-wing Greeks and the Turks co-operated, but right-wing Greeks, backed by the Greek Orthodox Church, opposed the proposals. In 1949 the Communists changed sides and supported the demand for Enosis. Athens now began to support this too, having earlier not been interested. Turkey on the other hand feared for the Turkish minority. From 1950, a movement known as E.O.K.A., Revolutionary Organization of Cypriot Struggle, led by Archbishop Makarios, was to employ increasingly terrorist means to gain independence, if not union with Greece. The former was eventually to be achieved in 1957, after much bitterness, struggle and bloodshed.

Palestine

The movement known as Zionism, that is the creation of a Jewish state in Palestine for persecuted Jews, arose in the late nineteenth century. Anti-semitism was once again becoming a problem in Europe, as it had been periodically for the previous 1900 years. In 1896 Theodore Herz published a book called *The Jewish State*, putting forward a Zionist case. Various wealthy Jewish families subscribed money and a number of Jews settled in Palestine under the Turks before 1914. The British government during the war adopted a double policy, which depended for its success on Arab-Jewish friendship. It actively supported Arab nationalism, for example T. E. Lawrence helped to organize the defeat of the Turks with the help of the desert Arabs. At the same time in 1917 it issued the Balfour Declaration, which viewed with favour the establishment in Palestine of 'a national home for the Jewish people'. In 1919 Britain was granted the mandate, by the League of Nations, to bring this about, but no national home could be created peacefully unless with Arab consent. They were hardly likely to have fought to win their independence from the Turks in order to be placed under alien Jews and this consent has in fact never been won. Thus Britain committed herself to an almost insoluble problem.

The Jewish community in Palestine in 1914 numbered about 100,000. In 1922 it has risen by 50% and it remained almost stationary for the next ten years. The country was divided into six districts, each under a District Commissioner. In 1927 the Jewish community was organized under a Chief Rabbi, a General Council and an Elected Assembly. English, Hebrew and Arabic were the official languages of Palestine.

During the 1930's Jewish immigration greatly accelerated, due to renewed anti-semitism in Germany and elsewhere. At the same time the differences in dynamism between the traditional Arab inhabitants and the forceful, vital and usually socialist Jews, became more pronounced. This clash is admirably shown by Arthur Koestler in his novel *Thieves in the Night*. Both Jews and Moslems regard Jerusalem as a sacred city and violent religious feeling here led to riots. In 1936 the Arab population rebelled and British troops were sent to restore order. A Royal Commission under Lord Peel followed, which declared that the mandate was unworkable and was becoming more so, as Arab nationalism developed as a force. The report therefore recommended the partition of Palestine, with the modern thriving Jewish cities of Tel Aviv and Haifa going to the Jews, as well as a partitioned Jerusalem.

The British government wished to adopt the recommendations of the report with League of Nations approval. Unfortunately both Jews and Arabs denounced it and so the government took the fateful decision of trying to maintain the *status quo* and work an unworkable system. Jewish immigration would therefore have to be limited to 75,000 a year just at a moment of violent anti-semitism through much of Europe. Powerful Jewish forces in America condemned this quota and it led to shiploads of illegal migrants being refused admission in the years just before the war began. Meanwhile Britain tried to keep the Arab countries friendly since so much of her oil depended on them. A Round Table Conference was tried in London in March 1939, which suggested that once the Jewish population reached one-third of the total population in Palestine, all immigration should cease. The Jewish answer to this was increased activites by terrorist organizations, Hagana and

February 1948. Jewish terrorists blow up the offices of the *Palestine Post*, a British newspaper in Jerusalem

Irgun, against both British and Arab. Individually the British colonial administrators seem to have preferred the Arab native to his thrusting Jewish counterpart, who was turning the desert back to fertility by superhuman efforts. When war began Britain was using methods reminiscent of Black and Tan days to maintain her position in an area now strategically vital.

In 1945 the Labour government hoped to be able to solve the problem, but without recognizing the full validity of the Balfour Declaration this was no longer possible. To do so would be to turn the Arab world against Britain and her interest. Ernest Bevin was thus the target of violent abuse, particularly since, when in opposition, the Labour Party had appeared to favour Zionism. His first move was to bring about an Anglo-American commission of enquiry, whose report was promptly rejected by Jews and Arabs, as well as by President Truman. Then followed a United Nations enquiry in 1947, which confirmed the Peel Report's recommendations for partition. This was eventually accepted by the necessary two-thirds majority in the General Assembly and Britain agreed to withdraw. As she did so, Jews and Arabs moved in and a state of war between the Arab states and the newly proclaimed Israel followed. A United Nations mediator Count Bernadotte tried, until his murder in September 1948, to bring about a settlement. Gradually Israel's frontiers became stabilized and she won recognition as a new nation, although not from the Arab states. Spasmodic fighting continued until January 1949. By then Palestine was effectively partitioned between Israel, Jordan and Egypt, four-fifths going to the victorious Israelis.

Africa

The emergence of Africa, as her various peoples have demanded and sometimes won political independence, is mainly a story of the 1950's and 1960's. Thus, strictly speaking, we have not here to devote much space to it. In 1945, the pattern of European power in Africa was still much as it had been in 1900, except that the German colonies had become mandated territories under British, French, Belgian or South African control. Kenya and the Rhodesias had developed rapidly between the wars, acquiring a white-settler population, which opened up large-scale farming, tobacco-growing and copper-mining, using cheap African labour. The Europeans in Southern Rhodesia in 1923 received the status of a self-governing colony, with the crown retaining rights over defence and over the fate of the native peoples. All other British possessions were either crown colonies, protectorates, or mandated territories. On the west coast, known before modern medicine as the 'white man's grave', no European settlement was made: commercial and mining firms opened up the colony, but land ownerships remained with the inhabitants. In Central and East Africa, as European settlers increased in number, racial distrust developed.

During the war East and West African soldiers fought and died alongside Europeans, towards the end of the war a number of Africans receiving the King's Commission in the army. This war experience was crucial, as mentioned in Chapter 15, since Africans would hardly be likely to accept a position of racial inferiority again. The Gold Coast, a colony whose contacts with Europe go back to the sixteenth century and slavery days, experienced serious riots of dissatisfied ex-soldiers calling for self-government in 1948. An all-African committee under Mr Justice Coussey recommended constitutional reforms and a new Constitution was put forward. Federal elections were held, and the state of Ghana came into being, under its first Prime Minister Kwame Nkrumah, obtaining full independence in 1957. The process had been rapid and the experiment proved successful, even though parliamentary democracy soon proved unworkable. Ghana's lead inspired movements of nationalism throughout the continent. Her huge neighbour Nigeria was already quietly following her lead from 1949 onwards, and other West African colonies were to follow.

But in Kenya hatred for the European settlers led to violence and bloodshed, the most notorious example of which was the Kikuyu tribe's attempt from 1952 onwards to win back their highland farmlands. An extreme group condemned the Christian Church as an instrument of colonialism and revived a pagan cult known as Mau-Mau. Some thirty-two European civilians and many loyal tribesmen were to be murdered by these extremists and many thousands of Africans were killed or imprisoned in return before order was restored in 1957. Yet by 1951 the Colonial Office in London had undoubtedly been converted to the idea of African self-government. Gradually the politicians were to follow and it then only remained to convince European settlers in Africa.

West Indies

Before the Second World War various British West Indian colonies had been achieving constitutional reforms by which Legislative Councils would be elected on a franchise which ignored colour. Jamaica became largely self-governing in 1944, and in 1947, at Montego Bay in Jamaica, there was held the first conference for federation and self-government of the British West Indies. A Closer Association Committee was formed and in 1953 a Caribbean Commission reported, recommending a Federal Constitution, a Federal revenue and Customs union, and a Federal Civil Service. The first Federal Parliament was to be opened in 1958, but Federation was to run into great difficulties and opposition from the larger islands. The result is that it is impossible to forecast (1963) what will be the fate of these British possessions. Probably the larger colonies will achieve separate Dominion status and the smaller ones remain crown colonies, for economic not racial reasons. The 1950's were to see the phenomenon of extensive immigration from the West Indies to Britain. Most of the migrants easily found work in industry and on the railways. But some colour prejudice was to arise: there were to be housing difficulties and even some rioting, and in 1961 the British government was going to seek powers to control this flow of unskilled labour.

But if this was to reflect the continuation of a 'colour bar' in Britain, still great changes had taken place in the decades 1930–1950 in methods of colonial administration. Successive governments, from the time of the Simon Commission's report in 1930, had accepted that the coloured peoples of the Empire (some hundreds of millions) had a right to receive political independence on non-racial terms and at the earliest rather than the latest possible moment.

19

Foreign affairs 1945–1951

Obviously what dominates the history of these post-war years far more than the 'liquidation of the British Empire' is the failure of the United Nations and the collapse of the war-time alliance. Within three years of the war ending the U.S.A. and Britain were on the brink of war with the U.S.S.R. Up to the time of writing (1963) they have seldom since been far from it.

The first years of the United Nations

During the war Winston Churchill had put forward a scheme for three Regional Councils: Europe, America and the Pacific, as successors to the League of Nations. But it was not acceptable and the United Nations had come into being at San Francisco in 1945. Britain's own early attitude was soured when her policy in Palestine was attacked without workable alternatives being suggested. But she was prepared to work with the United Nations, and when in July 1948 the General Assembly agreed on partition of Palestine, she acquiesced. Unfortunately Russia was to prove far less tractable.

In 1945 there were fifty-one states represented in the General Assembly (in 1961 there were 101). Twenty of these were Latin American states, which at that time could be counted on to support U.S. policy. Thus the U.S.A. could be sure of never receiving a two-thirds vote against her.

This situation was radically to alter in the 1950's, with the emergence of the Afro-Asian bloc, but it may help to explain why Russia so distrusted the United Nations and tended to use the veto in the Security Council so consistently. She knew that the Assembly was no more than a possible forum for propaganda, while the Security Council could be used to restrict the U.S.A. and the 'imperialist powers', which Russia still profoundly distrusted in 1945.

A clash between Western and Eastern powers soon came. A Conference of Foreign Ministers (Soviet, American and British) was held in London in September 1945, but it could reach little agreement on such matters as the desire of Russia to make a new alliance with Turkey; the continuance of Russian troops in Northern Iran (Azerbaijan); Russian refusal to allow U.N.R.R.A. agents to enter either the U.S.S.R. or the new Russian-dominated satellites of Roumania, Bulgaria, Hungary and Poland; the presence of British troops in Greece, to prevent Communist revolution there. All these matters were raised again when the Security Council and General Assembly met in London in January 1946. Other issues at that meeting were the presence of British troops in Syria and the Lebanon and the attempt by the Dutch to regain control in Indonesia. American policy in this early post-war period was to withdraw once again from world affairs into isolation and the British Foreign Secretary, Ernest Bevin, took the lead in the early discussions. The Foreign Secretaries met again in the summer of 1946 to discuss Danube trade, the Yugoslav frontier and an Austrian peace treaty. Up to now, although there was deep mistrust, there was no open division. This developed during the year 1946–1947, as the two giants, the U.S.A. and the U.S.S.R., slowly began to convince each other of mutual hostility.

The development of the East–West blocs

In March 1946 Churchill had made a speech at Fulton, Missouri, in which he called for a stronger link between Britain and the U.S.A.: a fraternal association, in view of the developing 'iron-curtain' across Europe. But the time was not yet ripe. American feeling against British 'colonialism' was still strong, especially over Palestine. Nevertheless in the same month American observers joined the French and British in Greece to oversee the elections. It was their first post-war intervention in Europe: Britain, deprived of Lend-Lease, was financially no longer able to meet the commitments she had taken on. The economies of the other West European powers were very weak and this in many places was leading to successful Communist agitation, especially in France and Italy, while in Greece the civil war between Royalists and Communists still simmered in the hills. In Czechoslovakia the left-wing parties, dominated by the Communists, won the general election of 1946 and this was to lead to the Communist seizure of power in 1947. At the end of 1946 it was agreed that the British and American zones in Germany be linked from 1 January 1947, since Britain could no longer afford the whole cost of occupation.

In February 1947 the British government felt obliged, through financial shortages, to renounce its commitments in Greece: undertaken since 1944 to keep some form of law and order against communist brigands, aided by Yugoslavia, Albania and Bulgaria. President Truman on 12 March then announced the 'Truman Doctrine' against the 'threat of totalitarianism': Greece and Turkey were to receive American aid and attempts were to be made to win back Yugoslavia from Communism under Marshal Tito. The third Foreign Ministers' Conference was meeting when the Truman doctrine was announced, and needless to say it collapsed. America had become convinced of Communist aggression; Stalin on his side had become convinced of an equally aggressive American policy.

The Americans quickly moved to a policy of 'containment' of the Communist threat by the building up of secure regimes from Norway to Japan to counter Russia. In the Far East great American efforts were made to bolster up the corrupt regime of Chiang Kai-shek and in Europe there was announced on 5 June 1947 the Marshall Plan. American aid was offered to any European state which was willing to collaborate and to plan the best use of the money on an international rather than national basis. Ernest Bevin hoped that the Russian satellite states would come into the scheme, but Stalin and Molotov prevented this. The Organization for European Economic Co-operation (O.E.E.C.) came into being, which began to bring about the economic recovery of Western Europe. Its long-term aim was to build up a large Free Trade area consisting of all the recipient states. This was to be partly realized in the 1950's by the Common Market scheme and it might have been realized earlier if Britain had not at the time convinced herself of the need to maintain her insularity. Meanwhile the Russians saw the whole Marshall Plan simply as a means to revive Germany as a bulwark against themselves. They replied to it by forming the Cominform in October 1947, whose function was to co-ordinate the Communist parties of Europe, whether or not they were yet under direct Soviet control. The term 'Cold War' began to be used in July 1947. By the end of the year the initiative for Western policy had passed from Britain to the U.S.A. 'From 1947 onwards, the fact that mattered most in international relations between the great powers was not what the intentions of each side really were, but what the other side believed them to be' (C. M. Woodhouse, *British Foreign Policy since the Second World War*).

Berlin air-lift

In March 1947 Britain and France had signed a treaty of alliance with each other at Dunkirk. Its significance was probably not great, but in March 1948 it was extended into the Brussels Agreement between Britain, France, Belgium, the Netherlands and Luxembourg. It was nominally aimed at possible German aggression, but was equally applicable to Russia. A month earlier, in February, the Communist Party in Czechoslovakia had seized full power and imprisoned its political enemies. Also in February, Britain, the U.S.A. and France had discussed the future of their West German zones and the Soviet reply to this latter was a

Peoples' Congress which met in the Soviet zone of Germany in March, as a preliminary to the granting of a constitution to the Russian-occupied zone. In April a conference of six Western powers met in Frankfurt to plan a Constitution for the three Western zones and in June 1948 the United States Senate agreed to grant military aid to the Brussels Treaty powers, thus foreshadowing the North Atlantic Treaty Organization. On the other side eight Communist ministers met to discuss the future of Germany, the result of their meeting being the decision to close the land route between Berlin and the Allied zones. Russia as yet had no atomic weapons, and it is thought that this alone may have deterred her at this point from any more aggressive action. The air-link was not touched and from July 1948 until May 1949 the Western zone of Berlin depended on an air-lift for its essential imports and exports. The people of Berlin suffered considerably in these months from food and coal shortages, but the co-operative effort needed to make this air-lift successful led to far closer alliance between the Western powers. On 4 April 1949 the North Atlantic Treaty was signed, an extension of the Brussels Treaty of the previous year. In May the Berlin overland routes were reopened and the Foreign Ministers once more met. But during May and June 1949 they again failed to reach agreement on the future either of Berlin or of Germany. Both sides remained stubborn and an uneasy *status quo* survived.

Both East and West Germany received constitutions in 1949: the German Federal Republic (West) and the German Democratic Republic (East). In August the Catholic centre party (Christian Democratic Union) of Dr Adenauer won the first Federal general election. The Western capital was to be Bonn and in September the Western powers ended the state of war with Germany. In October a provisional East German government was set up under Herr Ulbricht and the Soviet government theoretically ended its military occupation of Germany, though not of East Berlin. Both sides accused each other of being the first to re-employ Nazis. The flow of refugees from Eastern Germany to the West continued.

N.A.T.O. was designed as a defensive organization for resisting aggression. Unfortunately, however, it has also been seen by some Western statesmen as a potentially offensive weapon for bringing about the reunification of Germany. All the powers of the Atlantic seaboard, except Eire and Spain, were original members, together with the U.S.A., Canada, and the Mediterranean powers of Italy, Greece and Turkey. It was to have its headquarters in Paris (S.H.A.P.E.), all members contributing towards mutual defence. It is not easy to estimate the actual effect of N.A.T.O. on Russian policy. During 1949 Russia perfected her own atomic bomb and she also had considerable difficulties with her European satellites, especially Yugoslavia under Tito.

Towards a United Europe

Perhaps one effect of the growing power of both the U.S.A. and the U.S.S.R. was to stimulate the movement for a United Europe. In 1946 Churchill had spoken at Zürich of the need for a kind of 'United States of Europe', and in 1947, while still in opposition, he had helped to found a 'United Europe Committee'. In May 1948 he was one of the sponsors of the Congress of Europe, which met at The Hague. The first actual move towards union was the Benelux Customs Union between Belgium, Luxembourg and the Netherlands. It was followed by the defence agreements of the Brussels Treaty already referred to. In August 1949 the Council of Europe met for the first time, choosing as its seat the ancient city of Strasbourg, for so long fought over by the French and German powers. Its declared aim was to bring about genuine unification into a United Europe. West Germany joined in November 1949 and in May 1950 the Schuman Plan appeared for the creation of a European Coal and Steel Community, which came into being in April 1951. In October 1950 came the Pleven Plan for a European Defence Community. The Schuman plan was to lead to the European Economic Community (or Common Market) and to Euratom in 1957. The Pleven Plan failed; but West

West Germany was offered membership of N.A.T.O. The two main obstacles to a faster growth of a United Western Europe were Britain and France. The former was reluctant to participate in any economic union with Europe; the latter in any military union with Germany. Britain's reluctance continued even when Churchill, who had helped initiate closer union, became Prime Minister again in 1951. This reluctance was to last until the decision in 1961 to seek membership of the Common Market. France gradually became reconciled to co-operation with Germany, especially after the return to power in 1958 of General de Gaulle.

British trade links and defence costs

Before continuing this sketch of foreign affairs it might be worth remembering that Britain lives by trade and that her traditional foreign policy has always been to protect British interests abroad in the interests of that trade. In this way Britain has perhaps been less ideologically involved in the Cold War than has the U.S.A. The most obvious example of this is the decision of the British government in 1950 to recognize the Communist government as the legal government of China and not that of Chiang Kai-shek. Thus Britain has been able to trade with China and protect her interests there to a certain extent, while for the U.S.A. this is still (1963) impossible, largely for ideological and emotional reasons.

When the war ended Britain had 5,000,000 men under arms and 4,000,000 civilians working on war production. She had troops stationed in Germany, Japan, Austria, Italy (around disputed Trieste), Greece, Palestine, Iran, Egypt, South-East Asia and Africa. The aim was to reduce the armed forces to about 1,100,000 by December 1946 by a process of demobilization according to length of service, similar to that used in 1919, although National Service would continue. The problem was going to be to decide how much Britain could afford to spend on defence, while her government was seeking to introduce greater social justice at home and with most pre-war overseas assets gone. In fact the cost of defence was reduced from some £1,667,000,000 for 1946–1947 to less than £700,000,000 for 1948–1949. This was only enough if commitments in Europe and the Far East were drastically reduced, and the Berlin air-lift and the threat of war produced a reversal of policy. The costs of research towards the possession of thermo-nuclear armament (hydrogen bomb) and the outbreak of the Korean War in 1950, caused the cost of defence once more to rise as the Labour government became convinced of the need for an independent deterrent. As we saw, the split in the Labour Party which resulted, together with the reduction in social services necessary to off-set the Defence Bill, helped the Labour Party to be defeated in 1951. The estimates for defence for 1951–1952 were up to £1,300,000,000.

The Korean War 1950–1953

Korea is geographically a peninsula of the Chinese mainland, but its cultural traditions are in many ways different. It was annexed by Japan in 1894 and in 1943 the Allies agreed that it should be liberated on Japan's defeat. Russia entered the war against Japan on 8 August 1945 and the war ended on 12 September, but that gave Russia the chance

U.S. troops on North Korean front

to drive Japan from Manchuria and from North Korea. American troops entered Korea from the south and a rough line of demarcation was agreed upon along the 38th parallel. A Communist government was set up in North Korea and in South Korea a somewhat unsavoury right-wing government headed by Synghman Rhee was recognized by the U.S.A. and also by the United Nations.

In 1949 the Communist Chinese People's Republic was victorious in China, driving the Kuomintang into Formosa. In 1950 Britain and Russia recognized the new government, but not the United States. The Republic applied for membership of the United Nations, where the Kuomintang still held the position of permament membership of the Security Council, and was refused. Russia, in protest, temporarily walked out of the Security Council.

Meanwhile, both Russian and American forces had been withdrawn from Korea in 1949. The Americans had left an advisory commission, and both Korean governments obtained military and economic aid from their respective patrons. Frequent border incidents now ensued, until the North Koreans, allegedly in revenge against one of these from the south, crossed the frontier into South Korea in large numbers. South Korea was unprepared, but had been promised American aid if this should happen. This she at once obtained. President Truman sent aid from Japan and then asked the United Nations to approve. Russia being temporarily absent from the Security Council, this approval was given.

So began the Korean War, which was to last actively until the 1951 truce, but which would not be ended by armistice until 1953. Some 25,000 Americans were to be killed and some 600 British. Many thousands of Chinese 'volunteers', who came to North Korea's help, were also to be killed. It is impossible to know how many thousand Koreans died, either in fighting or as a result of the war. Out of it was to come in 1954 the S.E.A.T.O. organization to prevent Chinese aggression in South-East Asia and also the A.N.Z.U.S. pact of 1951 (in which Britain had no part), but which was designed by the U.S.A. to strengthen her position in the Pacific by links with Australia and New Zealand. British trade in the area was badly affected by the insistence by the U.S.A. on a trade embargo against China and North Korea. But public opinion in Britain was solidly behind the Labour and Conservative governments, who supported this war by the United Nations against aggression. At the same time Britain also put strong pressure on the U.S.A. to prevent her taking the offensive against China: Attlee flying to Washington in December 1950 to dissuade President Truman from using atomic bombs against China, who was openly helping North Korea. (Churchill and Eden were to make the same journey to persuade President Eisenhower to veto a similar policy in 1954 over Indo-China).

Colombo Plan

One indirect result of the Korean War was the Colombo Plan in 1950, an achievement of Ernest Bevin, who believed that the way to peace in South-East Asia was through economic and social development. It was published in November 1950 and by it Britain, Australia, Canada, New Zealand, India, Pakistan, Burma, Malaya, Indonesia, Ceylon and Japan, with the U.S.A. as an associate, agreed to give one another technical and economic aid. One of the main ways this has in practice operated is through the provision of university and technological education by the more advanced countries, particularly Britain, for great numbers of Asiatic students.

Britain and the new nations

As we have seen, during the years 1945–1951 the North Atlantic Alliance came into being and Britain passed the initiative to a somewhat reluctant America. But Britain was also involved in the creation of a number of new states. From her former empire came such powers as India and Pakistan; from earlier mandates came Jordan and Iraq and, much more painfully, Israel, Syria and Lebanon were assisted to their freedom from the French mandatory control by British interventions. In Indonesia Britain withdrew her support for the Dutch in their efforts to re-impose control and she applauded the American decision in the Philippines to hand over long-promised independence. Yet there remained a number of areas where, for strategic or trade reasons, Britain could not withdraw. An example of the former is Singapore and of the latter the Persian Gulf area, on which British oil supplies still depend, as they have done since 1914.

Persian oil dispute

It will be recalled that before the First World War the British Navy went over from coal to oil, and that Britain acquired a majority of shares in the Anglo-Persian Oil Company, now B.P. When the Ottoman Empire collapsed in 1918 Britain became the mandatory power in Iraq (large oil deposits) and Jordan (no oil, but a pipeline, today carrying 44,000 tons a day to the sea). Along the Gulf of Aden and the Persian Gulf there were a number of sheikdoms whose feudal regimes were upheld by British treaties and/or occupation: examples of these are the Aden protectorate; Bahrein (B.P. refinery since 1930 producing 1,000,000 tons of oil a year); and Kuwait (in 1961 producing over half the oil annually used in Britain).

In 1951 Iran's main income came from royalties from the Anglo-Iranian oil-field, with its large refinery at Abadan. In March of that year General Razmara, dictator of Iran, was murdered by nationalists, whose leader, Mussadiq, became Prime Minister. He announced the nationalization of the oil-field in April, but the oil company and the British Foreign Secretary, Herbert Morrison, refused to recognize this. Six months passed in fruitless negotiation, and then the refinery was closed. Mussadiq remained in power, although Iran's economic position suffered. He was supported by the Communist Tudeh Party. It was not until 1953 that he was overthrown by a right-wing revolution and that the good relations with Britain were restored, the refinery being reopened in 1954.

H.M.S. *Mauritius* anchored off oil refineries at Abadan

Thus there has been a tendency in this area for Britain, because of her economic interests, to support existing, sometimes reactionary, governments and to try to hold back the nationalist enthusiasms, which elsewhere she has cautiously supported. Yet, dependent as she must be for long on Middle East oil, Britain must clearly come to terms with the nationalists, who know as well as anybody that their countries depend on oil revenues for their own prosperity.

Labour Foreign Secretaries

When Attlee formed his government in April 1945 Ernest Bevin became both Foreign Secretary and the Minister in charge of co-ordinating all external affairs. He was a supporter of the United Nations, although he became somewhat disillusioned with what he regarded as its failure to be realistic over the Palestine problem. He was largely responsible for the Brussels Treaty and for putting the Marshall Plan into effect. He was deeply saddened by the failure of Russia to co-operate, having looked forward to the day when disarmament would be complete. He for long remained convinced that with a little more co-operation it would be possible to 'open up our countries to inspection, all of us' that 'light and knowledge might come in and passports and visas disappear'. One of his last acts as Foreign Minister was to put forward the Colombo Plan. In March 1951 ill-health forced him to hand over to Herbert Morrison in the middle of the Korean War.

Morrison only held the office until the October election, but it fell to him to face the Abadan crisis, as well as American criticism for the flight to Russia, in May 1951, of two Foreign Office officials, Burgess and Maclean. In October, at the end of his time in office, Egypt inflicted a rebuff on Britain by refusing to join a Middle East Defence Organization. This Egyptian problem was a legacy for the Conservatives and it was to lead eventually to the Suez crisis and the tragic intervention of 1956. At the time, Morrison was violently denounced for his handling of various situations, but, seen in retrospect, we can appreciate that few of his problems were easily soluble and that he hardly had time to sort them out before his party was defeated at the October general election.

20

Britain 1906–1951: prospect and retrospect

In 1906 H. G. Wells had written of what he saw in Britain as a 'spectacle of forces running to waste, of people who use and do not replace; the story of a country hectic with a wasting, aimless fever of trade and money-making and pleasure seeking'. By 1951, in spite of this harsh judgment, Britain had fought and won two world wars; she was heavily in debt to the U.S.A.; she was in the process of handing over her empire to its original inhabitants and was fighting the Korean War; she was in the midst of a financial crisis, but was nevertheless staging the Festival of Britain. Life was still hectic, but at least more people had the chance to join in the process of waste. In fact, without such waste no great industrial nation could now survive, so great had become the productive power of the machine. Britain retained her class-consciousness (nicknamed by one writer the 'pox Britannica'); there were still old and poor people insufficiently provided for and many slums and unconquered diseases. Other countries, notably Sweden, had carried the idea of a Welfare State further. But in a number of basic social matters great progress had been made, and probably for most boys and girls the future in 1951 was far more exciting and held far more chances, if nuclear war was avoided, than it had done for their grandfathers two generations earlier.

Changing patterns of living

(i) *Housing*. After the war the L.C.C. did not repeats it between-wars scheme of vast estates outside London.

The jitter-bug was the popular dance of 1951

Instead came the Putney and Roehampton schemes of subsidized flats: great pencil blocks dominating the west-London skyline and built in the grounds of defunct Victorian and Edwardian mansions. These flats, using new building techniques, were to be prototypes for great numbers of local government housing schemes up and down the country.

The rebuilding of the centres of bombed cities such as Plymouth, Coventry and the City of London was planned and begun soon after the war, although not completed until the 1950's and later. Architecturally these schemes varied from 'traditional' to 'modern', depending on local views and prejudices. Plans for fourteen New Towns were approved, such as Crawley, Stevenage and Basildon, and work on them began; both architecturally and socially exciting experiments. Unfortunately, as between the wars, it was the lush and favoured south which gained most from these experiments, compared with heavily industrialized northern and midland Britain, where rehousing remained a pressing need into the 1960's—acres of back-to-back houses, many built in the 1830's and 1840's, if not before, and 5,000,000 of them, it is estimated, still without a bath.

(ii) *Transport and Communications.* Probably new methods of communication and quicker means of transport are the most obvious developments of the half-century affecting social habits. By 1951 nearly every household had acquired a wireless-set and during the next decade a television-set would be added. By 1961 few households did not possess either a motor-car, a motor-bicycle or a motor-scooter (the fashion for the latter was to invade Britain from Italy in the 1950's). In 1945, with the vast impetus given by war research and with the invention of the jet engine, there was little that was not envisaged for air-travel. At once commercial companies began to operate transatlantic services and B.E.A. provided quick flights both within Britain and all over Europe. In the 1950's, when currency restrictions were raised, the holiday abroad was to become increasingly popular for those sections of the middle-class who before had never looked beyond Brighton; by 1961, but for international price control, it would have been possible to introduce air-fares which would have seriously undercut rail and sea communications. In 1938 Mr Chamberlain's flights to Germany had made history, but during and after the war prime ministers, and especially foreign secretaries, were scarcely ever out of an aeroplane. It is hard to estimate the importance which this change has had on the conduct of diplomatic affairs. Even so the effect of increased air-travel on everyday social life is probably not as revolutionary as had been that of the steam locomotive and steam ship a century earlier.

(iii) *The arts and entertainment.* In 1906 the music hall, the theatre and the public house were the main centres of popular entertainment, together with occasional boxing matches and, of course, horse-racing. The music hall was at the height of its popularity. Drunkenness in public was still extremely common.

Between the wars the music hall died and the hey-day of the actor-managers in the theatre came to an end. Association Football developed as mass entertainment and dog-racing, the movies and the B.B.C. arrived. The public house declined somewhat as an attraction, partly perhaps owing to the 1921 licensing laws. After the war came television, which dealt a heavy blow at the popular cinema. But contrary to the prophets of doom, it raised, if anything, the general critical standards of the public towards acting and stimulated the output of plays. Never, not even in the eighteenth century, had there existed such a voracious patron for playwrights and plays, and television can claim at least some of the credit for the emergence of an exciting new school of writers in the fifties, such as Pinter, Wesker, Osborne and Simpson.

Unfortunately it was to prove less kind to its rival, sound radio, especially the B.B.C. Third Programme. This had been inaugurated in 1946 and was quickly accepted throughout the world as one of the finest of radio programmes, designed specifically for a small percentage of highly discerning listeners. It patronized plays, discussions and talks which might never have gained a hearing in more popular programmes, but which unfortunately were often quite expensive. In the 1950's this programme was to be severely axed as television costs continued to mount.

(iv) *Consumer goods.* Some changes in the pattern of living in the 1950's were developments of what had already begun in the 1930's: more motor-cars meant larger and faster roads, including the first motorway; the increasing production of labour-saving devices for the home meant a spread down the social scale of refrigerators and washing-machines, bought through hire-purchase, as well as the introduction of central heating which would end that early-morning chore of cleaning the grate; the development of the American-type chain-store meant particularly the spread of the self-service grocery with its packaged goods including now 'sliced bread'. The ending in 1955 of the B.B.C. television monopoly would introduce commercial advertising through television and with it a fierce debate on the rights and wrongs of such methods of mass persuasion. As industrial production and the standard of living rose, so too would the need for more power and water; hence the 1950's were to see the first atomic power station and numerous schemes up and down the country for water reservoirs to feed the great cities.

The Festival of Britain

We mentioned in Chapter 16 the important step which the government took during the war in taking state-sponsoring of the arts beyond the owning of galleries (the National Gallery was purchased by Parliament in 1824) and of museums (the British Museum dates from a Parliamentary grant of 1753). From 1945, through the Arts Council of Great Britain, this government patronage was continued and expanded. There were many who thought that the grants made were ludicrously small in comparison with government expenditure on defence, but at least some payment was made. It enabled some remarkable art exhibitions to be held; it ensured that Covent Garden Opera House was developed into one of the finest opera houses in the world; it helped, by judicious subsidies, to keep many amateur choirs and orchestras afloat.

In 1951 the government staged a Festival of Britain, whose aim was to encourage overseas visitors and to show something of what post-war Britain was capable. Practically every town and village staged something, the Arts Council supporting no less than 386 artistic events in England, 86 in Scotland and 44 in Wales. There were 22 Festivals of the Arts, one of the most enterprising being that of York.

The centre of the Festival was London. Part of the South Bank of the Thames, at that time a run-down, seedy survival from Victorian London, was cleared. The Festival Concert Hall was built and so were numerous temporary buildings, using new techniques and materials, in which were housed a variety of exhibitions. It was a triumph for the architects, who obtained startling effects, within very

The Festival site on the South Bank in London, 1951. Note the new architectural forms

limited space. At the same time in Battersea Park an enterprising fun-fair was built and there was staged an exhibition of Henry Moore's sculpture which was not this time tarred and feathered. There were numerous theatrical events in London, and in Manchester the Free Trade Hall was reopened. The Festival marked a triumph for the first ten years of the existence of C.E.M.A. and the Arts Council, which now received something like £1,000,000 a year from the Exchequer.

Medicine and the Health Service

Obviously there are many aspects of change which one might consider in a review of the first half of the twentieth century. Possibly none is more important than the achievements of medical science, even though in some ways the most important results of this progress have been seen less in Britain itself than in Asia and Africa, where it has resulted in vast rises in population. In Britain its result has been to make life easier and more pleasant and to raise somewhat one's chances of reaching pensionable age.

Some of the most dreaded diseases and scourges have been conquered. Surgery has learnt to perform miracles, especially in the field of brain surgery and plastic surgery, which recreated whole new exteriors to bodies mutilated by the Second World War. Research on blood revealed the existence of different blood groups (and in 1940 of the Rhesus factor) and the development of blood-banks, with their supplies of grouped blood, reduced the numbers of deaths from loss of blood during the Second World War and increased the scope of surgery; so too have developments in anaesthetics.

The advances in pharmaceutical medicine during the century have been perhaps the most startling; producing both drugs which prevent the development of a disease, as well as whole classes of drugs to fight diseases already contracted.

By 1939 immunization by innoculation with vaccine could be obtained against a whole series of diseases previously fatal, such as diphtheria, cholera, bubonic plague, tetanus, typhoid and yellow fever. Research against numerous intractable virus diseases such as poliomyelitis was to be carried on after the war, and the Salk vaccine perfected in the 1950's. The disease of malaria was defeated first by preventive measures against mosquito-breeding and then in the 1940's by the preventive drugs mepacrine and later paludrine, which prevent the disease developing. This has helped to make tropical Africa a possible future centre of civilization. The development of a class of drugs called anti-histamine drugs has enabled a number of previously intractable states to become curable, for example a number of allergies, and the discovery of insulin in 1922 made diabetes a disease no longer to be feared. During the pre-war period a number of nutritive diseases such as beri-beri, rickets and scurvy came to be understood, even though in many parts of the under-developed world they cannot be cured, owing to food shortages.

In 1935 came news of the effectiveness of a red chemical dye 'prontosil' against numerous streptococcal infections. This was followed by a whole group of sulphonamides such as sulphanilamide and sulphapyridine, by the action of which, for example, Churchill was cured during the war of two serious attacks of pneumonia. The antibiotic powers of the mould penicillin were first discovered in 1927–1928 by Fleming and they were developed by two pharmacologists, Chain and Florey, into a 'highly therapeutic agent' by the end of the war, capable of saving thousands of lives. Since then other antibiotics such as streptomycin, chloramphenicol and the tetracyelines have been isolated from various species of the fungus streptomyces. These are active against many kinds of bacteria which are not sensitive to penicillin.

Thus in one lifetime such diseases as tuberculosis, malaria and yellow fever, pneumonia and diabetes, leprosy and osteomyelitis, to name only a few, have all yielded to the work of the pharmacologists.

Considerable advances have been made in the study of mental health since the break-through by Sigmund Freud early in the century, but it is a subject about which there remains great ignorance.

Certain virus diseases continue to beat all the efforts of medical research and so, above all, does cancer, which continues to increase its number of victims, especially as medicine steadily increases the average length of life. Yet nothing has more increased the pleasure of living for more people in Britain than have the phenomenal advances made by medical research in all its fields, and it is almost impossible to realize just how ignorant in medicine men were a mere century ago. But, of course, such advances cost money.

Health Service charges

The government estimates of the likely cost of a National Health Service (made during the war and published in a White Paper in 1944) were £147,000,000. In its first year the Service actually cost £388,000,000, of which some £305,000,000 were borne by the Exchequer, £36,000,000 from National Health Insurance and the remainder from miscellaneous sources. By 1959 the total was £726,000,000 and still rising, due to the development and expansion of the hospital service as well as to the increased drug bill. It was to help defray some of these costs that Mr Gaitskell in 1951 introduced part payment for spectacles and dentures, a slight economy, saving some £5,000,000. The 1952 budget of Mr Butler was to impose a 1*s* per prescription payment, a charge of up to £1 for dental treatment for all over twenty-one, except expectant mothers, and increased payments for spectacles and dentures. These charges saved another £11,000,000. In 1957 the 1*s* per prescription charge became a 1*s* charge per item, while the rate of insurance contributions was doubled. These increased charges saved another £6,000,000 a year. In 1961 there were to be further increases which raised another £13,000,000 on the previous year 1960–1961. Under these, prescription charges were to rise from 1*s* to 2*s* per item; denture and spectacle charges were to be raised again; health clinic orange juice, cod-liver oil and vitamins were all to cost more. At the same time contributions from National Insurance were again to be raised by 1*s* per week (10*d* for the employee and 2*d* for the employer).

In 1949, 2,900,000 in-patients passed through hospitals; in 1959, 4,000,000. Of course, the service cost more but the vast majority were willing to make their contribution that so excellent a service could continue to expand.

Trade unions

One of the most important changes to have taken place in our period is in the power and position of the trade unions. In 1906 they finally won legal powers to strike, but at that time many of the leaders of the movement, if not the rank and file, were militant Marxist Syndicalists who equated government with the employer class and thought of their job as one to devise the best ways of fighting these powers. Gradually things changed. In the 1914–1918 war, the government sought trade-union help and co-operation. Although later deterioration led to the General Strike of 1926, new patterns began to emerge from 1927 onwards, with trade unionists coming on to the planning side of industry. Slowly their whole attitude began to change. At the same time, careers in trade-union administration began to attract men with administrative ability who had never worked their way up from the bottom, as the earlier leaders did. So many of the basic demands of the trade unions for greater social welfare having become accepted by all parties, the political cohesion of the movement began to come to an end.

Some features of trade unionism in the 1950's were to be: an increasing apathy and distrust by rank and file of the official leaders of many unions; a number of unions allowing their executives to become controlled by Communists; the occurrence of a number of unofficial strikes, which reflected lack of contact between the rank and file and the leaders; a number of strikes resulting from quarrels between unions, for example over questions of demarcation between unions. It was clear that the movement was divided on whether it wished for further socialization, while at the same time it lost many leaders who accepted posts on public corporations partly through salary inducements. The largest unions dominated the T.U.C. and the Labour Party Conference. At the same time only 184 trade unions were affiliated to the T.U.C. in 1959. One reason why more had not joined may have been the long connection of the Congress with the Labour Party. A problem of the future is certainly going to be the growth of the so-called white-collar trade unions and the shrinkage of what are called in the U.S.A. the blue-collar unions (manual workers), as automation and industralization continue to develop.

Nationalized Boards

During the half-century various public corporations came into being: for example the Port of London Authority, the B.B.C., the British Transport Commission, the National Coal Board. There was great diversity in their organization and also in the degree and methods of government control.

The essence of a nationalized industry is that it provides an important service, for example, power, transport or entertainment, on a non-profit-making basis. It should be financially self-supporting, although perhaps in need of government finance for heavy programmes of modernization. Centralization makes possible effective planning, capital development, research, marketing and standardization. But it can also lead to excessive interference by bureaucracy and hence to frustration. All such industries have to try to find a balance between centralization and managerial decentralization. As party politics went out of these industries in the 1950's, so were they more able to sort themselves out.

Society and Education

Britain faced the second half of the twentieth century in a mood in many ways far healthier than at the beginning. There was less wealth, but it was more evenly distributed. There was less poverty, less drunkenness, but better housing and more education. There was less hypocrisy, if also less church-going. There was a greater popular appreciation of the arts. Above all, there was less class hatred, if still plenty of class ambition. The great fear of a social cataclysm in which the 'proletariat' or 'artisan class' would overthrow the social order (a fear at least as old as the seventeenth century) had gradually subsided and the anonymous face of the man in the crowd no longer threatened violence. More probably it reflected social ambition and a search for status for himself and his children. In a highly competitive society, which Britain remained in spite of the welfare provided by the state, this meant qualifications. For many parents education in the 1950's was not an end in itself but a means to the end of 'getting ahead': children were crammed for the eleven-plus in order to scramble into a grammar school; once there they must reach the sixth form and then squeeze into a university, in order to gain the qualification which would enable them 'to succeed'. Alternatively their parents might somehow find the money to finance ten years of preparatory and public-school education for its continuing class appeal. By 1961 critics were arguing that the whole educational system was wasteful of ability, encouraging class-consciousness and retarding Britain's attempts to come to terms with the second half of the twentieth century. One solution offered by some and opposed by others was a comprehensive system of education from primary to university level, with a vast expansion scheme for the latter. Social critics have been blaming education for society's evils, while seeking their solution through educational reform, for as long as civilization has existed and in mid-twentieth-century Britain there is no lack of such critics. Unfortunately education costs money and if Britain is to solve her remaining social problems by further improved education she must first solve her financial and economic problems to provide the necessary means.

"Must I Teach You Another Lesson, Children?"

A cartoon by Vicky pleading for world understanding

Ten pocket biographies

Henry Herbert Asquith (1852–1928)

First Earl of Oxford and Asquith

He was the second son of Joseph Asquith, a nonconformist Yorkshire wool-spinner and weaver, and he was educated at the City of London School, from which he won a scholarship to Balliol College, Oxford. Its famous master, Jowett, predicted a brilliant career for him, and he soon became established as a London barrister with sufficient savings in 1886 to consider entering Parliament. He was elected that year and in 1888 devoted himself to helping Parnell clear his name of implication in the Phoenix Park murders. In 1892 he became Home Secretary in Mr Gladstone's last government. After its fall he attacked Chamberlain's policy which led up to the Boer War of 1899–1902, yet he supported the war itself, unlike his party leader, Campbell-Bannerman. In December 1905 he became Chancellor of the Exchequer, and was determined to maintain Free Trade. He introduced old-age pensions in 1908, although he had suddenly, on 6 April, become Prime Minister on Campbell-Bannerman's retirement. He showed himself a cabinet chairman of great skill and had the full support of King George V in the crisis of 1911.

Over the three pre-war problems of industrial unrest, women's suffrage and Ireland, however, he gave little lead, and was opposed at all times to the use of violence. He was vaguely sympathetic with the demands of industrial workers; he genuinely believed that women would lose rather than gain by direct participation in politics; over the Irish problem it seems difficult to excuse him from the charge of vacillation, in that Sir Edward Carson and the Unionists were allowed to build up their private army unchallenged.

On the question of entry into war in 1914 he made the following points in cabinet: Great Britain has no obligation towards either France or Russia; but she is tied by friendship to France; if the latter were wiped out as a great power, Britain would suffer; Britain cannot allow Germany the use of the Channel ports; Britain has an obligation to Belgium. Thus he believed Britain should enter, without having any idea how long the war would last. He was very disappointed that peace did not follow the First Battle of the Marne in September 1914.

The failure of the Dardanelles venture early in 1915 led to his forming a Coalition government. In 1916, after the Dublin rising, he wanted to introduce Home Rule at once, but was prevented by the Conservatives in his cabinet. He had accepted conscription in 1916 with great reluctance. At the same time all criticism over the Battle of the Somme was directed at Asquith, who loyally supported and covered up for colleagues and service chiefs.

During the year a dispute had developed between him and Lloyd George, Bonar Law and the Conservatives, over the creation of an effective War Cabinet. The Conservative newspapers became highly critical of his leadership and the Conservative ministers threatened to resign if he did not reconstruct his government. Lloyd George did in fact resign, whereupon Asquith decided to follow. Lloyd George, with the support of Bonar Law, Balfour, the Conservatives and Labour formed his government, which Asquith refused to join. The split was widened in May 1918 by the 'Maurice Debate', over General Sir Frederick Maurice's charges that Haig had been dangerously weakened by the shortage of troops under his command at the time of the German offensive in March 1918. Lloyd George never forgave Asquith for attacking him in this debate. At the 'Coupon Election' he was branded as 'the man who had conspired against the government' and he lost his seat. He was not invited to Versailles.

He attacked the Black and Tan methods in Ireland, but in 1923 the quarrel between the two leaders was officially

A caricature of Asquith and MacDonald by Will Dyson, 1913. The left wing of the Labour movement disliked MacDonald for his moderate views

patched over. He led the Liberal Party which supported the Labour government of 1924, but again lost his seat in the election of October 1924. The quarrel with Lloyd George reopened, particularly over the Lloyd George Trust Fund (money obtained in the days of the Coalition for sale of honours). He resigned his party leadership in 1926 and died on 15 February 1928, having been made a peer by George V in 1925. He was a man of great ability and integrity who devoted his life to 'government of the people', but who never perhaps completely accepted the democratic methods necessary for 'government by the people'.

David Lloyd George (1863–1945)

First Earl Lloyd George of Dwyfor

Born in Manchester, he was brought up, on the death of his schoolmaster father, by his uncle, Richard Lloyd, in Llanystumdwy, Caernarvonshire. He was educated at a village school and then articled as a solicitor's clerk. He passed his law finals in 1884 with honours and won a reputation in Criccieth as an able lawyer, a staunch Baptist and an opponent of the established Church of Wales. In 1889 he entered the new County Council politics and a year later won a Parliamentary by-election, aged twenty-seven. One of his early causes, the disestablishment of the Church of Wales, was defeated by the House of Lords in 1895.

He tended always to support small nations and regarded the Boer War as a national crime, having to escape from an angry crowd on one occasion disguised as a policeman. He entered the Liberal government of December 1905 as President of the Board of Trade and was responsible for a number of important Acts. In 1908 he succeeded Asquith as Chancellor of the Exchequer and his People's Budget of 1909, with its land values tax (abandoned in 1920), precipitated a crisis with the House of Lords. Lloyd George, embittered by that House's treatment of many Liberal reforms in 1893–1895, as well as more recently, determined to reduce its powers. The Parliament Act of 1911 was followed by the National Health and Unemployment Insurance Scheme and the disestablishment of the Church of Wales.

In 1912–1913 he was involved in a financial scandal concerned with his purchase of shares in the American Marconi Company, but he survived. He supported Home Rule for Ireland and deplored Asquith's handling of the crisis in 1914. He supported Britain's entry into war in that year, particularly as it was to help a threatened small nation. His budget of November 1914 doubled income tax and introduced paper money to replace sovereigns.

In 1915 he quarrelled with the General Staff, supporting Churchill's aim of attacking 'the enemy where he is weakest' by 'a policy of side-shows', for example Gallipoli. But in May 1915 he became Minister of Munitions in the new government, showing great energy, mobilizing the chemical industry and persuading the trade unions to accept women in industry. On 6 July 1916 he replaced Kitchener as Secretary for War and at once clashed with the generals, particularly the C.I.G.S., Sir William Robertson. Following Asquith's resignation, Lloyd George became Prime Minister on 7 December 1916. He created a small War Cabinet with a large secretariat, and several new ministries, for example Food, Labour and Shipping. He wanted the Allied plans to be co-ordinated, from France to Mesopotamia; but he was not even to see a supreme commander in France until 1918, while complete co-ordination was never achieved. After Passchendaele and Caporetto in the autumn of 1917 he had great problems. These increased with the 1918 German offensive begun on 21 March. On 7 May Asquith proposed his enquiry into the conduct of the war, which Lloyd George regarded as a stab in the back at a time of high casualties, food shortages and air-raids. He worked desperately to rally the country until the successful Allied offensive began in August 1918. It led to victory, which was followed by the 'Coupon Election', revealing the fatal split in the Liberal Party.

Lloyd George's methods in Paris helped to build a bridge between the idealism of Wilson and the hard realism of Clemenceau. He was anxious to see European trade and industry restarted 'if only to prevent the spread of Bolshevism', although he kept a sense of proportion about the latter. He obtained a trade agreement with Russia in March 1921 and in July started negotiations with the Sinn Fein in Ireland. But the Black and Tan methods had counted against him and so did the assassination of Sir Henry Wilson by Sinn Feiners in London in June 1922. The Irish Treaty of 1921, the Chanak crisis and a scandal over the sale of honours caused his downfall. His own attitude to honours was that they were meaningless and that if people were foolish enough to want to buy them he would not stop them.

During the 1920's he used the Lloyd George Trust Fund to finance research on such problems as unemployment, coal, roads and land-ownership. He was not a socialist, but thought public utilities and social services should be provided by public-controlled corporations, the first of which he had created as the Port of London Authority. He supported J. M. Keynes's ideas of expansionist remedies for unemployment, but none of this helped him to win votes.

In the 1930's he handed the leadership of the party to Sir Herbert Samuel. He farmed in Surrey, wrote memoirs and formed a small independent Liberal Party of himself, his son, his daughter and his son's brother-in-law. He had opposed French militarism in the 1920's and believed the Versailles Treaty had been unfair to Germany, but from 1936 onwards he attacked the policy of appeasement towards Germany. In 1940 he refused a cabinet post, accepted an earldom in 1945, but died in March of that year. A man of enormous energy and charm, with a quick wit and very retentive memory, he was not without ideals. The small nation, the poor, the oppressed and world peace were all causes for which he was prepared to fight. Distrusted by the Conservatives, yet opposed to socialism, it was in many ways a tragedy that he never wielded effective power again after 1922.

Ramsay MacDonald (1866–1937)

Of all the twentieth-century prime ministers, he came from the humblest origins. He was born at Lossiemouth, Morayshire, the son of Anne Ramsay and John Macdonald, a ploughman: his parents never married. His mother somehow found the 8*d* a month needed for school at Drainie, where at sixteen he became a pupil teacher. In 1885 he went to Bristol to find work, but his health broke down and he had for a while to return to Scotland. He moved to London where he was extremely poor for a while, living on oatmeal sent from home and earning no more than 10*s* a week. He joined the Birkbeck Institute, to study science in the evenings, and also the Fabian Society. He became private secretary to Thomas Lough, a Gladstonian Liberal M.P., and in 1895 himself began to stand for Parliament, for the Independent Labour Party. In 1896 he made a very happy marriage; his wife, Mary Gladstone, being the daughter of a wealthy London scientist and philanthropist, a founder of the Y.M.C.A. and also an F.R.S. From now on financial matters ceased to worry MacDonald and foreign travel and public affairs took all his time, while his family home became a centre of Fabian activities. In 1900 he became secretary of the Labour Representation Committee, which changed its name to the Labour Party in 1906, when he was elected to Parliament for Leicester.

The death of his wife in 1911 was a terrible blow to him. From now on he began to be accused of remoteness and of distant behaviour, which sprang partly in fact from a certain social shyness. During the First World War he became the victim of violent abuse. Although he said that 'those who can enlist ought to enlist, those who are working in munition factories should do so whole-heartedly', he was mercilessly smeared by the press as pro-German and a pacifist; he was portrayed as 'all that the average citizen dislikes and mistrusts most'. He was defeated in the 'Coupon Election' of 1918, 'the most unpopular man in England'.

But he now came under attack from the Communist Party, who called him only 'lukewarm', and public opinion swung back to his favour. In 1922 he was elected to Parliament again, became the leader of the Parliamentary Labour Party and, in January 1924, Prime Minister and Foreign Secretary.

His aim was to reduce world tension. He succeeded in reducing that between France and Germany; launched the Dawes Plan; drew up the abortive Geneva Protocol; but fell from office because his efforts to improve relations with Russia were suspect.

He was not enthusiastic about the General Strike in 1926, being always opposed to violence and extremism and in 1929 he formed his second government. He was active in seeking disarmament and chaired the first Indian Round Table Conference in 1930. His cabinet split in 1931 on the economic measures to be taken against the flight of capital from London and he formed the National government. He ceased to lead the Labour Party and was accused of yielding to the 'aristocratic embrace'.

Believing as he did in disarmament, he was reluctant to agree to the need for 'appeasement with rearmament'. Yet he helped to draft the vital White Paper on Defence in 1935. He resigned as Prime Minister in that year and from the government in 1937, dying in November. A charming, sensitive man, it was said of him that with increasing power he became more and more autocratic and intolerant, but this may have been unfair. Certainly he drifted far from his humble origins, developing a profound interest in and knowledge of literature and the arts. Probably no other Labour figure could have made the Labour Party as acceptable to public opinion as he did in his two periods of office.

Stanley Baldwin (1867–1947)

First Earl Baldwin of Bewdley

He was born in Bewdley in Worcestershire, son of a well-to-do iron-founding family, and was educated at Harrow and Cambridge. On the death of his father he entered Parliament for the Bewdley division of Worcestershire in 1908. Bonar Law was a friend of the family and in 1916 Baldwin became his Parliamentary Private Secretary. In 1917 he became joint Financial Secretary to the Treasury and in 1919 he gave 20% of his personal fortune (some £150,000) to the nation for cancellation of the War Debt and urged others to do the same.

He entered the Coalition cabinet in 1921 as President of

the Board of Trade, but felt 'inarticulate and uncomfortable' in this cabinet of 'first-class brains' whose apparent levity seems to have shocked him. Lloyd George he found a dynamic force which might 'crush you, but it is not necessarily right'. He therefore supported Bonar Law and the Conservative Party revolt in October 1922. He became Chancellor of the Exchequer, and when Bonar Law resigned in the spring of 1923 he succeeded him as Prime Minister, determined to be 'English instead of Welsh; plain instead of brilliant'. His apparent plainness and provincialism certainly won him popular approval.

He believed that protection was necessary in 1923, calling a surprise general election, even though this cost him his office for a year. He returned as Prime Minister in October 1924, head of a united Conservative Party. He dedicated himself to 'binding together all classes of our people', and, in spite of the General Strike in May 1926, there is some evidence that he helped towards that reduction in class hatreds, which began in the late 1920's. In 1926 he presided over the historic Imperial Conference, from which developed the 1931 Statute of Westminister, and he supported the Simon Commission's recommendations that India acquire Dominion status. Although defeated in the election of 1929, his personal popularity, 'trusted and acceptable', remained.

He became Lord President of the Council in August 1931. After the Ottawa Conference, when all the Free Traders left the National Government, it was dominated by the Conservative Party which he led. At a time of strong pacifist feeling in the country Baldwin faced a genuine dilemma on the question of defence in these years. Heavy rearmament was delayed until March 1936, the year of the death of George V, the Rhineland occupation, the fall of Abyssinia, rioting in Palestine and the Civil War in Spain. He was ordered to rest by his doctors this year, but in the abdication crisis he asserted his solid provincial respectability and obliged the King to give way. In May 1937 he retired and accepted an earldom. His popularity had been waning during the decade and he was to be increasingly blamed for Britain's failures, especially at the time of the air-raids of 1940–1941 (the Blitz).

A sincerely religious man and a skilful party manager, he held a united party together from 1924 to his retirement and made a definite contribution towards achieving his aim of 'taking the bitterness out of political life'. He lived through the war, but took no part, being in his last years the victim of much popular abuse and misunderstanding.

A. Neville Chamberlain (1869–1940)

The eldest child and only son of Joseph Chamberlain by his second wife, he was not at first destined for politics at all. Educated at Rugby School, he went briefly to an accountant's office and then to the West Indies to manage unsuccessfully a family estate in the Bahamas. He returned in 1897 and entered Birmingham city politics, specializing in health questions. In 1917 he became Director-general of National Service for Labour in Industry, but after seven months he returned to Birmingham, having been given inadequate powers and incurring the dislike of Lloyd George.

In 1918 he entered the House of Commons, aged nearly fifty, supporting the Coalition but refusing to serve under Lloyd George. He supported the Carlton Club revolt of 1922 and became Paymaster-General, Minister of Health and Chancellor of the Exchequer in quick succession. In October 1924 he was offered the Exchequer again, but preferred the Ministry of Health, being very interested in housing and local government problems. He showed great ability in handling the Rating and Valuation Act of 1925 and the Local Government Act of 1929, which recast the financial relations between national and local government. His department was responsible for building nearly 1,000,000 houses in four and a half years.

Chamberlain opposed the 'Safety First' Conservative election policy in 1929 but in 1931 returned to the Ministry of Health; then in November he became Chancellor of the

Exchequer. He showed great skill in handling problems of imperial trade, war debts and reparations, and in 1932 introduced a 10% general tariff. At the same time a low bank rate made money cheap for loans, thus stimulating building; but he did not favour a wide programme of public works as adopted by President Roosevelt in the U.S.A.

From 1935 he took an active part in foreign affairs. The 1936 budget provided £1,500,000,000 for defence, in accordance with the now accepted rearmament programme. In 1937 he succeeded Baldwin as Prime Minister, and, believing that peace could not be kept without the co-operation of Hitler and Mussolini, he established contact with both. He was more successful with the latter, who, after Eden's resignation in February 1938, agreed to conversations, since in spite of his Axis Pact he was alarmed at Hitler's expansionist aims in South-East Europe.

France was allied to both Czechoslovakia and Poland, but the French were very unsure and Chamberlain did not believe that they could would intervene in Eastern Europe. At the same time he believed British opinion would not support a British venture there either and so he sought to appease rather than oppose German aims in Austria and Czechoslovakia. The crisis over the latter in September 1938 was felt at the time to have been ably handled by Chamberlain: he was praised in Parliament for averting war, general criticism only coming later. In November 1938 a violent anti-Jewish pogrom in Germany occurred and Chamberlain pressed on with rearmament and civil defence.

After March 1939 his policy hardened, following the siezure of Prague. Appeasement had been 'wantonly shattered', he said in his Birmingham speech and on 31 March Britain joined France in guaranteeing Poland's frontiers, and followed by guaranteeing those of Greece and Turkey. The Polish guarantee however really depended on Russian help and the Poles were determined to avoid this if possible; so it seemed were the British. Negotiations with Russia made no progress and on 21 August 1939 the news was announced of the Russo-German pact. Chamberlain still made desperate efforts, but it was too late and Poland was invaded on 1 September. On 3 September he announced that Britain was at war. There was apparently no plan of attack and there was virtually no fighting on the Franco-German front while Poland was extinguished. After the unsuccessful expedition to Norway in April 1940 the government's majority fell to eighty-one. On 10 May Chamberlain resigned, but joined the new government, which he served until shortly before his death in November 1940.

His real political interests were in social reform. Although increasingly involved in foreign affairs, it was more from a sense of duty than from interest or profound knowledge. He seems to have been a forceful and determined personality who fought hard for peace; so hard that when Britain finally went to war all were united in believing it both just and necessary.

Churchill forms his Coalition Cabinet; Churchill, Attlee, Chamberlain, Eden and Bevin are here included

Ernest Bevin (1881-1951)

Born at Winsford, Somerset, and an orphan when seven years old, he went to Bristol to find work. He earned 1*s* a day in a restaurant, became a van-boy and then a van-driver. He educated himself and became the champion of Bristol's unemployed in the days before government relief. He soon concentrated his interests on the dockers, still one of the worst paid and most hazardous forms of unskilled labour. At twenty he was a paid Dockers' Union official and in 1913 became assistant national organizer of the Dockers' Union. In 1916 he joined the government's Port and Transit Commission, but in 1919 the dockers, no longer under government supervision, clashed with the employers and Bevin brilliantly conducted their case for a wage increase before a government tribunal, earning the title of the Dockers' K.C. In 1920 he spoke in an interview with Lloyd George on behalf of the Trade Union Council of Action against the government's proposed support of Poland's war against Soviet Russia, which happily ended soon after at the Treaty of Riga.

He now created the giant National Transport and General Workers' Union out of thirty-two separate unions, and was its secretary from 1921 until 1940. In 1921 he reluctantly supported the decision of the Triple Alliance not to support the miners' strike, a decision which caused much bitterness. He was one of the leading unionists seeking an honourable solution to the General Strike in 1926 and afterwards he supported the crucial talks of 1927–1928 between the T.U.C and powerful groups of industrialists led by Sir Alfred Mond, resulting in a greatly improved industrial atmosphere. He was also a member of the joint employers/unions mission to the U.S.A. in 1927, and sat on the Macmillan Commission on finance just before the depression. In all this he was seeking to break down the simple class division of employee v. employer, inherited from early nineteenth-century capitalism but now no longer applicable. In the

1930's he was an active supporter of the I.L.O. in Geneva, one of the most successful League of Nations organizations, which the United Nations took over.

In May 1940 he became Minister of Labour and National Service and later joined the War Cabinet. He organized man-power to make Britain in 1943 the most highly mobilized of the belligerent countries. His influence in keeping industrial strife to a minimum in the war was decisive.

In July 1945 he became Foreign Secretary, having been keenly interested in the problems involved through most of the war. He obtained peace treaties with Italy, Bulgaria, Roumania, Hungary and Finland but, deeply mistrusting the Russian post-war behaviour, he began to work for a system of alliances among the Western nations. Bevin wanted an association of sovereign states from America and Europe, such as developed as N.A.T.O., but he treated schemes for European Union with suspicion. Thus, though he deplored visas and passports, he was no enthusiast for the Council of Europe. At the same time he was strongly criticized for his failure to find a peaceful solution in Palestine. The prospect of a shipload of Jews returning to Europe in 1945 shocked many and Bevin was accused by both sides of breaking his word. But fundamentally the Palestine problem had been insoluble ever since the Balfour Declaration of 1917, unless Arabs would accept returning Jews. Even though Israel came into being, it has remained in a state of cold war with the rest of the Arab states.

In 1950 Bevin launched the Colombo Plan, following a Commonwealth Foreign Ministers' Conference; but ill-health forced him to resign in March 1951. He was a realist and an optimist. Having seen in his lifetime the end of violence in Britain's industrial disputes, he always hoped the same thing was possible in international affairs. He lost the support of the extremists in his own party when Foreign Secretary, but won that of the great majority of the country, who regarded him with affection and with confidence, as he strove to solve the great problems of the post-war and Cold War years.

Aneurin Bevan (1897–1960)

Born one of thirteen children at Tredegar, Monmouthshire, the son of a coal-miner of traditional Welsh Baptist background, he worked in the mines from the age of thirteen for seven years. His father was a socialist and founder of Tredegar Working Mens' Medical Aid Society. He ignored his call-up papers in 1916, never believing in the Kaiser's War, and having become an active trade unionist. He now

During the war, Aneurin Bevan continually criticized Churchill's coalition government and was only with difficulty persuaded to toe the party line

contracted a disease, nystagmus, which prevented further underground work and he was sent by his union to London to study for two years at the Central Labour College. Returning to Wales after the war, he found it impossible to obtain work due to his active socialist views; but he was forced on a colliery by his union as a check-weighman. He was now elected to his local Urban District Council and to the Council of the South Wales Miners' Federation.

He actively supported the General Strike in 1926 and was elected a County Councillor in 1928. Next year he entered Parliament for Ebbw Vale and during the 1930's spoke regularly on miners' questions. He was expelled from the Labour Party for a few months in 1939 for his support of Sir Stafford Cripps's Popular Front movement of Socialists, Liberals and Communists; but he and Cripps were re-admitted after the war began. In the later years of the war he was a consistent critic of the government, acting particularly as a watch-dog for individual liberties, always in danger at such times. In 1944 he challenged the Defence Regulation IAa which imposed heavy penalties for strikes in 'essential' industries. He was required by the Labour Party to give written assurance of loyalty, which he did.

In 1945 he became Minister of Health and was responsible for the various acts of legislation already discussed (Chapter 17). He was loyal to his Prime Minister, Attlee, but never seems to have established deep mutual understanding with him. He wrote regularly for the left-wing periodical *Tribune*, which was often highly critical of the government. As a colourful figure of extreme views he was anathema to the Conservative press, who, to use one example, turned his description of nineteenth-century Welsh coal-owners as 'lower than vermin' into a general attack against the whole middle class.

In January 1951 he became Minister of Labour, but resigned in April, owing to the health charges. He became leader of a dissident group of 'Bevanites' who published a pamphlet *Going our Way* and who forcefully attacked the Labour Party's support of the new government's foreign policy. He was to be nearly expelled again from the Labour Party, but from 1956 was to establish better relations with Mr Gaitskell, even reversing his opinion of H-bombs, which he now considered necessary, to prevent a Foreign Minister walking 'naked into the conference room'. He became deputy leader of the Labour Party before contracting cancer and dying at the early age of sixty-three.

His was a warm and generous personality, full of personal charm. He had a wide knowledge of literature and the arts and it was said of him 'he loved the good things of life and there were few things on which he could not talk with considerable knowledge and none on which he could not talk attractively'. He was no demagogue and, contrary to popular opinion, he neither enjoyed nor was good at public speaking. But in the House of Commons it was said that he had only one rival for brilliance of repartee, and that was Winston Churchill.

Clement Attlee (1883–   )

First Earl Attlee

Born in Putney, he was educated at Haileybury and University College, Oxford, where he was a conservative in politics. Through working at Haileybury House with boys of the Stepney slums, he became interested in social problems and influenced by the writings of William Morris and John Ruskin. He was called to the bar in 1905, became a socialist, in 1910 secretary of Toynbee Hall (a social centre in the East End of London) and in 1913 a lecturer at the London School of Economics. He joined the army when war broke out and reached the rank of major, serving at Gallipoli. After the war he returned to academic work; became Mayor of Stepney in 1919; and entered Parliament in 1922, as Labour M.P. for the Limehouse division of Stepney.

He became Parliamentary Secretary to Ramsay MacDonald and in 1924 and 1929 held minor offices. He was a member of the Simon Commission on India and became Deputy Leader of the Opposition in 1931 under Lansbury, whom he succeeded in 1935. Over the Spanish Civil War he at first supported the Republican government; going to Spain, he was very impressed with the government troops led by Miaja. He was convinced that without Fascist foreign intervention the Republic could have survived without going Communist and he therefore felt the British government should have taken a stronger line against foreign intervention.

He opposed the diplomatic efforts of 1937–1939 to establish closer relations with Italy; yet he also opposed the efforts of Sir Stafford Cripps in these years to establish his 'popular front'. At the beginning of the war he remained in opposition until May 1940, when he became Lord Privy Seal, Vice-Chairman of the War Cabinet and Leader of the House of Commons. In 1942 he became deputy Prime Minister and Secretary of State for the Dominions. In April 1945 he took part in the founding of the United Nations and in July was at Potsdam, when he learnt of his Party's victory. He returned to the conference on 28 July with Ernest Bevin as his Foreign Secretary.

In November 1945 he travelled to Washington to try to persuade President Truman to arrange for the continuation of joint research in atomic and rocket projects. Being unsuccessful, in spite of British research which had made the atomic bombs possible, he decided on the need for a separate British research programme.

There were two grave dangers in 1945: famine in Europe and revolution in the Empire. World food production in 1945–1946 was 12% below that of 1939. He urged the U.S.A. and Australia to help, while rationing bread in Britain in July 1946 (never rationed in the war) and maintaining other food rationing, in order to aid Europe. His other great decision was to grant self-government to much of the Empire at once. Over India he was actively and constantly engaged from 1945 until the passing of the India Independence Act of 1947, taking personal responsibility for the appointment of Mountbatten as last Viceroy and for the time-table of withdrawal. The danger of massacre had been rising in India for some time. There is some ground for believing that the death-roll would have been higher not lower if independence and partition had not come when they did.

In 1947 during the sustained fuel and financial crisis,

Sir Stafford Cripps seems for a while to have lost confidence in him and to have tried to make Bevin his successor. But Attlee survived and never lost the friendship of either man, a considerable personal feat. Cripps became Chancellor of the Exchequer and the government ran its course.

After the 1950 election Attlee again went to Washington in December to persuade President Truman against provoking a major with war China by using atomic bombs in the Korean struggle. This time he was successful and thus helped to avert a third world war.

Early in 1951 he developed a duodenal ulcer and had to enter hospital. With Cripps and Bevin dying, he still hoped to avert a split in his cabinet, but this illness prevented him and he decided instead on a second general election. He resigned when the result was published and became Leader of the Opposition, accepting a peerage in 1955. He is a brilliant co-ordinator and showed a masterly skill during his ten years in senior cabinet office. As a leader he held his colleagues together, particularly when under criticism, and he was a master at getting government committees to work to some purpose.

R. Anthony Eden (1899–   )

First Earl of Avon

Born in County Durham, the son of Sir William Eden, he was educated at Eton, from where he joined the King's Royal Rifle Corps in France in September 1915. At twenty he was a brigade major and had won the M.C. He then went to Oxford, where he read Persian and Arabic, taking no obvious interest in politics. He stood for Parliament, unsuccessfully in November 1922 and successfully at the next election in 1923 for Warwick and Leamington. He became the Parliamentary Secretary of Austen Chamberlain and thus gained his interest in foreign affairs. On the formation of the National government in 1931 he became

Under-Secretary of State for Foreign Affairs under Lord Reading. In 1932 he led the British delegation to the Geneva disarmament conference and in 1934, when only thirty-seven, he became Lord Privy Seal. He was seconded to the Foreign Office, under Sir John Simon, a curious and unprecedented arrangement. He was active in 1934 at Geneva, among other things trying to heal a rift between Italy and Yugoslavia over the assassination of King Alexander of Yugoslavia, while on a state visit to France. He now became Minister without Portfolio for League of Nations Affairs and was busy in all the capitals of Europe, meeting Hitler, Stalin, Pilsudski and other European politicians. In Italy he offered Mussolini a possible compromise solution for his African ambitions, but without success. Mussolini at this time seems to have been apprehensive of Hitler and the Stresa Pact, although Eden was unwell at the time of the actual conference. After the British-German Naval Pact later in 1935, Eden travelled to France and Italy, trying to restore confidence in Britain's Foreign Secretary, Sir Samuel Hoare. The latter resigned over the Hoare-Laval Pact and Eden succeeded him, expected by all 'to uphold the League and the cause of collective security'. After the German occupation of the Rhineland it became Chamberlain's basic policy to seek to detach Mussolini from his German agreement of 1936. Eden at first supported the policy of 'economic and political appeasement', one result of which was the successful ending in 1937 of pirate sinkings in the Mediterranean, but he would not support appeasement if it meant allowing the 'impression to gain currency abroad that we yield to constant pressure'. He therefore resigned in February 1938.

He rejoined Chamberlain's Government in September 1939 as Dominions Secretary, became Secretary for War in May 1940 and Foreign Secretary again in December 1940, when Lord Halifax went to Washington as ambassador. He attended conferences throughout the war, especially after Britain ceased to stand alone: for example in Moscow, Cairo, Washington, Teheran. In 1942 he signed a twenty-year peace treaty with the U.S.S.R. and he was deeply involved in the steps leading to the San Francisco conference and the United Nations.

After the defeat of the Conservatives in 1945, he became Deputy Leader of the Opposition and in 1951 Foreign Secretary again, in Churchill's last government. He inherited vast problems: in the Middle East the Persian oil dispute; and in the Far East the Korean War. The ending of this war in 1953 and of the Indo-Chinese War a year later owed much to his skill. In 1955 he was to become Prime Minister and to take part in a 'summit conference' at Geneva. But ill-health was now increasingly to plague him. Problems of Middle East oil and Egyptian nationalism were to lead to a decision to challenge the Egyptian nationalization of the Suez Canal (July 1956). This nationalization had led to war between Israel and Egypt, who refused passage to Israeli ships. Britain and France decided to intervene, although condemned by the U.S.A. and the United Nations. At this point Eden's health was to collapse and he was to undergo a series of operations. He resigned in January 1957 and embarked on a prolonged convalescence. His career is still a controversial one. But all seem agreed that as a negotiator he was highly skilled, both during the war and when at the height of his powers 1951–1956, before being struck down by ill-health.

Sir Winston Churchill, O.M. (1874–1965)

He was born at Blenheim Palace, the first son of Lord Randolph Churchill (himself the third son of the sixth Duke of Marlborough) and of Jennie Jerome, an American heiress. He was educated at Harrow and Sandhurst, joining the 4th Hussars in 1895. He managed to be seconded to a Cuban civil war in 1896, returning with a taste for cigars, and the habit of a siesta and the Spanish Order of Military Merit. Next he was posted to India, where he fought on the North-West frontier and first began to read widely. In

1898 he was posted to Egypt where, under Kitchener, he fought in the battle of Omdurman, taking part in one of the last cavalry charges in history and sending home dispatches to the London *Morning Post*. He now resigned his commission, lost a Parliamentary by-election, and went out to the Boer War in 1899 as war correspondent for the same paper. Here he had many adventures, including capture, escape and joining in the relief of Ladysmith. In 1900 he returned to England and was elected Conservative M.P. for Oldham.

He attacked the government's army policy and on the question of Free Trade decided in 1904 to join the Liberals in opposition, beginning his long association with Lloyd George. In 1906 he was Under-Secretary of State for the Colonies in the new Liberal government and entered the cabinet in 1908, as President of the Board of Trade, two years later becoming Home Secretary. He conducted the siege of Sidney Street and handled the syndicalist strikes with vigour, before going in 1911 to the Admiralty, where he was responsible for continuing the naval expansion and beginning the change from coal to oil. In 1913 he offered Germany a year's 'naval holiday' but was unsuccessful. In July 1914 there was a trial mobilization of the navy. Afterwards, Churchill and the First Sea Lord, Prince Louis of Battenburg (father of Lord Louis Mountbatten), kept the fleets at sea. On 4 August he signalled, 'Commence hostilities against Germany.'

In the early months of the war he concerned himself with two new weapons: tanks and aeroplanes, the Royal Flying Corps having been founded in 1912 partly by his efforts. In October 1914 he personally organized the defence of Antwerp and in November recalled Fisher to replace Battenburg (compelled to retire because of his German origin). After the failure of the Dardanelles scheme, Fisher resigned and the Conservatives refused to join a coalition unless Churchill left the Admiralty. He became Chancellor of the Duchy of Lancaster and then in the autumn of 1915 went to France as commanding officer of the 6th Royal Scots Fusiliers. He seems to have been one of the few who enjoyed his winter in the trenches, constantly challenging the Germans opposite to minor skirmishes and exterminating the lice in his battalion. In March 1916 his unit was amalgamated with another and he returned to politics. In July 1917 he became Minister of Munitions, working very closely with Lloyd George for the rest of the war. His great contribution was the mass-production of tanks, aircraft and bombs, all of which were to be used in the great Allied offensive, which won the war in 1918.

In the new Coalition government of 1918 he was given to the War Office and made responsible for demobilization. He became preoccupied with the Russian problem: seeking to give the maximum possible aid to anti-Bolshevist groups wherever they were to be found. He disagreed somewhat with Lloyd George here, who was less antagonistic to the Revolution and determined to avoid the cost of a full-scale undertaking. In the end British troops were all withdrawn.

He supported Lloyd George's efforts to find a settlement in Ireland in 1921, winning the confidence of Michael Collins, who paid tribute to his help in establishing the Free State. Unlike many of his cabinet colleagues, he had never been an Ulsterman, nor a supporter of the Unionists.

He lost his Parliamentary seat in 1922 and did not get another until October 1924 when he won Epping, again a Conservative. As Chancellor of the Exchequer 1924–1929 he was responsible for the restoration of the pre-1914 gold standard, but only on the advice of the Treasury and City financiers. The industrial disputes, predicted by J. M. Keynes, duly followed, culminating in the General Strike. Churchill pressed for vigorous action against 'the enemy', by which he meant the T.U.C. and Organized Labour. He founded and personally edited the *British Gazette*, whose circulation rose to 2,000,000 in eight days.

He left office in 1929 and did not join the National government, calling Ramsay MacDonald a 'boneless wonder'. He thought that 'to abandon India to the rule of the Brahmins', as this government seemed about to do, 'would be an act of cruel and wicked negligence', owing to their attitude to the untouchables and to Moslems. Over this question of India he remained firm and thus stayed out of office.

In 1932 he argued that it would be better to reopen questions like Danzig and the Corridor 'while the victor nations have ample superiority', than to disarm; instead he pressed for a large air-force as a deterrent against a re-arming Germany. During the 1930's he published a number of books, including his classic Life of the First Duke of Marlborough.

After rearmament began in 1936 he was still critical of the National government, and from 1938 onwards was advocating a pact with Soviet Russia to resist 'an act of Nazi aggression'. His attitude to the U.S.S.R. had changed considerably: he now regarded it as definitely the lesser of two evils. On 3 September he returned to the Admiralty, arguing that if Britain survived the winter 1939–1940 without any large-scale or important loss 'we should have gained the first campaign of the war, since our strength is mounting rapidly'.

As Prime Minister from 10 May he worked tirelessly: touring bombed cities in a private uniform of battle-dress, hat, cigar and walking-stick; dictating for long hours; and speaking continually in Parliament or on the radio, to keep up morale. Already he was planning two years ahead for the offensive. In November 1940 he paid tribute to Chamberlain for his 'love of peace, toil for peace, strife for peace and pursuit of peace'.

On 19 December 1940 he announced the capture of thousands of Italian prisoners in Libya, the conquest of which was complete by February 1941. It was a bold decision to send troops to Egypt while the bombs were still falling on Britain and the danger of invasion had not fully gone. Equally bold was his decision to honour promises to Greece in the spring of 1941, at the cost of a setback in Libya. He was strongly attacked in Parliament for this decision. When Germany invaded Russia in June 1941, he offered 'any technical or economic assistance which is in our power and which is likely to be of service'.

In August 1941, before the U.S.A. entered the war, he met President Roosevelt off Newfoundland. They published an eight-point declaration, the Atlantic Charter, which formally associated the U.S.A. with the Allies (see Appendix II).

Japan attacked British colonies in Malaya, Singapore and Hong Kong on 7 December 1941. Churchill declared war and summoned Parliament by radio. On the same day came Pearl Harbour and the American entry into the war. Three days later Churchill had to announce the loss of the two great ships H.M.S. *Prince of Wales* and H.M.S. *Repulse*, sunk by Japanese aircraft.

He now began his series of world tours to co-ordinate the planning and fighting of the war. At the same time, early in 1942, he had to meet strong criticism. In Parliament Sir William Beveridge criticized the congested, lumbering cabinet, 'lacking in speed and decision'. Abroad, Russia pressed for a 'second front now', which Churchill condemned as absurd. He answered home criticism by creating a Ministry of Production and reorganizing the cabinet, making Sir Stafford Cripps Lord Privy Seal and leader of the House of Commons and promoting Attlee to be deputy Prime Minister. In Moscow he persuaded Stalin to abandon his demands and succeeded in establishing mutual confidence. But at home criticism was resumed as the summer months of 1942 brought continued failure, culminating in the fall of Tobruk in June 1942, when Churchill was in Washington. Clement Davies listed the long line of disasters and twenty-five M.P.'s voted against the government, whose reputation stood at its lowest at this point. The invasion of North Africa in the autumn of 1942 took some of the strain off Russia, against whom were pitted over 240 divisions, and by the end of the year the successes of war brought an end to the criticism of Churchill.

In 1943, with victory in sight, there began the long debate on the Beveridge Report (published in December 1942) and the future of Britain. Churchill reminded the House that in 1910 he and Lloyd George had begun much that the report now recommended should be completed. He was all in favour 'of bringing the magic of averages to the rescue of millions' and therefore supported Beveridge. The year also saw conferences at Casablanca, Quebec and Teheran.

1944 saw the Normandy landings, Churchill himself landing in France on D Day + 6. It also saw the beginning of the problem of the refugee governments in London. Many of these were more right-wing than were the partisan forces fighting internally for liberation, for example in France, Yugoslavia and Greece. Tension in the latter led Churchill to fly to a liberated Athens in December 1944 to try to end the civil war there. The visit led to a compromise and a slow restoration of peace.

In 1945 there was the Yalta Conference in February, which discussed Poland and Eastern Europe as well as the proposed United Nations. The problem of the refugee governments was particularly difficult in Eastern Europe: the Communist Party had far too firm a grip by 1945 to make a restoration of the neo-Fascist regimes of 1939 possible, even if the Allies had wanted it, which on the whole they did not.

In March Churchill was again in France and he fired a shell into Germany on which he had chalked 'Hitler personally'. At 3 p.m. on Tuesday 8 May he announced victory in Europe. Wild scenes of rejoicing took place, with dancing and singing in the streets all through the night. But on 23 May Churchill resigned as Prime Minister and brought the Coalition to an end. He formed a caretaker government, with a cabinet of sixteen Conservatives, which organized the general election. In spite of his great vigour, his special train and tremendous scenes of personal popularity, the Conservatives lost the election and Churchill resigned in the middle of the Potsdam Conference, to the bewilderment of both Russian and American opinion.

During the next six years he made a number of important international speeches. His personal relations with Attlee were very cordial after working for five years together. As he himself said, 'things can never be quite the same again' after this coalition of Conservative and Labour. The bitterness of the 1920's was a thing impossible now to imagine. Churchill might inveigh against 'the horrors of socialism', but he knew, as well as any, that this was now little more than shadow-boxing. In opposition he opposed, as was his

When the Conservatives won the election in October 1951 they inherited from Labour a number of very tough problems. Churchill, Eden and Attlee are here included

duty; attacking some measures of nationalization, the speed of the Indian hand-over and 'government incompetence' on various occasions. But he gave his support to Ernest Bevin and his foreign policy, Bevin being a man who had won his friendship and admiration during the war. He also travelled, wrote his memoirs, painted, bred cattle, registered his colours as a horse-breeder and enjoyed himself as an amateur bricklayer. In 1951 he resumed office as

Prime Minister, which post he held until 1955 in spite of suffering a stroke in these years.

Unquestionably the greatest man of the ten here considered (his nearest equal being Lloyd George), he was never a rigid party man in politics. He was always a fighter, obviously enjoying power and also enjoying life. The forty-five years covered in this book are inevitably coloured by his personality. Politically he may have made mistakes and there have been times when he was wrong, but as a war minister he had the confidence of the country more than any British leader ever did before: more than Pitt the Younger or Lloyd George. Unconventional and in many ways a radical, he watched with approval, in the first half of the twentieth century, the growth of the Welfare State from its infancy to maturity.

APPENDIX I

President Wilson's Fourteen Points

(a brief summary)

(i) Open covenants of peace, to be openly arrived at.
(ii) Freedom of navigation of the seas, in peace or war.
(iii) The removal of all economic barriers to international trade.
(iv) Reduction of armaments to lowest point consistent with domestic safety.
(v) Adjustment of colonial claims, bearing in mind the needs of colonial peoples.
(vi) Evacuation of all Russian territory. Russia to be free to develop, to be given all possible assistance, and to be welcomed into the League of Nations.
(vii) Belgium to be evacuated and her pre-war government restored.
(viii) France to be evacuated and Alsace-Lorraine to be restored.
(ix) Italy's frontiers to be adjusted along lines of nationality.
(x) The peoples of Austria-Hungary to have the freest opportunity to develop autonomously.
(xi) Occupied territories in the Balkans to be evacuated and Serbia given access to the sea.
(xii) Turkish portions of the Ottoman Empire to be allowed to retain sovereignty but other nationalities to be allowed independence. The Dardanelles to be open to all nations.
(xiii) An independent Poland to be created with access to the sea.
(xiv) A general association of the nations to be formed.

APPENDIX II

The Atlantic Charter

(*a brief summary*)

(i) Britain and the U.S.A. seek no aggrandizement, territorial or otherwise.

(ii) They seek no territorial changes not in accord with the freely expressed wishes of the people concerned.

(iii) They respect the right of all people to choose the form of government they want, and wish self-government to be restored to those forcibly deprived of it.

(iv) They wish to see free access by all nations, victor or vanquished, to trade and raw materials of the world.

(v) They wish to see fullest economic collaboration to secure improved labour standards, economic advancement and social security.

(vi) After the destruction of Nazi tyranny they wish to see all men everywhere living out their lives in freedom from fear and from want.

(vii) Such freedom should enable all men to traverse the high seas without hindrance.

(viii) They believe all nations of the world must come to abandon the use of force. They believe the disarmament of nations which threaten aggression, essential. But pending the establishment of a permanent system of general security they will lighten for peace-loving peoples the crushing burden of armaments.

Index

ABYSSINIA: division of, 180; Stresa Pact 1935, 193; admitted League of Nations 1923, 194; Italian attack 1935, 194; occupied by Britain 1941, 234

Acts of Parliament: Acquisition of Land 1919, 120; Aerial Navigation 1911, 56; Agricultural Land Utilization 1931, 219; Agricultural Marketing 1931, 219; 1933, 219; Agricultural Wages 1924, 162; Agriculture 1920, 120; 1937, 219; 1947, 279–80; Artisans Dwellings 1875, 27; British Shipping Assistance 1935, 174; 'Cat and Mouse' 1913, 62; Catering 1943, 260; Children and Young Persons 1908, 186; 1933, 186; Civil Defence 1937, 189, 256; Coal Mining Industry 1911, 56; 1919, 140; 1920, 140; 1929, 148; 1930, 173; Nationalization 1946, 276; Coal Miners' Minimum Wages 1912, 58; Conspiracy and Protection of Property, 1875, 27; County Council 1888, 27; Criminal Law Amendment 1871, 27; Defence of the Realm 1914, 94, 120; Disestablishment of Welsh Church 1914, 36, 58, 59; Education (Balfour) 1902, 25, 38; 1907, 40; 1918, 101; 1944, 186, 260–1; Emergency Powers 1939, 206, 251–2; Factory 1937, 187; Family Allowances 1945, 261; Financing Anglo-Persian Oil Co. 1914, 49; Government of South Africa 1909, 50; Housing: Addison 1919, 119; Wheatley 1924, 132, 210; 1935 and 1936, 186; Town Planning 1943, 280; Town and Country Planning 1944, 260, 280; 1947, 280; 1946, 281; 1949, 281; New Towns 1946, 280; Import Duties 1932, 168–9; India 1935, 176, 294; Legal Aid and Advice 1949, 286–7; Licensing 1872, 28; 1904, 28; Licensing Bill 1909, 39; see also D.O.R.A.; Livestock Industry 1937, 219; Local Government 1929, 146; 1948, 286; Maternity and Child Welfare 1818, 263; Merchant Shipping 1906, 37; Milk 1934, 186; National Assistance 1948, 286; National Health Service 1946, 284–5; National Unemployment Insurance 1911, 56, 57; 1920, 119; 1922, 125; 1927, 145; 1934, 176, 186; 1946, 282–4; Nationalization of Electricity 1947, 278; Nationalization of Gas 1948, 278; Official Secrets 1911, 56; Parish Councils 1894, 36; Parliament 1911, 43, 45; Amended 1949, 282; Parliamentary Incomes 1911, 56; Physical Training 1937, 213; Port of London Authority 1906, 37; Prevention of Crimes 1909, 40; Public Health 1848 and 1876, 27; 1936, 186; Representation of the People 1918, 101; 1928, 146; 1948, 282; Safeguarding of Industries 1921, 127; School Meals 1906, 39; Shops 1911, 56; Smallholdings (England) 1908, 120; Smallholders (England) 1926, 121; Smallholders (Scotland)

Acts of Parliament—*contd.*
1911, 56; Territorial and Reserve Forces 1907, 46, 47; Trade Boards 1909, 42; 1918, 99; Trade Disputes 1906, 28, 37; 1927, 144; and Repeal of, 282; Trade Union 1871, 27; 1913, 59; Unemployed Workers' Dependents 1921, 125; Wheat 1932, 219; Women Councillors 1911, 56; Workmen's Compensation 1906, 37
Afghanistan: in Anglo-Russian Agreement 1907, 75; and British Foreign Policy 1918, 110
Africa: Second Boer War 1899–1902, 16; and Tariff Reform League, 17; and British Imperialism, 19; South Africa after Boer War, 31, 49–51; German Colonies, 69; Division of Portuguese Africa 1914, 72–3; Portion of French Congo ceded to Germany 1911, 76; North Africa 1940, 234; 1942, 242–3; and Bandung Conference 1955, 289; South Africa as Member of Commonwealth, 290; 1945 and after, 304–6
Agriculture: 1914–1918, 99–100; Food Production Committees 1915, 100; County Agricultural Committees 1915, 100; Food Production Department 1917, 100; Wages Board 1918, 100; Food Control Board 1916, 100; Lloyd George's Policy 1919, 120; in the 1920's, 162; in the 1930's, 218–19, 279; During Second World War, 252, 279; Agriculture Act 1947, 279–80
Albania: 1912–1914, 78–9; In 1939, 190
Albert I (Belgium): 70
Allenby, General: and Arab Independence 1917–1918, 102–5
Amery, Leo: Attitude to General Strike 1925, 141; In Coalition Government 1940, 255
Architecture: In 1920's, 160; In 1930's, 211
Army: Haldane's Reforms, 45–7; Mobilization, 85, 89; Battle conditions, 93; Battle of Passchendaele, 103; and Rearmament 1936–1939, 188; and Dunkirk, 231–2
Art: In 1920's, 160; Dadaism and Surrealism 1930's, 215
Arts Council of Great Britain: originates from C.E.M.A. 1945, 264; Picasso-Matisse Exhibition 1945–1946, 266; Festival of Britain 1951, 325–6
Asia: Colombo Plan 1950, 317; Bandung Conference in Java 1955, 289
Asquith, H. H.: as Prime Minister 1908, 38; and Parliament Bill 1910, 43–4; Irish Policy 1912–1914, 64–6; Home Rule Policy 1914, 113; Resigns from Goverment 1916, 94; In General Election 1918, 117; 1922–1923, 129; Works with Labour Party 1923, 131–2; Resigns 1926, 135; Pocket Biography, 335–7
Attlee, Clement: Leader of Labour Party 1935, 182; In Coalition War Cabinet 1940, 253; Prime Minister and Minister of Defence 1945, 271–2; Cabinet 1945, 271; Against Truman's War Policy 1950, 317; and Dissolution of Parliament 1951, 288; Pocket Biography, 351–3
Atlantic Charter: United Nations Declaration 1941, 250, 364

Auden, W. H.: 215, 217, 221
Australia: and Tariff Reform League, 17; Galipolli, 90; in Depression 1929, 165; Troops withdrawn from Middle East, 241; as a Commonwealth, 289–92
Austria-Hungary (Habsburg Empire): and Nationalism, 29; Bismarck Alliance 1879, 73; Triple Alliance 1882, 74; Annexation of Bosnia and Herzegovina 1908, 78; End of Austro-Russian Co-operation 1908, 78; In Balkan Wars 1912–1913, 79; Events leading to First World War, 80–1; Ultimatum to Serbia 1914, 66; War with Serbia 1914, 69; War Aims, 83; Mobilization, 85; Retreat from Russians 1916, 92; Caporetto 1917, 103; Vittorio Veneto 1918, 105; End of Empire—Treaty of Versailles, 121
Austria: Republic founded 1918, 105; Annexation of, 1938, 199–211

BALDWIN, Stanley: As President of Board of Trade 1921, 127; As Chancellor of Exchequer 1922–1923, 129; Forms Government 1923, 130; Loses General Election 1923, 131; Wins General Election 1924, 135; Character, 136; Locarno Pact 1925, 137; Crisis in Mining Industry 1925, 140–1; and General Strike 1925, 142–4; and Russian Relations 1927, 145; and Reform Bill 1928, 146; and General Election 1929, 147; in National Government 1931, 149–50; Lord President in Cabinet, 166; becomes Prime Minister 1935, 177; attitude to Foreign Affairs, 178; resignation of Hoare, 181; resignation and character, 184; Pocket Biography, 342–4
Balfour, A. J.: Prime Minister 1902, 16; Balfour Act 1902, 25; formed Tariff Reform League 1903, 17; resignation from Conservative Government 1905, 19; and Parliament Bill 1911, 44; Resignation from Leadership of Unionist Party 1911, 58; Coalition Foreign Secretary 1918, 117; and Chanak Crisis 1922, 128; and Imperial Conference 1926, 290; and Balfour Declaration 1917, 302
The Balkans: the Balkan Wars 1912–1913, 78–80; 1914, 69; Alliances before 1914, 73–4; in First World War, 84, 92; occupation by Germany 1941, 234
Beaverbrook, Viscount: 1916–1917, 94; Carlton Club Revolt, 128; Minister for Aircraft Production 1940, 255
Belgium: British Policy on, 1914, 70; in Africa, 73; Mobilization 1914, 81; Invasion of, 81–3; the Western Front 1914, 85–6; 1917, 102–3; War Reparations 1919, 122; Occupation of Ruhr 1923, 130; in 1938, 191; attacked by Germany 1940, 231
Berlin Air Lift: 1948–1949, 311–13
Bevan, Aneurin: As Minister of Health, 272, 281–8; Pocket Biography, 349–51
Beveridge, Sir William: National Health Scheme recommendation 1942, 259; attacks Government, 359

Bevin, Ernest: Labour Leader 1921, 124; and General Strike 1925, 143; and National Government 1931, 149; Policy in Labour Party 1935, 182; Minister of Labour and National Service 1940, 255, 259; and Catering Bill 1943, 260; as Foreign Secretary 1945, 271, 319–20; in United Nations 1946, 309; Colombo Plan 1950, 317, 320; resigns 1951, 287; Pocket Biography, 347–8
Birkenhead, Lord: Lord Chancellor 1918, 117; Irish Policy 1919, 114; and Chanak Crisis 1922, 128; Secretary for India 1925, 135
Boer War, Second: 1899–1902, Peace of Vereeniging, 16; Losses, 31; Army inefficiency, 45; Concentration Camps, 49
Booth, Charles: 20, 26
Boothby, Robert: 147, 168
Botha, General: First Cabinet, 50–1
British Broadcasting Company: and Religion, 156–7; in 1920's, 157–9; in General Strike 1925, 142; in 1930's, 214; Television begun 1936, 214; during Second World War, 259; Promenade Concerts 1942, 265; Third Programme begun 1946, 324; loses Television Monopoly 1955, 325
British Fascist Party: 148, 219–20
British Transport Commission: created 1947, 277
Bulgaria: Balkan Wars 1912–1913, 78–9; in First World War 1917, 90; Salonika and Armistice 1918, 105; in 1939, 190; Satellite of Russia 1945, 209
Burma: British offensive in, 1944, 240, 247; 1944–1948, 296–7
Burnham Committee: Founded 1918, 102
Burns, John: 37
Butler, R. A.: Minister of Education 1942, 260

Campbell, Roy: 217
Campbell-Bannerman: Liberal Leader, 50; on South Africa, 50; Prime Minister 1906, 37–8
Canada: and Tariff Reform League, 17; Battle of Vimy Ridge, 103; as Member of Commonwealth, 290–2
Carson, Sir Edward: Ulster Leader 1910, 64–5
Ceylon: 1943–1952, 297–8
Chamberlain, Austen: Chancellor of the Exchequer 1918, 117; and Chanak Crisis 1922, 128; and General Election 1923, 131; Foreign Secretary 1925, 135; and Locarno Pact 1925, 137
Chamberlain, Joseph: Leader of Liberal Unionists 1886, 16; affiliated with Conservative Party 1895, 16; forms Tariff Reform League, 17–19; Old Age Pension Scheme, 26; seeks German Alliance 1901, 74; Colonial Secretary 1906, 50
Chamberlain, Neville: attitude to General Strike 1926, 141; Minister of Health 1925, 145; Local Government Bill 1928, 146; in National Government 1931, 149; Minister of Health (Cabinet 1931), 166; Chancellor of the Exchequer (Second Cabinet) National Government 1931, 168; introduced Import Duties Bill 1932, 168; views on League of Nations, 178; Prime Minister 1937, 184; character

and policy, 185, 207, and re-armament, 188; Czechoslovakian policy 1938, 201–4; meets Hitler (Sept. 15, 1938) (Sept. 23, 1938), 202; and Godesberg Memorandum Sept. 1938, 203; and Munich Conference Sept. 1938, 203; recognition of Franco's Fascist Government in Spain 1939, 204; reviews Foreign Policy 1939, 205; declares War on Germany Sept. 3, 1939, 206; forms War Cabinet 1939, 251; Fall of Government 1940, 253; in Coalition War Cabinet 1940, 253; resignation and death of, 1940, 255; Pocket Biography, 344–6

Chanak Crisis 1922: 127–9

Chiang Kai-shek: Leader of Kuomintang 1920, 248; attitude to communism, 249; Teheran Conference 1943, 250

China: Suzerainty over Tibet 1907, 75; German attitude to, 1911, 73; 1920–1950, 248–9; and United Nations Security Council 1945, 250; Hong Kong, 299; and Communist Aid to North Korea, 317

Churchill, Sir Winston: Reaction to Tariff Reform League, 19; President of Board of Trade 1908, 38; Trade Boards Bill 1909, 42; Home Secretary 1910, 52; and Tonypandy Strikes 1910, 54; First Lord of the Admiralty 1911, 48; and Anglo-Persian Oil Company, 49; National Insurance Bill, Part II, 1911, 57; Policy on Ireland 1912, 64–5; and Dardanelles campaign 1914, 87–90; description of a battle 1915, 93; Minister of Munitions 1917, 94; Secretary for War 1918, 111, 117; Policy in Ireland 1919, 114; Chanak Crisis 1922, 128–9; fails to be elected 1923, 131; Chancellor of the Exchequer 1924, 135; Policy in General Strike 1926, 141–2; and Welfare Legislation 1925–1929, 145–6; Policy on India, 176; attitude to Abdication of Edward VIII, 183; attitude to re-armament 1933, 187; against appeasement 1938, 199; joins Government 1939, 231; negotiations with France, 232; First Lord of the Admiralty 1939, 251; Prime Minister 1940, 253; career of, 253–4; Leader of Conservative Party 1940, 255; Policy 1943, 243; Fulton Speech 1946, 309; Zürich Speech 1946, 313; Prime Minister 1951, 288; Pocket Biography, 355–62

Cinema: in 1920's, 159; in 1930's, 215; effects of television after 1945, 324

Coalition Government 1940: Churchill's War Cabinet, 253, 254–5; Home Guard May 1940, 255–6; Air Raid Precautions 1940, 256–7; E.N.S.A. created 1940, 258, 259; C.E.M.A. 1940, 258, 259, 264–6; evacuation of civilians 1939–1941, 262; National Fire Service 1941, 257; Clothes Rationing 1941, 257; A.T.S., W.A.A.F., W.R.N.S. 1941, 258; Ministry of Fuel created 1942, 257; Ministry of Production created 1942, 258; Beveridge National Health Report 1942, 259–60; Social Legislation 1940–1945, 262–3; Tuberculosis Allowance Scheme 1943, 263; Family

Coalition Government 1940 —*contd.*
Allowance Act 1945, 267; falls 1945, 267
Coal Mining Industry: 1911–1912 Strikes, 54–6; in 1914–1918 War, 98; and Black Friday, 124; and General Strike 1925, 139–144; in 1930's, 172–3; Nationalization 1947, 274, 276–7; see also Coal Mining Industry Acts
Communications: Electric Telegraph, Telephone and Wireless Telegraphy, 35; Electric Grid System, 152
Communism: (in Russia) Bolshevik Revolution 1917 and establishment of Bolshevik Regime 1917–1919, 109–12; under Stalin 1924–1935, 192–3; (in China), 248–9; (in Germany), 190–1; (in Malaya), 298–9; (in Italy), 190; (in Spain), 190, 198; (in Persia), 318; (in Czechoslovakia), 310–11
Communist Party in Britain: formed 1920, 99, 118; increased membership 1921, 124; *The Workers' Weekly* 1924, 134; the Zinoviev letter 1925, 135; arrests for Incitement to Mutiny 1925, 140; expansion of, 1930's, 174; attitude during Second World War, 259
Conservative Party: and Disraeli's Policy on Housing 1875, 26; up to 1902, 16; Balfour Act 1902, 25; Policy on Licensing until 1904, 28; and General Election 1906, 17; attitude to democracy 1906, 19; Legislative failures until 1906, 36; Naval Policy 1906, 40; opposition to Budget 1909, 41; and South African problem 1900–1909, 50; and General Election 1910, 43–4; opposition to National Insurance Act 1911, 56; Conference on Ireland 1914, 66; Policy on War Reparations, 123; and Chanak Crisis 1922, 127–8; General Election 1922, 129; 1923, 131; General Election 1924 and Zinoviev letter, 135; Baldwin's Cabinet 1924, 135–6; Government Policy on Industry 1925, 139; Government Legislation 1925–1929, 145–6; General Election 1929, 147; Policy in Depression, 167; aversion to Planned Economy and Nationalization, 175; National Government formed 1931, 149–50; National Government re-formed 1935, 177; Policy in General Election 1935, 179; War Cabinet 1939, 251; Evacuation of Civilians 1939, 251; Conscription 1939, 206; Government Legislation 1939–1940, 251, 252, 263; failure of aid to Norway 1940, 231; and Chamberlain's resignation 1940, 253; Churchill becomes Party Leader 1940, 255; and British Transport Commission 1947, 277; and General Election 1950, 287–8; and Iron and Steel Bill 1951, 279; wins General Election 1951, 288
Cooper, Duff: In Coalition Government 1940, 255
Cosgrave, W. T.: Prime Minister of Irish Free State 1922, 115–16; Government fell 1932, 183
County Councils: Created 1888, 25, 27
Cripps, Sir Stafford: Member of Socialist League, 181; President of Board of Trade 1945, 272;

Chancellor of Exchequer 1947, 274; resigned 1950, 288
Curzon, Lord: in War Cabinet 1915, 94; Foreign Secretary 1923, 129; not asked to be Prime Minister 1923, 130; Lord President of Council 1926, 135
Cyprus: 1878–1957, 300–1
Czar Nicholas II: 77
Czechoslovakia: British Government Policy for, 1935, 180; by 1938, 190, 227; British Policy of Appeasement 1938, 201–4; and Godesberg Memorandum Sept. 1938, 203; and Munich Conference Sept. 1938, 203; invaded by Germany 1939, 205; falls to Communism, 310–11

DALI, Salvador: 215–16
Dalton, Hugh: Chancellor of Exchequer 1945, 272; resigns 1947, 274
Dawes Plan: 132–3; and Depression 1929, 165
Day Lewis, Cecil: 217, 267
De Gaulle, General: forms Free French Movement 1940, 232; 314
De la Warr, Lord: President of Board of Education (C.E.M.A.) 1939, 264
De Valera, Eamonn: imprisonment 1917, 1918, 113; escape from prison 1919, 114; meets Lloyd George 1921, 115; Republican Party Leader 1921, 116; Prime Minister 1932, 116, 183
Denmark: attacked by Germany 1940, 230–1
Disraeli: 1868 election, 16; Legislation under, 1874–1880, 22; Housing Policy 1874–1880, 26
EDEN, Anthony: Minister without Portfolio 1935, 178; Foreign Secretary 1935–1938, 178, 181; resigned from Office 1938, 185; joins Government 1939, 231; Dominions Secretary 1939, 251; Pocket Biography, 353–5
Education: Universal Primary Schooling 1870, 22; before 1906, 24–5; Education Bill 1906, 38; school meals and medical attention 1906–1907, 40; Education Act 1918, 101–2; school-leaving age raised 1929, 148; in 1920's 154–6; in 1930's 210; after 1945, 331–2
Edward VII: character, 15, 43; in Ireland 1903, 30; appoints Asquith Prime Minister 1908, 38; advice on Budget 1909, 42–3; death of, 1910, 43
Edward VIII: abdication of, 182
Egypt: and Fashoda Incident 1898, 74; British advance from, 1917, 102; in 1940, 234; German offensive in, June 1942, 241; British offensive in, Oct. 1942, 242–3; 1922–1956, 300
Eisenhower, General: Combined Western Commander, 242; Supreme Allied Commander 1944, 244
Eliot, T. S.: *The Waste Land* 1923, 160; *Murder in the Cathedral* 1935, 215
Epstein: in 1920's, 160
Ernst, Max: 216
Europe: Towards a United Europe 1946–1958, 313–14

FABIAN Society: G. B. Shaw and *Major Barbara*, 20; founded 1884, 21–2; and Poor Law and unemployment, 26

Falkenhayn, General: replaced General von Moltke 1914, 86; victories on Russian Front 1916, 92; replaced by Ludendorff 1916, 102
Family Allowances: Unemployed Workers' Dependents Act 1921, 125; widows and orphans 1925, 145; Family Allowances Act 1945, 261; National Insurance Act 1946, 284
Far East: Britain's Policy towards, 1890's, 74; German attitude to China 1911, 73; collapse of European power in, 1941, 239; emergence of coloured peoples, 240–1; Allied offensive in, 1943, 247–8; after the Second World War, 248–9
Fascism: in Italy, 190; British Union of Fascists founded 1932, 219
Fashions: in 1920's, 162; in 1930's, 172, 213
Faulkner, William: in 1920's, 161
Financial Crisis 1931: 149
First World War: 1914–1918, 84–105; Western Front, 85–6, 91–3, 102–3; Russian Front, 87, 92, 96, 103–4; Turkey, 87, 105; Gallipoli, 89–90, 105; Italian Front, 103, 105; Government changes, 93–4; D.O.R.A., 94–5; Air Warfare, 95–6; War at Sea, 96–7; American entry 1917, 97; Labour Party and War, 98–9; Caporetto, 105
Fisher, Sir John: Fisher-Cawdor Programme, 40, 48; First Sea Lord 1904, 47, 90
Fitzgerald, Scott: 161
Fleming, Alexander: 218, 328
Foch, General: Supreme Commander of Allied Armies 1918, 104, 105
Forster, W. E.: 24
France: humiliation of, 1870–1871, 29; Berlin Conference 1884, 73; Alliance sought by Russia, 74; Entente Agreement 1904, 74; Moroccan Crisis 1905, 75; Loans to Russia 1905–1906, 77; Agreement with Germany over Morocco 1909, 76; Recognition of French position in Morocco 1911, 76; Naval Defence Agreement with, 1912, 48; in Balkan War 1914, 69; English traditional hostility to, 70; relaxation of economic rivalry before 1914, 72; Serbian Crisis 1914, 80; German Declaration of War on, 1914, 82; War Aims 1914, 83; see First World War 1914–1918, 84–105; Occupation of the Ruhr 1923, 130; Hoare-Laval Pact 1935, 180; in 1938, 190; Daladier supports Chamberlain over Czechoslovakia 1938, 202; and Godesberg Memorandum Sept. 1938, 203; and Munich Conference Sept. 1938, 203; in 1939, 228; German attack on, 1940, 231–2; Pétain's Policy 1940, 234; Member of United Nations Security Council 1945, 250
Franchise: Suffragettes, 31–2, 56, 60–2, 101; Fourth Reform Act 1918 and Emancipation of Women, 101; Representation of the People Bill 1928, 146
Franco, General: Aid from Italy, 196; flies to Morocco, 197; recognized by Britain, 198, 199
Free Trade: Tariff Reform League 1903, 17–19; Safeguarding of Industries Act 1921, 127;

Labour Legislation 1924, 132; Liberal Election Programme 1929, 147

GAITSKELL, Hugh: Chancellor of Exchequer 1950, 287, 350
Gandhi, Mahatma: discussion of Independence, 176; 1919–1948, 294–6
Gascoyne, David: 267
Geddes Acts: 126
George V: Succession to Throne 1910, 43; Parliament Bill Conferences 1910, 44; intervenes in Irish Crisis 1913, 65, 66; appoints Bonar Law Prime Minister 1922, 129; appoints Baldwin Prime Minister 1923, 130; intervenes during General Strike 1926, 142, 144; meets Ramsay MacDonald 1931, 164; Silver Jubilee 1935, 177; Death of, 1936, 182
George VI: Succession to Throne 1936, 183; Coronation of, 1937, 184
Germany: Naval expansion 1895–1914, 40, 47–9; Disarmament Conference 1907, 40; Economic expansion 1890–1914, 71–2; Alliances 1879–1914, 73–6; Balkan Wars 1912–1913, 78–9; Serbian Crisis 1914, 80; Schlieffen Plan 1914, 70, 81, 85, 86, 87; Mobilization and Invasion of Belgium, 81, 85; Submarine Warfare, 84, 96–7; on Russian Front 1914–1915, 87; gas warfare 1915, 91; offensive on Western Front 1916, 91–2; air warfare 1914–1918, 95–6; on Western Front 1917, 102–3; on Italian Front 1917, 103–4; on Western Front 1918, 104–5; Armistice 1918, 105; War Reparations 1919, 121–2; economic collapse 1929, 148; in Depression 1929–1933, 165; during 1930's, 190–2; and reviving Nationalism 1935, 193; rearmament and the Rhineland 1930's, 196; The Axis 1936 and 1937, 200; invasion and annexation of Austria 1938, 201; invasion of Czechoslovakia 1939, 204; mutual Pact of Non-Aggression with Russia 1939, 206, 229–30; in 1939, 225–7; The Axis 1939, 228; annexation of Poland 1939, 230; attacks Norway and Denmark 1940, 230–1; Battle of Britain 1940, 232–4; Control in Mediterranean, 234; Offensive in Balkan Peninsula 1941, 234–5; invades Russia 1941, 235, 238; Battle of the Atlantic, 236–7; situation in 1941, 238–9; captures Tobruk 1942, 241; reaches Stalingrad 1942, 241; Russian counter-offensive 1942, 241–2; 1943, 243–4; Allied offensive in Normandy 1944, 244–6; last counter-attack 1944, 246; surrenders 1945, 246; Berlin Air Lift 1948, 311; new Constitutions 1949, 312–13; West Germany joins N.A.T.O., 314
Gielgud, John: 160
Gladstone: in General Election 1868, 16; First Ministry 1868–1874, 22; and Licensing Act 1872, 28; and First Home Rule Bill 1886, 62; and Irish Land Acts 1870 and 1881, 62
Gold Standard: returned to, 1925, 135; end of, 1931, 166
Graves, Robert: 217
Greece: and Balkan Wars 1912, 78–9; Armistice 1916, 105; and Anatolia, 127; by 1939, 190

Greene, Graham: 217
Greenwood, Arthur: in Coalition War Cabinet 1940, 253
Grey, Sir Edward: Foreign Secretary 1905–1916, 38, 70; and Anglo-Russian Agreement 1907, 75; attitude to Serbian Crisis 1914, 80, 82
Griffith, Arthur: 112, 115
Griffiths, James: 282, 286

HAIG, General Douglas: 93, 103, 104
Haldane, Lord R. B.: Secretary for War 1906, 37, 38; character and policy, 46; created Territorial Army and reorganized Regular Army, 46–7; and mobilization 1914, 85; Lord Chancellor 1924, 132
Halifax, Lord: discussion of Indian Independence, 1931–1935, 176; Foreign Secretary 1938, 185; meets Hitler 1937, 200; opposes Godesberg Memorandum Sept. 1938, 203; in War Cabinet 1939, 251; in Coalition War Cabinet 1940, 253; Ambassador to U.S.A., 354
Hemingway, Ernest: 103, 161
Henderson, Arthur: in War Cabinet 1915, 94; emissary to Russia 1917, 109
Hitler, Adolf: rise to power, 191; and reoccupation of the Rhineland, 196; and murder of Dollfuss 1934, 199; and annexation of Czechoslovakia 1938, 202; and Munich Conference Sept. 1938, 203; General Policy before 1939, 225–7; Policy 1940, 232; 1941, 238–9; attempted assassination of, 1944, 245; committed suicide 1945, 246
Hoare, Sir Samuel: Foreign Secretary 1935, 177; and Stresa Pact 1935, 193; Hoare-Laval Pact, 180–1, 194, 354; Lord Privy Seal 1939, 204; in War Cabinet 1939, 251
Holland: by 1938, 191; attacked by Germany 1940, 231
Hore Belisha: 188, 251
Housing: Slum Clearance before 1900, 26–7; housing in 1920's, 152; in 1930's, 170, 171, 210–11; Bevan's Housing Policy 1945–1951, 281–2; Post-War Policy, 321–3; see also Housing Acts
Hungary: Annexation of, 1938, 199–201; in 1939, 190; as satellite of Russia 1945, 309
Huxley, Aldous: 161, 221

IMPERIAL Conference: 1911, 290; 1926, 146; Statute of Westminster 1931, 176
India: steps towards independence 1931–1935, 176; 1906–1958, 292–6
Industry: Tertiary employment and consumer goods, 171, 172; Shipbuilding in 1920's, 139, 173; 1929–1933, 165; in 1930's, 174; Textiles, 139, 172–3; Iron and Steel, 139, 172–3, 278–9; see also Coal Mining
Ireland: Land Purchase Act 1903, 30; effects of, 63; Irish Nationalists in 1906 Government, 16; Religion in, 29; before 1906 and the Act of Union, 30–1; Liberal attitude to Home Rule 1906, 30; Conservative attitude to Home Rule 1910, 44; General Election 1910, Irish Nationalists, 43; Third Home Rule Bill 1912,

58; Ulster and opposition to Home Rule, 63–6; origins of Sinn Fein, 63, 112; Coupon Election 1918, Irish Nationalists, 113; First Ulster Parliament 1921, 115; Establishment of Irish Free State, 112–16; Republican reaction to abdication, 183; Republican General Policy 1930's, 183–4; became Eire 1937, 184; in 1949, 292
Irwin, Lord: see Halifax, Lord
Isherwood, Christopher: 215, 221
Italy: Unification of, 1860, 28; occupation of Tripoli 1911, 76; Italian Front 1916, 102, 103–5; invasion of Abyssinia 1935, 180; The Axis 1936 and 1937, 200; and Spanish Civil War 1936, 197–8; The Axis 1939, 228; occupation of Albania 1939, 206; enters War 1940, 234; and control of Mediterranean, 234–5; fall of Mussolini's Government, 243

JAPAN: Anglo-Japanese Treaty 1902, 74; defeats Russia 1905, 75; and Pearl Harbour 1941, 239–40; control in Far East, 240; Hiroshima and Nagasaki 1945, 247, 272
Joyce, James: 112, 160

KEYNES, J. M.: opposed return to Gold Standard 1925, 135; economic theory in 1930's, 174–5; President of Arts Council 1945, 264; seeks U.S. Financial Aid 1945, 273
Kiel Canal: 47
Kitchener, Lord: asked to command the War 1914, 89; Policy in Turkey and Gallipoli 1915, 89–90; death of, 1916, 93
Koestler, Arthur: *Darkness at Noon*, 192; *Thieves in the Night*, 302
Korea: War in, 1950–1953, 315–17

LABOUR Party: and Chinese Miners 1905, 19; origins of, 22; Trade Disputes Act 1906, 37; and Welfare Legislation 1906, 39; and General Election 1910, 43; 1911, 44; and Trade Union Act 1913, 59–60; in Coalition Government 1915–1918, 98–9; attitude to War 1917, 109; Programme and Constitution 1918, 116–17; and General Election 1922, 129; attitude to French occupation of the Ruhr 1923, 130; and General Election 1923, 131; First Government 1924, 132–5; reaction to General Strike Reprisals, 143; effects of General Strike on, 1926, 144; attitude to Conservative Russian Policy 1927, 145; reaction to Local Government Bill 1927, 146; and General Election 1929, 147; Policy in Depression 1929–1933, 167; and Keynes's Economic Theory, 174–5; and National Government reformed 1935, 177; Policy in General Election 1935, 179; General Policy in 1930's, 181–2; influence of Spanish Civil War, 182; Policy 1938, 199; Election Programme 1945, 271; wins General Election 1945, 267–8; Government Policy in Far East 1945–1951, 299–300; Attlee's Post-War Cabinet,

Labour Party—*contd.*
1945, 271; Demobilization 1945–1946, 273, 314; European Policy 1945–1950, 273–4, 314–15; Government Legislation 1945–1951, 272–285; seeks U.S. Financial Aid 1945, 272–3; Crisis of 1947, 274–5; Agricultural Policy 1945–1951, 279–80; Palestinian Policy 1945–1951, 279–80; wins General Election 1950, 287–8; effect of Korean War 1950, 287; loses General Election 1951, 288; Korean War 1950–1953, 315–17; and Persian Oil Dispute 1951, 318; and Festival of Britain 1951, 325–6
Lansbury, George: 179, 182
Laski, Harold: 181
Law, Bonar: Leader of Unionist Party 1911, 58; attitude to Ireland 1911–1914, 64–6; in Cabinet 1915, 94; Lord Privy Seal 1918, 117; and Chanak Crisis 1922, 128; Prime Minister 1922, 129; death of, 1923, 130
Lawrence, D. H.: *Sons and Lovers* 1913, 161
Lawrence, T. E.: 102
League of Nations: Formed 1920, 123; Proposals for Pacific Settlement of International Disputes 1924, 133; and Germany, 137; 1934 Peace Ballot, votes for, 179
Lenin: and Bolshevik Revolution 1917, 109; establishment of Bolshevism and War of Allied Intervention, 110–12; death of, 192
Liberal National Party: 179
Liberal Party: Newcastle Party Conference 1891, 36; and General Election 1868, 16; and Licensing Act 1904, 28; Election promises 1906, 26; wins General Election 1906, 17; and South Africa 1906–1909, 31, 49–51; and Suffragettes 1906, 32; and retirement of Campbell-Bannerman 1908, 38; Government Naval Policy 1906–1908, 40–1, 48; wins General Election 1910, 43; Government Legislation 1910, 52; later Legislation 1911, 56, 60; and Conference on Ireland 1914, 66; and General Election 1918, 117; and Chanak Crisis 1922, 127–9; and General Election 1923, 131–2; 1929, 147; and National Government 1931, 149–50; and Policy in Depression, 167; and Policy in Second Cabinet, 168; aversion to Planned Economy and Nationalization, 175; Policy in General Election 1935, 179
Lloyd George: President of Board of Trade 1906, 37; Chancellor of Exchequer 1908, 38; and Budget 1909, 41–2; and Parliament Bill 1910, 44; and strike conciliation 1911, 55; and National Insurance Act 1911, 56; advice on Irish problem 1912, 64; Conference on Irish problem 1914, 66; and Cabinet division on Gallipoli 1914, 87; Minister of Munitions 1915, 98; at War Office 1916, 93; Prime Minister 1916, 94; and Food Production Department 1917, 100; and General Election 1918, 117; Policy on Ireland 1919, 114; Agricultural Policy 1919, 120, 162; Mining policy 1919, 140; and Treaty of Versailles 1919, 122; and League of

Nations 1920, 123; and Black Friday 1921, 124; leaves Conservative Party 1922, 127; and Chanak Crisis 1922, 128; and General Election 1923, 131; attacks Labour Policy 1924, 133; and General Election 1929, 147; and General Election 1935, 179; Pocket Biography, 338–40
Locarno Pact: 137, 146
Ludendorff, General: replaces Falkenhayn 1916, 102; Austrian offensive 1917, 103

MACARTHUR, General: occupation of Japan 1945, 248
MacDonald, Ramsay: first Secretary of Labour Representation Committee 1900, 22; Prime Minister of first Labour Government 1924, 132; Foreign Policy 1924, 132–3; fall of Labour Government 1924, 133–5; Prime Minister second Labour Government 1929, 147; Legislation 1929–1931, 147–8; and Committee of National Expenditure 1931, 139; Prime Minister of National Government 1931, 150; character of, 164; Cabinet of 1931, 166; forms second Cabinet 1931, 168; becomes Lord President of Cabinet 1935, 177; attitude to German menace 1935, 193; defeated in General Election 1935, 180; leaves Government 1937, 180; death of, 1937, 184; Pocket Biography, 340–2
MacNeice, Louis: 217, 267
Macedonia: Partition of, 79
Malaya: 1940–1947, 298–9; and Singapore, 299
May Report: 1931 Committee on National Expenditure, 149
Means Test: introduction of, 166–7; and Unemployment Act 1934, 176; effect of, 209; abolition of, 263
Medicine: advances in surgery, 327; pharmaceutical research, 327–8
Mesopotamia: German interests in, 1914, 72
Middle East: in Balkan War 1914, 69; economic rivalry in, 1914, 71; agreements with Britain, France and Germany 1914, 72; Arab nationalism in 1914–18, 84, 102
Mitchell, R. J.: 188
Molotov: and Russo-German Pact, 229–30
Moltke, General von: Chief of German Staff 1914, 86; replaced by Falkenhayn 1914, 86
Montenegro: in the Balkan Wars 1912–1913, 78
Montgomery, General: offensive in Egypt 1942, 242, 243; offensive in Normandy 1944, 244
Moore, Henry: in 1920's, 160; C.E.M.A. Exhibition of 1942, 266; Festival of Britain Exhibition 1951, 326
Morocco: French and German rivalry in, before 1914, 72; Crisis 1905–1911, 75–6; outbreak of Spanish Civil War, 1936, 197; in 1940, 234
Morrison, Herbert: Home Secretary 1941, 259; Lord President of Council 1945, 271; Foreign Secretary 1951, 318, 320
Mosley, Sir Oswald: Member of Labour Party 1924, 134; founded British Union of

Mosley, Sir Oswald—*contd.* Fascists 1932, 219, 148; interned 1939–1943, 252
Mountbatten, Lord Louis: Supreme Commander, South-East Asia 1944, 247; last Viceroy of India 1947, 295
Mussolini: and annexation of Abyssinia, 194; and Spanish Civil War, 196; occupies Albania 1939, 206; Government overthrown 1943, 243

NATIONAL Declaration Committee: and Peace Ballot, 179
National Government: formed, 149–50; first Cabinet, 166; second Cabinet, 168; wins General Election 1931, 167; re-forms 1935, 177; Foreign Affairs 1935–1938, 178; General Election 1935, 179; Rearmament Policy, 180, 187
National Health Service: created 1946, 284–5; charges, 329
National Labour Party: and General Election 1935, 179
Nationalist Boer Party: in South Africa, 51
Nationalization: of Bank of England 1945, 275–6; of Coal Mines 1947, 276–7; of Transport 1947, 277; of Electricity and Gas 1947 and 1948, 278; of Iron and Steel 1951, 278–9; control of Nationalized Industries, 331
Navy: Cawdor-Fisher Plan 1906–1914, 40–1, 47–8; at Gallipoli 1915, 89–90; in Battle of Jutland 1916, 96; Mutiny at Invergordon 1931, 166; Bilateral Agreement with Germany 1935, 193; Rearmament 1937, 188; in Battle of Atlantic, 236–7
Nazi Party: first formed, 130; rise of, 165; methods of, 190, 192; anti-Semitism and Hitler, 191; and murder of Dollfuss, Austria 1934, 199; and Austrian agitation 1938, 200; in Germany 1939, 225–7
Nehru, Pandit: 1939–1948, 295–6
New Zealand: and Tariff Reform League 1903, 17; troops at Gallipoli 1915, 90; in depression 1929, 165; as Member of Commonwealth, 289–92
Nicholson, Ben: 160
North Atlantic Treaty Organization: signed 1949, 312; aims of, 313
Norway: attacked by Germany 1940, 230–1; failure of Narvik landing, 231

OLD Age Benefits: Royal Commission for pension scheme 1895, 25–6; and Budget 1908, 38; contributory pensions scheme 1925, 145, 286
Old Vic Theatre: 160, 266
Olivier, Laurence: 160
Opera: Sadler's Wells, 215; Glyndebourne, 215; Covent Garden, 325
Organization for European Economic Co-operation: 1947, 311
Orwell, George: 209, 217
Ottawa Conference: 1932, 169, 170, 219

PALESTINE: British Government Policy for, 180; 1896–1949, 301–4
Pankhurst, Emmeline and Christabel: 32, 60–2
Peace of Vereeniging: 1902, 16, 31, 50

Peace Pledge Union: development of, 179
People's Budget: 1909, 41–2
Persia: Anglo-Russian Pact 1907, 75; British and Russian rivalry in, 1914, 72; Oil Dispute 1951, 318
Pétain: commands French Army 1916, 103; forms Vichy Government 1940, 232
Piper, John: C.E.M.A. Exhibition 1942, 266
Poland: created 1920, 110; and Treaty of Riga 1921, 111; by 1939, 190, 227–8; and Czechoslovakia, 203; seeks British protection 1939, 205; War in, 1939, 206; annexation of, 1939, 230; Russian advance through, 1944, 246; as satellite of Russia 1945, 309
Poor Law System 1834: workhouses, 26; and National Insurance Act 1911, 57; and Poor Law Guardians, 126; ending of, 1948, 286
Press: in 1906, 32–3; *Daily Herald* formed 1912, 54; in 1920's 157–8; in Zinoviev letter 1924, 135; in General Strike 1926, 142; in 1930's, 213–14
Priestley, J. B.: views on England, 208; in 1930's, 215, 216

REARMAMENT: in 1930's 187–9
Reith, John: 142, 158
Religion: in 1920's, 156–7; and Pacifism, 179; in 1930's, 219
Ribbentrop, von: German Foreign Minister, 193; talks with Eden 1937, 200; and Russo-German Pact 1939, 230
Richardson, Ralph: 160
Rommel, General: Commands German troops in Africa 1941, 234; advances to El Alamein 1942, 241
Roosevelt, F. D.: attitude to Second World War, 235–6; death of, 1945, 247
Roumania: acceded to Triple Alliance 1883, 74; in the Balkan Wars 1912–1913, 79; collapse of, 1916, 92; by 1939, 190; as satellite of Russia 1945, 309
Rowntree, Seebohm: 33, 144
Russia: in 1891 seeks alliance with France, 74; in 1900, 29; and Moroccan crisis 1905, 75; defeated by Japan 1905, 75; first Revolution 1905, 75; Anglo-Russian Pact 1907, 75; and Turkey 1908, 78; under Czar Nicholas II 1894–1917, 77; and Balkan Wars 1912–1913, 78–80; British rivalry in Persia 1914, 72; mobilization 1914, 81, 85; Russian Front 1914–1915, 87; Russian offensive, Pripet and Pruth 1916, 92; Treaty of Brest-Litovsk 1918, 104, 109; War of Allied Intervention in 1918, 109–12; Britain ends negotiations 1925, 137; British anti-Russian demonstrations 1927, 145; during 1930's, 192; admission to League of Nations 1934, 193; and Pacts with France and Czechoslovakia 1935, 193; and Spanish Civil War 1936, 197–8; seeks Conference on Czechoslovakia 1939, 206, 229–300; and annexation of Poland 1939, 230; invaded by Germany 1941, 235, 238; counter-offensive 1942, 241–2; 1943, 243–4; advance through Poland 1944,

Russia—*contd.*
246; surrounds Berlin 1945, 246, in United Nations Security Council, 250; Foreign Policy 1946, 309; and 'Cominform' 1947, 311; and Berlin Air Lift 1948–1949, 311–13; and Korean War 1950–1953, 315–17
Rutherford, Lord: 217–18

SADLER'S, Wells: 160, 215, 266
Salisbury, Lord: Leader of Conservative Party 1880, 16; attitude to Turkey 1885, 74; and Education Act 1891, 24; Prime Minister 1895–1905, 16; seeks new alliances 1899–1902, 29
Samuel, Sir Herbert: Chairman of Royal Commission on Mining 1925, 140, 144; and General Council of T.U.C. 1925, 142–3; in National Government 1931, 149–50; resignation from Office 1932, 168–9; and General Election 1935, 179
Sarajevo: assassination of Archduke Ferdinand, 80
Scandinavia: by 1938, 191
Schuschnigg: talks with Hitler 1938, 200–1
Scientific Discovery: in 1930's, 217–18
Scotland: Smallholders Act 1911, 56; 'Battle of George Square' 1919, 118
Second World War: Germany attacks Poland 1939, 230; Germany attacks Norway and Denmark 1940, 230–1; Germany attacks Holland and Belgium 1940, 231; Dunkirk 1940, 231–2; Battle of Britain 1940, 232–4; evacuation 1939–1940, 233; Italy enters War 1940, 234; Taranto Nov. 1940, 234; Cape Matapan March 1941, 234; North Africa 1940–1941, 234–5; German offensive in Balkan Peninsula and Africa 1941, 234–5; Britain occupies Iraq, Syria and Lebanon 1941, 235; Cash and Carry Bill 1940, 235; Lend Lease 1941, 236, 257; Battle of the Atlantic 236–7; America enters War 1941, 239; Pearl Harbour and War in Far East, 239–41; Allied position 1941–1942, 241–3; Dieppe Raid 1942, 242; offensive in Egypt 1942, 242–3; end of War in Africa 1943, 243; Allied offensive in Italy 1943, 243–4; German offensive 1942, 241; Russian counter-offensive 1942, 241–2; 1943, 243–4; Teheran meeting 1943, 244; British offensive in France 1943, 244–6; Allied offensive in Italy 1944, 235; V1 and V2 missiles, 245; Battle of the Bulge Dec. 1944, 246; the Yalta Conference 1945, 246; Potsdam Conference 1945, 246; Far Eastern offensive 1943, 247–8; War in Asia 1944, 247–8; Hiroshima and Nagasaki 1945, 247
Serbia: and Balkan Wars 1912–1913, 69; War with Austria 1914, 69, 80–3; collapses 1916, 90
Shaw, G. B.: 20
Sheppard, Rev. Dick: 157, 179
Sickness Benefits: Friendly Societies before 1900, 25; National Insurance Act 1911, 56–7; and Beveridge Report, 259; and National Health Service, 284
Simon, Sir John: 168, 177, 251, 394

Sinclair, Sir Archibald: 168, 255
Slim, General: Burma offensive 1944, 247
Smith, Matthew: in 1920's, 160
Smuts, General: rise to power in Transvaal 1906, 50–1; in War Coalition Cabinet 1916, 94
Snowden, Philip: Chancellor of the Exchequer 1924, 132; 1929, 148; (Cabinet 1931), 149–50, 166; Lord Privy Seal (Second Cabinet National Government 1931), 168, 169
Socialist League: founded 1932, 181
Social Survey: circa 1900, 15, 23–4; in 1920's, 151–63; in 1930's 171–2, 211–13; after 1945, 323–5
Spain: under de Rivera, 197; Civil War 1936, 196–9; in 1939, 190; evacuation of foreign troops, 200
Spencer, Stanley: in 1920's, 160
Spender, Stephen: 215, 217, 267
Stalin, J.: in 1930's, 193; views on Godesberg Memorandum 1938, 203
Stein, Gertrude: 161
Stresa Pact: 193–4
Strikes: Great London Dock Strike 1889, 23, 37, 53; Taff Vale Case 1901, 28; Railway Strike in Newcastle 1910, 53; Cotton Strike in Lancs. 1910, 53; Tonypandy 1910, 54; National Seamen 1911, 55; Firemen 1911, 55; London Carmen 1911, 55; Railwaymen 1911, 55; Miners' Federation 1912, 56; Dockers 1912, 56; General 1926, 136, 137, 138, 141, 343, 347
Sutherland, Graham: C.E.M.A. Exhibition 1942, 266
Switzerland: By 1938, 190
Syndicalist Movement: origins of, 53–4; effects of, 1912, 56

TAFF Vale Case: 28, 36
Tariff Reform: Tariff Reform League formed 1903, 17; protection 1921, 126–7; Import Duties Bill 1932, 168–9
Temple, William: 144, 157
Theatre: in 1920's, 159, 160; in 1930's, 215; after 1945, 324
Thomas, Dylan: 267
Tibet: Chinese suzerainty 1907, 75
Tirpitz, Admiral: as Minister of the Marine 1897, 47–9; Naval Policy 1905–1909, 40, 74
Trade Unions: 1893–1906, 22; 1824–1906, 27–8; Trade Disputes Act 1906, 37; Tonypandy Strike 1910, 54; form Triple Alliance, 54–5; Trade Union Act 1913, 59–60; Policy during 1914–1918 War, 98–9; and British Communist Party, 118; and Black Friday, 124; and Royal Commission on Mining, 140–1; in General Strike, 142–3; development of, 329–30
Transport: Motor Car, 33, 34; Aeroplanes—Development 1905–1912, 34–5; Airships in 1920's, 153; emergence of B.O.A.C. in 1930's, 175, 277; B.E.A., 277; after 1945, 323; formation of underground electric railway, 34; railways in 1920's, 152; methods of and conditions in 1920's, 153; development of Diesel in Ireland, 153; London Passenger Transport Board in 1930's,

Transport—*contd.*
175; Traffic problems in 1930's, 217; Nationalization of, 1947, 277; after 1945, 324
Trevelyan, Sir Charles: Member of Socialist League, 181
Truman, President: elected 1945, 247; Doctrine of 1947, 310; Korean War Policy 1950, 317
Turkey: by 1900, 29, 74, 76; revolution in, 1908, 77–8; in Balkan Wars 1912–1913, 78–9; Britain's attitude to, 1914, 71; in 1914–1918 War, 84, 87–90, 105; and Peace Conference 1919, 121; and Chanak Crisis 1920–1922, 127–8; during Second World War, 243

UNEMPLOYMENT Assistance Board 1934, 176
Unemployment Figures: 1920–1921, 124; 1921–1922, 127; 1929–1930, 147, 148; in 1920's, 152; 1931, 149; 1933, 169; 1938, 169, 186; in 1930's, 209
Unemployment Relief: Workmen's Compensation Act 1906, 37; National Insurance Act 1911, 56–7; Insurance Act 1920, 119; 1922, 125; cuts in Relief 1931, 166; restoration of Relief 1934, 176; in 1930's, 209; addition of agricultural workers 1936, 186; addition of domestic servants 1938, 186
United Nations: Declaration 1942, 250; Teheran Conference 1943, 250; Moscow Declaration 1943, 250; Dumbarton Oaks 1944, 250; San Francisco 1945, 250; Enquiry into Palestine 1947, 304, 308; 1945–1950, 308–9; Conference of Foreign Ministers 1945, 309; Security Council and General Assembly 1946, 309
United States of America: enters War 1917, 97; in France 1917, 104; Château Thierry 1918, 104; under General Foch 1918, 105; and War Debts 1923, 129; and Gold Standard 1925, 136; Cash and Carry Bill 1940, 235; attitude to and entry into Second World War 1941, 235; Lend Lease 1941, 236, 272; declares War on Japan 1941, 239–40; and United Nations Security Council 1945, 250; Foreign Policy 1946, 309; Truman Doctrine 1947, 310; Marshall Plan 1947, 310–11; Korean War 1950–1953, 315–17

VICTORIA, Queen: 15
Versailles, Treaty of: 121–3, 191, 196

WALL Street Crash: 136, 148, 163, 165, 167
War of Allied Intervention in Russia: 1917, 109–12
Wavell, General: Commands British Troops in North Africa 1940–1941, 234
Waugh, Evelyn: 161
West Indies: 306; Immigration to Britain in 1950's, 306–7
Whittle, Frank: 218
Wilhelm II, Kaiser: dismisses Bismarck 1890, 74; and Moroccan Crisis 1905, 75; and Imperialism 1914, 73; attitude to Britain 1914, 79; Policy in Serbian Crisis 1914, 80; flees to Holland 1918, 105

Wilson, Harold: resigns from Labour Government 1951, 288
Wilson, General Sir Henry: 65, 114, 339
Wilson, President: 97, 105, 122, 123
Women's Social and Political Union: 32, 60
Wood, Kingsley: Air Minister in War Cabinet 1939, 251; Taxation Policy 1940, 257
Woolf, Virginia: 161

YUGOSLAVIA: by 1939, 190